ALL DOGS
GO TO KEVIN

ALL DOGS GO TO KEVIN

Everything Three Dogs Taught Me
(That I Didn't Learn in Veterinary School)

DR. JESSICA VOGELSANG

GRAND CENTRAL
PUBLISHING

NEW YORK   BOSTON

Grand Central Publishing
Hachette Book Group
1290 Avenue of the Americas
New York, NY 10104

www.HachetteBookGroup.com

Printed in the United States of America

RRD-C

First Edition: July 2015
10 9 8 7 6 5 4 3 2 1

Grand Central Publishing is a division of Hachette Book Group, Inc. The Grand Central Publishing name and logo is a trademark of Hachette Book Group, Inc.

The Hachette Speakers Bureau provides a wide range of authors for speaking events. To find out more, go to www.hachettespeakersbureau.com or call (866) 376-6591.

The publisher is not responsible for websites (or their content) that are not owned by the publisher.

Library of Congress Cataloging-in-Publication Data has been applied for.

ISBN 978-1-4555-5493-5 (hardcover) / ISBN 978-1-4555-5492-8 (ebook) / ISBN 978-14789-0415-1 (audio download) / ISBN 978-1-4789-3483-7 (audio book)

*To the misfits, the miscreants, the
misunderstood, the freaks and geeks and socially
inept, and the dogs who love them.*

PREFACE

It took me a moment to realize that the choking intake of air I was hearing was the sound of my husband crying. It was an unfamiliar sound; in ten years of marriage, I had never encountered it. Silently, I watched the spreading pool dampen his pillow until it almost matched my own. Brian thought I had fallen asleep, but how could I? Hours earlier his best friend, Kevin, had died.

After they said good-bye to Kevin in the ICU, his friends and family gathered at his favorite Mexican joint to pour a margarita in his honor and share some of their favorite memories. There were plenty to choose from: You had to hand it to the guy for managing to pour a whole lot of living into forty short, occasionally debauched years. They smiled as they told the one about the silver flute, the one about the pirate ship, and the one about the time Blue Öyster Cult showed up at their house. Then, as the adrenaline wore off and the reality of the day set in, they all wandered home, where spouses like me asked them uselessly what we could do.

"I'm OK," Brian said, faking a tired smile. "I'm all right."

"Do you want to talk?" I asked.

"No."

Preface

I wouldn't have known what to say anyway. Brian sat on the couch and flipped on the Discovery Channel, rubbing his temples. When I went to bed, he stayed put while I pulled the covers up to my chin and stared at the ceiling.

Eventually, he slid in beside me and put his head down. I opened my eyes and stared at his back, my hand hovering as I debated whether to put it on his shoulder.

But before I could decide, I heard an old familiar sound approaching from the hallway: thump-thump-thump, the approaching sound of my black Lab Kekoa and her bull-whip tail. She paused only long enough to sniff the ground and make sure there were no loose crumbs on the floor before making a beeline for my husband's side of the bed.

She slid her face along the edge of the mattress and rested her nose next to Brian's, her tongue snaking out to kiss him on the nose. Only then, in that quiet moment in a pitch-black room, was he finally able to let the loss sink in.

I brought my hand back down to my side and closed my eyes, trying not to let my sniffle give me away, and went back to sleep. Kekoa had this one.

Dog the First:
TAFFY

The spirit of enlightenment first shone upon me in a pile of incandescent dog poop.

I had spent most of the afternoon angrily lecturing my Lhasa Apso Taffy for destroying my newly purchased sixty-four-pack of Crayolas. A bona fide wax junkie, Taffy was unable to resist the temptation and destroyed half the contents while I was at school learning whatever it is third graders learn. I came home to find paper shavings and crayon nubs strewn about my bedroom, and one satisfied-looking dog with green teeth.

"I wanted those crayons," I said to her. "I needed those crayons."

Taffy licked her stained lips, unimpressed. Bits of wax stuck in her beard like confetti.

By the time I finished picking wrapper remnants out of the carpet, Taffy was prancing back and forth in her interpretive I-have-to-potty dance. I leashed her up for a walk, grumbling as she merrily pulled me along. Halfway up the street, we ran into old Mr. Rillsworth, standing at the end of his driveway with his arms folded across his chest.

He peered down his long nose at me. "Are you the child whose dog is relieving itself in my driveway?" he asked in a sonorous voice.

"No," I lied. I don't know what it was about the Rillsworth driveway, a simple concrete affair much like every other one along the street, but Taffy saw it as irresistible, a throne fit for a queen. I did my best to be a responsible child by picking up after her almost every time, but sometimes I just forgot.

Mr. Rillsworth pushed the sleeves of his cardigan up over his forearms and pursed his lips, unconvinced. "Someone," he huffed, "has been leaving piles of dog refuse at the end of my driveway, and this morning I stepped in one." He rubbed the sole of his loafer on the concrete in distaste. "That is unacceptable."

"Yes, sir. But it wasn't me, sir." My palms were sweating. He looked like the type who might pull a switch out of the garage. We were at a standoff. His Siamese cat watched us silently from the window, licking her front paw. I was weighing the pros and cons of framing my sister when Taffy took matters into her own hands.

While I was defending my dubious honor, the ingested crayons had been snaking their way through Taffy's digestive tract. Bored with the conversation, Taffy chose that moment to prove her guilt and hunched over in the same place Mr. Rillsworth had been pointing to in his driveway. As he grimaced in disgust and my mouth fell open, Taffy produced a veritable work of art, a multihued cone of glory. It looked like a small tie-dyed ski hat.

I took advantage of the old man's shock to yank a bag out of my waistband and quickly scoop up the trophy. "See, sir?" I held my hand out, driving him back three feet toward his door. "It wasn't us. My dog poops rainbows." Before he could retort, we scampered away, earlier events forgiven. From that point on, Taffy and I were a team.

Some of us are born knowing just what to say to impress other people, to claim the world as the oyster we so richly deserve. The rest of us have dogs.

Unless you're my friend Kevin, of course, but that's a story for a little later.

CHAPTER 1

You'd think someone as antisocial as I am would have been surrounded by animals from an early age, but I was a latecomer to the realization that I was an animal person, because with the exception of my grandmother, nobody in my family actually liked animals.

From the time I was born, I was known as the "sensitive one" in the family. I spent a lot of time crying. Singing "Rock-a-Bye Baby" was banned when I was two, once my mother finally figured out the imagery of an infant crashing through the tree limbs was sending me into hysterics. Shortly after that, I announced I was never watching Tom and Jerry again because I felt sorry for the cat who was just trying to get something to eat. Other cartoon bans soon followed: Road Runner, then Sylvester and Tweety. Exasperated with all these failed attempts to keep me entertained in front of the TV, my mother eventually led me to the children's section of the library and told me to read whatever I wanted, which suited me just fine.

When I was four, my favorite place to hang out and collect my thoughts was under the kitchen sink, where I would curl up next to the Windex in complete darkness and ponder the mysteries of the universe. My mother would find me and tell me that the neighbors' kids were outside if I wanted to join them, and I would reply, "No thanks." When I got too big for the kitchen cabinet, I found my way into the cool cellar, flipping through our stacks of musty old *National Geographic* magazines, reading about Jane Goodall and dreaming of a life in the jungle among the chimps.

Instead of grounding me when I was in trouble, Mom would kick me out of the house and refuse to let me back in until dinner. "Go play!" she'd implore, closing the door then locking it behind her. I'd sigh, then wander across the yard to my grandparents' house where my grandfather was on permanent vigil in the foyer, reading history books. We would sit side by side for hours, reading; then I would come back home and pretend I had been riding my bike all afternoon. It wasn't that I disliked all the other kids in the neighborhood; it's just that I preferred books to people. They were easier to put away when you were done.

My mother was flummoxed at this development, having raised in my older sister, Kris, an archetypal extrovert who talked from sunrise to sunset. She tried multiple approaches to bring me out of my shell, with little success as the options in a dying mill town in early-1980s Massachusetts were pretty limited. Gymnastics was an utter disaster, ending with me on the floor in the fetal position with a bruised nose on my first day. Dance was only slightly better, though I was always in the back row during the recitals behind the willowy girls with the swingy ponytails and impeccable rhythm.

There's no joy in repeated attempts to squish yourself into

a mold that you know deep in your heart is not one you are meant to fill. I soon learned that the less I drew any sort of attention to myself, the less anyone would think to ask me to do something I hated. Team sports. Girl Scouts (couldn't handle the door-to-door cookie sales). Lest you think I was unhappy scurrying around the margins of society quiet as a mouse, I can assure you every day I evaded the notice of my fellow man was a victory, another day in my calm and peaceful fortress of inner solitude.

It didn't take me too long to finally discover the comfort of being surrounded by animals.

I was five when this was first revealed to me. "I have something to show you," said my dziadziu, the Polish word for "grandfather," in his heavy accent one afternoon. Eyes twinkling with excitement, he led me to the garage. I wondered what it could be. Candy, I decided. Those little ribbon candies that always stuck together in a big sticky, splintered mess. Or maybe a doll? Dziadziu and I were close, and I could always count on him to spoil me.

Dziadziu, a World War II refugee, was a deer hunter. Every winter, he, my father, and my uncle would retreat to the densely forested regions of Maine with heavy flannel and a shotgun rack, returning with a deer carcass strapped proudly to the front of the Buick—a lifeless, limp trophy resigned to its gruesome fate. Assuming I was one with nature the way the rest of the family was, Dziadziu thought I would be delighted and overcome with pride to see the gutted deer body hanging from the rafters. Not so much.

He slowly heaved up the heavy wooden garage door,

steered me through into the chilled concrete room, and there it hung, gutless, headless. No, wait—there, to the side—there was the head, waiting to be turned into a wall decoration. It regarded me dispassionately. *So these are humans, eh?* it seemed to ask.

Dziadziu, Dad, and my perpetual prankster uncle Ron waited for my reaction, unaware of the psychological trauma they were about to inflict.

As I stood there processing this sight, my uncle leaned down toward my trembling form, touched his whiskered cheek to my pale one, and whispered, "We killed Bambi." He grinned. I screeched.

My grandfather never quite figured out why I took off, screaming, into the arms of my grandmother, but this was the moment I learned I was an animal lover.

From that point on, seeing the signs of a kindred soul, my grandmother insulated me from the influence of my male relatives, letting me follow her around the yard as she laid out saucers of milk for the neighborhood cats, nursed baby birds with broken wings back to health, and whacked the neighborhood boys with a stick if they were teasing strays. Then she went home and cooked up venison stew. Her heart was kind, but pragmatic.

A year after the Bambi incident, I sat squished in the back of the family Chevette on a long car ride to Maine, off to visit family friends. Having tired of staring at the back of my father's headrest, I instead turned my attention to my seatmates. On the drive north, we had stopped by the market to pick up some lobsters. With little room to spare in the tiny car, they wound up perched next to me for the next three hours.

"Hello, Lobby," I said, addressing the box on the center seat. I peered in the holes, looking for a response. The lobster's claws were rubber-banded together, so there was none, save the soft *skritch skritch skritch* of its legs on the cardboard. "How are you today?"

In the back of my mind, I knew that establishing a personal relationship with my dinner was probably a bad idea, but I had nothing else to do. So we talked. Well, I talked, and the lobsters cruised around the box in search of an escape.

Their only escape came in the metaphorical sense, emerging from a boiling pot of water several hours later: changed, bright red, dead, and edible. I should have left the room once I saw the rolling bubbles, but I stood fast, determined to observe for myself the process. It wasn't my brightest idea.

"What's wrong?" asked my friend June a few hours later, wearing lobster claws on her hands like finger puppets. She raised them up to me, an eyeless, smelly marionette. "Tell me all about it," the claws clacked.

"I'd rather not," I replied, sniffling.

"Aren't you hungry?" she asked. "You didn't eat a thing tonight."

In New England, there's always a certain amount of confusion reserved for a person who doesn't like lobster. I've heard it's marvelous, but I wouldn't know.

We didn't have our first pet until I was eight and a neighbor's Lhasa Apso ended up with a litter of puppies they hadn't been planning on. Against my father's better judgment, he relented after intense lobbying from my sister and me, and allowed us to purchase one for $100. In return for this discount price, the neighbors made us wait for the last dog to be sold, ensuring we would have the most antisocial puppy— the one who'd spent most of her formative weeks cowering in the back of the whelping box. That is how we ended up with Taffy, a bundle of teeth in a perpetually anxious, furry body. She wasn't the "worst dog in the world" as Dad claimed, not really. She was just an introvert in an extroverted world. I got her immediately.

My mother had only agreed to the new family member in the hope of providing a bridge between her painfully shy youngest daughter and the rest of the world, but sadly it was not to be. Grumpy, kid-hating Taffy was born with one of those sweet fuzzy faces people found irresistible—and the temperament of a senior with a bad prostate. It must be a certain type of hellish existence to be a creature so utterly attractive to the one group of beings you want nothing to do with.

We were the wrong match from the get-go. She probably would have loved living with a sedate retiree who watched *Wheel of Fortune* on the couch while Taffy ate Milk-Bones. Sadly for her, she wound up in a house with one little girl who never gave up trying to stuff her into pink dog T-shirts, and another who dreamed of being a long-distance runner. Taffy, with her short temper and even shorter legs, found both activities atrocious.

From the tender age of eight weeks, Taffy made it clear that she was only marginally pleased with her living arrangements and would tolerate us solely for the purpose of acquiring food. As the designated dog feeder, I would wake up most mornings with her paws pressing on my chest, breathing doggy breath silently in my face as she willed me out of REM sleep in order to get her Kibbles 'n Bits.

Once she realized she was stuck with us, we settled into a routine. Her view: *You feed me, you walk me, don't stick your fingers in my bowl, and we'll get along fine.* Over time, this expanded: *You rub my belly, I'll crawl in your lap, we'll get along fine. I may even deign to lick your face, if there's gravy on it.* We came to an understanding, Taffy and I. You'd rather be left alone? Me too. Let's be alone together.

When Taffy was three months old, my father made an unexpected announcement: We were moving to California. As a nuclear engineer, Dad's rather specific niche mandated he follow the job opportunities where he could find them, and when Portsmouth's shipyards were shutting down he was offered two choices: Southern California or South Africa. Neither prospect pleased me, but my mother cast the deciding vote and Southern California it was. California, from what I could tell, was really weird, the home of fluorescent gym shorts and surfers named "Kade." I was forced to leave behind the warm, enveloping cocoon of my grandparents and a couple of close friends to start from scratch with a whole new group of acquaintances, a prospect that was, quite frankly, terrifying for an introverted third grader.

The transition from small-town New England to sleepy oceanside beach town was as bumpy as I had anticipated. Rachel and Rebecca, the two tall, grinning blond twins down the street, studied my pleated wool plaid skirts and knee-high argyle socks the same way one might study an orangutan at the zoo.

"Say sneaker," they demanded in unison.

"Sneakah," I'd respond in my heavy Boston accent, causing them to squeal in delight.

"Like, those are so weird," they'd say, pointing to my leather Mary Janes. "You should get these instead." They pranced around in hard plastic jelly shoes, pushing handfuls of rubber bangle bracelets up their arms. They were always moving, always talking. I did neither. Instead, I wrote letters to my friends in Massachusetts punctuated with sad faces scowling behind prison bars.

Rachel and Rebecca were friendly enough, too friendly if you asked me, but they tried, bless their hearts, to make me one of them. It never quite gelled. The plastic sandals gave me blisters. My mother refused to buy me LA Gear sneakers unless she could find them at a discount at Marshalls. The twins would ask me why I was mad at them whenever there was a two-second lull in the conversation. Spending time with these Southern California kids was just exhausting.

Taffy wasn't any more thrilled with the move than I was. As a long-haired Lhasa Apso, she chafed in the heat under the weight of all that fur. "Out for a drag?" the neighbors would respond when my sister walked by with an uncooperative dog sullenly lagging behind her. In addition, the year-round temperate weather translated to nonstop fleas, leaving us plugging our noses against a constant barrage of smelly flea dips and house bombs. Eventually my mother gave up and shaved

Taffy's fur into an all-over crew cut, solving both problems, which is how she remained for the next decade until Advantage came on the market.

The two of us spent a lot of time indoors, trying to shut out both fleas and chattering neighbor kids. My parents had rented the vacation home of a traveling businessman, which featured such 1980s excesses as zebra-print velvet wallpaper and the centerpiece of the entryway, a fully functional indoor waterfall. My father was too frugal to turn it on except for very special occasions, which were few and far between. For the entire year we lived there guests would open the front door to find themselves staring at a large, shallow ceramic bowl, empty save the splayed form of a small, bald dog resting on the cool flea-free surface. I'd join Taffy on occasion, staring up at the ever-present sun pouring through the skylight and wondering why I couldn't simply will myself to fit in just a tad bit more. In those moments of meditation, resting my hand on Taffy's back while we tried to sink farther into the floor, none of the outside chaos swirling about mattered. Our time together was easy.

Although I eventually traded my wool getups for more environmentally appropriate attire, I never quite mastered the knack of blending in with the crowd. After a while, I gave up the desire to assimilate and decided to go in the entirely opposite direction and wear my individuality like a hand-drawn flag, with varying degrees of success. "I'll just be oblivious to others' disdain" worked for a while, at least through elementary school. By then, my parents decided to make the move permanent by buying a house. I was stuck.

My lack of interest in the trends of my fellow classmates gave me a certain freedom to express myself in whatever get-ups caught my fancy, cringe-worthy or not. My favorite piece of clothing was an acid-washed cropped denim jacket featuring a self-drawn puffy paint white tiger that I modeled off a poster in my bedroom. I wore thick-framed black plastic glasses that were the only ones available capable of handling a lens of my extensive prescription, and kept my perpetually wild hair out of my face with a wide variety of scrunchies. I accessorized my attire with various small buttons I picked up in Spencer's Gifts featuring sassy sayings such as I'LL THINK OF YOU EVERY TIME I CLEAN UNDER THE BATHROOM SINK. It was the sort of eccentricity that is somewhat tolerated in eighty-five-year-old women, but less so in the cesspool of hormonal transformation known as junior high.

Sadly, I committed an error even more egregious than dressing funny: I had a big vocabulary. Having whiled away so many afternoons in universes painted by other people's words, I just ended up knowing a lot of them. So many, in fact, that my English teacher Mr. Small once accused me of plagiarizing a paper before realizing that that was simply how I talked. After that, Mr. Small ended up pushing me even harder to write more and better, letting me hide in the back of his classroom to bang away at a first-generation Apple during lunch breaks. My fellow students were not impressed with my hobby; they just assumed I was showing off by using words they didn't understand. At first, I was too oblivious to realize this was a problem, but it soon became apparent that I was easy prey. My magic puffy denim jacket was no armor against the verbal slings of a determined preteen.

Of all my peers, Mouth Breather Dan was the worst. Pale, slack-jawed, short, and freckled, he'd lurched through sixth grade without crossing my path any more than was necessary, but when junior high hit, he stretched out like a piece of chewing gum. Now he was pale, slack-jawed, tall, and freckled, a gangly ruler with a mop of greasy yellow hair who stared down at the world through his beady little eyes. I had no protection, no buddies to shield me, no understanding of how to stick up for myself. I hid behind my Coke-bottle glasses and buried my nose in my dog-eared *Hitchhiker's Guide to the Galaxy*, willing him to just go away.

It didn't work, of course. The less I fought, the more emboldened Mouth Breather Dan became, and soon enough everyone was joining him in target practice. Mornings at the bus stop became an endless torment of critiques about my hair, my skin, my body. All my deepest fears and insecurities were verified by the general population, engaged in a game of one-upmanship to vie for the guffaws of their pasty leader.

Taffy wasn't faring much better in life. Our new house was next door to a large German Shepherd who came running up to the chain-link fence, barking his head off, whenever we let Taffy outside. She walked up to the fence each and every time she saw him waiting for her, and when she did he lifted his leg and peed on her. My mother couldn't understand why Taffy didn't simply walk away, and grumbled to herself each night as she plunked the dog in the bathtub, but I got it. Letting the dog mark her was the only way to get him to shut up. Might as well get it over with as quickly as possible.

Taffy had urine to endure; I had words. "Am I really a lard-ass gargoyle?" I asked her one afternoon as I wiped tears from my face. I looked at my bookshelf, a messy pile of Piers Anthony fantasy novels and Invisible Woman 3-D models. I didn't care if anyone called me a nerd. I was; I never really saw that as a problem. But everything else? Maybe the rest of it was true too.

Taffy licked my cheek, and I knew that I might be a lard-ass gargoyle, but at least I was a lardass gargoyle with a dog who didn't care one way or the other. "You're my best friend," I told her, and she didn't deny it.

I decided to take Taffy for a walk to get some fresh air and let the puffiness recede from my eyes before I had to face Mom at dinner. She didn't know how to help me; letting her know how bad things were just seemed to make her sadder. We headed up the hill, around the block of neat two-story tract homes.

I heard the wheels of his skateboard before his nasal voice. "Hey, Gargoyle!" Mouth Breather Dan yelled, zooming by in his rolled-up jean shorts and trying to grab my scrunchie out of my hair. "Nice bow. Too bad it doesn't make you any less ugly."

Taffy ran under my feet, annoyed by the rattle of his skateboard wheels.

"Your dog's a lot better looking than you are," he said. He

stopped and leaned down, leering at her fuzzy muzzle. "I feel sorry for you."

She snapped at his face, coming an inch or two from his nose.

"AUGH! Get away from me, you stupid dog!" he yelled, and though Taffy tried, pulling in the other direction, in his panic Dan stepped backward onto his skateboard. It took his right foot with it, sending him spinning face-first onto the pavement. Scared by the screaming, Taffy left a little puddle seeping into Dan's sock as we backed away.

"I can't believe you were scared of that dog," his friend said as we walked away. "She's like, ten pounds. And cute." He leaned in toward me, opening his mouth for one last insult, then thought better of it and skated away. Taffy may have been a horrible little dog as far as the rest of the world was concerned, but she was perfect for me.

CHAPTER 2

During my shaky adolescent years, I maintained faith in the idea that life would eventually get a whole lot better. There was always something to look forward to: high school, which meant losing sight of Mouth Breather Dan in a crowded hallway; college, which meant moving away from that group entirely; and med school, where I could once and for all prove my worth to society. I'd decided to be a doctor by process of elimination, med school being the only option I could think of that my mother felt I was suited for and my dad felt would appropriately contribute to society. "Don't waste your time with the arts," he said, waving his hand dismissively when I floated the idea of majoring in journalism. "You can't make a living off that stuff."

Chasing your dreams and being your one true self and all those Oprah-ish platitudes never really figured into my dad's world, and I can't say I blame him. He'd grown up in a very different world than the one in which he'd raised me. His father, flinty Dziadziu, was placed in a Polish ghetto at the start of World War II, getting shuffled to a work camp and eventually a concentration camp due to his tendency to try smuggling guns inside the fence. Dziadziu survived his internment because his ability to speak three languages made him very useful, and they kept him around to witness horror after horror. "Education," he would tell us, tugging down the sleeves of his cardigan, "is the most important thing in life." Those long sleeves he perpetually wore covered the prison tattoo on his wrist. Dad was born in a displaced persons camp in West Germany and came to America on a boat, landing at Ellis Island after the war's end in 1952 with nothing but a small suitcase.

The mandate for immigrants was clear: Assimilate and make yourself useful. If they wanted to eat, they had to work: In the garden, growing vegetables. In the cellar, sewing their clothes. In class, learning English. In the textile factory mills of Lowell, inhaling dust. There was no safety net to fall back on if a job didn't pan out, no other family to ask for help, so it was pretty much work or starve. Self-reliance was woven into the family cloth from the get-go, industry your proof of worth. The American dream of working your way to a better life for your family was still shiny and optimistic in the national psyche when my dad was growing up. Dad joined the Navy and used the GI Bill to major in nuclear engineering, a practical, employable sort of field, and did exactly what he was supposed to: build a life safe and comfortable enough so that I had the luxuries of not having to grow my own food (thank goodness; I'd have starved) and of contemplating things like what I wanted to do with my life. Contemplation was fine up to a point, as long as it was followed up with practical action.

My mother's upbringing was less dramatic but a lot

louder—she was born into a rowdy Irish Catholic clan with forty-five aunts and uncles and an army of cousins too numerous to count. They were traditionalists, and her career choices after high school were fairly limited: nurse, secretary, teacher, or homemaker. Being accustomed to tending the various injuries caused by the never-ending scuffles in the family, Mom chose the nursing route. By the time I hit school, acceptable options for women in our circles had expanded slightly: doctor, lawyer, nurse, secretary, teacher, homemaker.

Only the first two options held any appeal. As I lacked the aggression required to be a lawyer, doctor was the most palatable option. A neurosurgeon or an orthopedic surgeon, preferably; the idea of actually having to converse with a patient was rather terrifying, so choosing a specialty where the patient would be unconscious for the majority of the interaction had a certain appeal.

"Perhaps," my mother suggested delicately, "you shouldn't put that on your college applications."

Fortunately for me, my insular tendencies had led to excellent grades, and like all good nerds, I had my pick of colleges. I wanted to go to a school with serious intellectual gravitas, the kind of place a think tank would go to cull their top scientists: Cal Tech, MIT, Harvey Mudd. (Those were the only interviews I had where I was asked whether I would feel comfortable developing a biological weapon.)

I was all set until the tuition estimates arrived. My parents were taken aback at the "expected parental contribution" portion of the admission packets. Unfortunately for me, Mom and Dad never got the memo that they were supposed to be contributing to my degree, so my visions of ivy-encrusted brick walls teeming with pasty intellectuals shrinking from the ray of light angling through the library windows were to be short-lived.

"Well," said Dad, "I went to school on the GI Bill."

"That's your plan, Dad? Have me enlist?"

"Well, no," he admitted. "But you should go to whatever school gives you the most financial aid. You applied to state schools, right?"

I had, but I wasn't thrilled at the thought. They were big. They were loud. They felt like the beach on the Fourth of July, a crowded, noisy place you were supposed to enjoy but secretly loathed. But it was all I had, until the letter from Loyola Marymount University arrived.

LMU was at the bottom of my list, a random liberal arts college I applied to only because my high school counselor went there and he seemed to like it. I didn't think I would have trouble getting in though it still annoyed me to no end that my parents opened the letter on my behalf.

"Look!" Mom shouted, waving the letter in my face. "Full scholarship! Can you believe it?"

Dad beamed. "I knew I liked that place."

I frowned. "No you didn't, Dad. It's the Catholic university, remember?"

Mom returned my frown. "Well, we're Catholic."

That was true, but only in the most technical sense. As

kids, my sister and I attended church weekly, yawning through Sunday school, squinting into the camera through tiny sheer veils at first communion, sitting in a mildewy wooden box trying to think of transgressions to confess to a tired-sounding priest. Our family's dedication fizzled over the years, though, as my father's indifference to the practice was revealed in countless stories about the ruler-happy nuns who dominated his early years in parochial school. After we moved away from New England, our attendance dropped dramatically. I held out long enough for the sacrament of Confirmation when I was fifteen, mostly to make my mother happy, and hadn't been back in a church since.

"We haven't been to church in three years, remember?"

As far as Dad was concerned, all was forgiven. "Well, kid, get praying. You've been delivered from student loans."

I couldn't argue with that. As an added bonus, LMU was close enough to home for weekend visits with my family and Taffy but far enough away that I could live in the dorms. I purposefully chose the quietest dorm on campus, hoping to surround myself with as much tranquility as possible for a college freshman. I was blessed with my wonderful room-mate Kathy, a sarcastic and cynical girl who was happy to sit in the dorm with me on the weekend watching *Beavis and Butt-Head* and sip Boone's Strawberry Hill instead of stumbling around campus with red plastic cups in search of kegs like the rest of the freshmen. We were refined that way. We stood together in solidarity against the terrifying scene before us, remaining aloof and above the fray. We were a team, best friends forever. Five months in, she dropped out, and I never heard from her again.

Kathy was replaced by Lisa, a midyear transfer who based her entire aesthetic off an encyclopedic knowledge of what a *Baywatch* extra should look like. We had nothing in common. I knew we were doomed from the second she laid eyes on my white tiger poster and declared tigers passé. It just went downhill from there.

Quiet lulls were not spaces of tranquility, but gaping holes Lisa felt compelled to fill with the sound of her voice. From the first moment she opened the door to the time we parted at the end of the school year, she never stopped chatting. About her breast implants. About the massive fairy wings tattooed on her back. About her bartending outfits, her Rollerblades, or her favorite step instructor at the gym. We were friendly but completely incompatible.

By the end of my freshman year, I was loving my biology classes but still struggling with finding my place at the school. I wondered if spiritual counseling was in order. Loyola Marymount was a Jesuit university, which in the hierarchy of Catholic denominations tended to attract a fairly worldly bunch: reformed alcoholics, men who had at one point been homeless, and Brother Joe, who had lived in Reno and dealt blackjack for five years before getting his heart broken and becoming a man of the cloth. I learned a lot from them.

Brother Joe was a far cry from the stuffy, nasal-voiced priests I had come to know and dread as a child in Boston. He set up a booth in the central plaza with a hand-lettered sign reading PSYCHIATRIC HELP 5 CENTS and waited for wayward students to meander over. On days I was feeling particularly lonely I would sit down and ask him about his days as a blackjack dealer.

"Maybe I should do that," I said. "Travel the world, meet people."

Brother Joe shook his finger at me. "That's not for you. You need to like people to do that."

"How do you know I don't like people?"

He gestured to the plaza. "There's a thousand kids your age sitting around, eating, talking, making plans, and you're here talking to this old guy."

"Well, you're more interesting," I said.

"No I'm not. I'm just older. Now skedaddle." God hath spoken through His resident blackjack dealer, and He sounded exactly like my mom: Go make a friend or something.

I had friends in the Greek scene, but their descriptions of rush sounded about as much fun as a naked march through city center. Fortunately, the school had an even better alternative: service organizations, a social/community service group hybrid, kind of like Jesuit fraternities and sororities. It was a much better fit.

The Loyola Marymount Belles met weekly to sign up for various volunteer events both off and on campus. Our adviser was a young priest slightly reminiscent of Christopher Reeve–era Clark Kent, a mild, gracious man who met with his flock of do-gooders every Tuesday and led us out to the Bread and Roses soup kitchen in Venice to feed the homeless. On

Sundays, we went grocery shopping and cooked dinner for a group of runaway teens in a halfway house in Hollywood, children whose lives were marred by abuse, drugs, and a general battering by the world. Expressing faith through service was integral to the Jesuit philosophy, and for the first time my family religion made sense.

One morning, I joined my fellow Belles at a retirement home to do a "day of beauty" for the residents. We set up shop in the main dining hall armed with curling irons, mirrors, and nail polish. One by one the residents entered, wheeled in by orderlies or tottering in on walkers.

The woman who was rolled across from me was suffering from late-stage dementia, unable to talk. Her wispy hair was too fragile for curling.

"Can you do her nails?" the nurse asked. I picked up the woman's chilly hand and examined her fingers, veins visible through her paper-thin skin. "Pink?" I asked. "Or red?" At that, a gentle squeeze.

"Ms. Atkinson was one of the top entertainment lawyers in Los Angeles," the nurse told me as I rubbed lotion onto her hands. "She founded one of the biggest agencies in Hollywood." She smiled fondly at her charge, who sat quietly staring at the other hand folded in her lap. "She doesn't remember everything, but she remembers that."

Ms. Atkinson patted her lap.

"And her little Poodle," said the nurse. "She always remembers her Poodle."

Now that I'd found a sense of community in the Belles, the college experience improved dramatically after my freshman year. I moved out of the dorm and into an apartment with two other biology majors I actually enjoyed being around. Away from Lisa's constant suggestions for how I could improve my hair, clothing, and feelings about plastic surgery, I was able to focus on my next step: getting into medical school. That lasted about a year and a half, until my stint at the morgue.

I was prepared for the academic rigors of medical school, but the one hurdle I couldn't see myself getting over was first-year cadaver lab. Just the thought gave me the willies.

"I don't know if I could dissect a dead person," I said to my mom in my junior year. "I don't know anything about death, really."

"You get used to it," she said with a shrug born of her nurse's pragmatism. "Why don't you volunteer with a mortician or something?" We have both always been decidedly unsentimental, and this was about as good a test as I was going to get.

So instead of volunteering at a hospital like a normal pre-med student, I went in search of the most disturbing, seedy, non-wimpy side of life to see if I was tough enough to take on dead bodies. And there, in the school's college career center intern binder, was my golden opportunity: "LA County Coroner. Unpaid internship, 16 weeks." Easy peasy, I thought, flipping my ponytail. I got this.

I arrived for my coroner interview promptly at nine a.m., entering the lobby and pausing a moment to admire the toe-tag key chains for sale at the gift shop. Yes, the LA County

Coroner has its own gift shop, complete with a Sherlock Bones mascot. I signed in and sat next to a nervous-looking man who was filling out paperwork.

"Who died?" he said to me.

"No one," I replied, affronted. We looked at each other in confusion, then reverted to silence.

Shortly thereafter, a tall, lean man with a ponytail and a 1970s Burt Reynolds mustache popped out of the back in a Tyvek suit and motioned for me to follow him. "You don't have to come in the main entrance to work here," he said, pressing a button for the elevator. "You can come in through the bay doors where the hearses pull up."

We walked down the whitish hall, flickering fluorescent lights hitting the sterile stainless-steel gurneys lining either side of the hallway like the effects in an old-school horror flick. We paused by a small office, and he led me inside.

"A lot of college kids come through here," he said. "It's not for the weak-stomached." He plopped into a wheeled desk chair and pulled a shoe box off the shelf behind him. "Here." He reached in, pulled out a Polaroid, and handed it to me.

"Gunshot, domestic dispute."

I studied the crime scene photo he gave me, nodded, then handed it back.

"Car accident, northbound 405.

"Elevator incident, construction site.

"Climbed into the bear enclosure at the LA Zoo."

Having satisfied himself that I could see such images

without passing out, he passed me along to the next level of the interview: the tour.

He handed me shoe covers and we padded toward the autopsy room. The hallway was eerily silent. I caught my first whiff of decay, a sweet, pervasive scent that sinks into your pores and makes you long for sunshine. He pushed the button for the autopsy room doors and with a quiet *whoosh*, I peered into the abyss.

I was strangely disappointed at how anticlimactic the scene before me turned out to be. I'd girded myself for something a little more, I don't know, somber. Instead, teams of pathologists were efficiently stripping waxy-looking plastic dummies—oh wait, those were dead people—of organs, weighing them, expertly slicing off bits of liver and brain and whatnot to be dumped into formaldehyde jars. Policemen needing to know the exact cause of death of Table 10 hung back, sipping coffee out of Styrofoam cups and pretending not to be grossed out.

I was simultaneously fascinated and repulsed.

Having surmised that I would be OK for a bit, Burt left me to my own devices and headed back to his office. I wandered further inside and found a pathologist happy to have an audience: Dr. Cortes, a jolly older man with a heavy Spanish accent and a bristling mustache. (There were lots of mustaches at the county coroner.) I helped him lift livers and bisect bladders, watching death and murder and disease reduced to formulaic dissection and paperwork, what was once a living, breathing human now simply a pile of evidence.

Dr. Cortes was patient and thorough with me, taking twice as long as he normally would to complete an autopsy. By the time we were finishing up, the rest of the employees had already departed for lunch, leaving the two of us alone in the room with the body of a seventy-two-year-old woman. "Here," Dr. Cortes said, handing me a yard-long bit of suture swathed onto a one-and-a-half-inch curved needle. "Why don't you sew this one up?"

"I don't know what to do," I protested. My mustachioed mentor passed me a mask with a splash guard and an apron.

"What?" he asked. "Didn't your momma ever teach you how to sew?" He moved his hand in a circular motion, holding an imaginary needle. "Just pull the sides shut, the funeral home's not picky." As I dubiously poked two sides of the Y-incision into place and started to pull, he told me he was going to lunch. "Be careful!" he said as he headed out the door. "She died of hepatitis!"

His merry laughter cut off as the doors hermetically sealed behind him, leaving me alone with the corpse, the wicked needle, and no way to tell whether or not he was joking.

For the next three months, I spent one Sunday a month surrounded by such strange characters, forcing myself to complete the internship out of not enjoyment but determination. If I can hang with dead people for a few months, I reasoned, I can handle anything. And I could. Until I found myself in the hallway with the plastic bag.

That morning, I passed by the processing room, where the bodies' possessions are noted and put aside for the next of kin, and noted a body still clad in Lee jeans and a pair of Keds. This being the mid-1990s, he was wearing the standard grunge uniform: flannel shirt, Pearl Jam T-shirt. His head, sadly, had not fared very well. I didn't look too closely. Cradled in his left elbow was a Vons plastic grocery bag.

"What's in the bag?" I asked, more to myself than anything.

"I don't know," answered a fellow intern passing by, a senior pre-med student at USC. "Why don't you look?"

Curiosity got the best of me. I picked up the bag and peered in, immediately regretting my decision. There are moments in your life that sear into your cranium, never to be unseen, much as you might wish you could. This was one of them.

I got light-headed. The intern checked the contents of the bag, then looked at the body on the table inquisitively. "Buckshot, maybe? Or car accident." He shrugged and continued on his way, unperturbed. That right there, that was a person who belonged here. I did not.

I slumped on the floor, ready to cry uncle. I didn't care if I was a wimp or not at that point, I just didn't want to come back here. "You have to learn to separate yourself emotionally from your job," Dr. Cortes had told me on my second day as he dispassionately surveyed a set of charred remains. "This, for example," he said as he grabbed a scalpel with a flourish, "is no longer a person. It is a crispy critter." I kept waiting for that wall to form between what I was doing and what I was feeling, but after several months I still hadn't gotten there.

Back in the autopsy room, Dr. Cortes tried to cheer me up.

"Here, little doctor!" he chirped, handing me a heavy set of gardening shears like he was Santa. "You can crack this one's chest!" I picked it up, surveyed it, and decided all these people were nuts. I shook my head and handed it back. "Oh no!" he said. "Someone didn't eat their Wheaties today!" I smiled weakly.

"Can I do it?" asked the other intern, elbowing in. "I'm good with a bone saw, too."

I headed outside for a few deep breaths of fresh air, which in downtown Los Angeles was a bit of a stretch. I wasn't sure what I was expecting out of this internship, but this wasn't it. As I pondered whether this was really the direction I wanted my life to go in, a small, calico cat darted out from behind an ambulance and twirled through my feet.

"I'm sorry," I told her. "I don't have any food."

She purred and let me rub her ears for a minute before sauntering away, away from the smell and the discarded remains of our mortal coils.

Shortly after, I sauntered away too.

The summer before my senior year of college, I found myself completely confused. The thought of applying to medical school was just not appealing anymore. I had spent enough time working in doctors' offices and watching surgeons grunt away as they threw their weight into hammering a hip replacement into a faceless bit of exposed leg that the luster had worn off the idea.

My mother encouraged me to talk to Dr. Banda, the pediatrician I'd gone to for years, who was also her boss. Here was a man with a true calling: He lived, breathed, and lived again for his work. He loved working with kids, especially teenagers.

"What do you think of the profession?" I asked him, looking for a pep talk. "Would you do it again if you could?"

"If I were just starting now?"

I nodded.

He mulled it over. "Nope. Don't get me wrong," he said, "I love what I do. I love being a doctor. But I hate the paperwork, the bureaucracy, of where this profession is going. It really takes the joy out of it."

I considered my options, and decided that perhaps my talents were better suited to a PhD program, where I could work on projects in the relative silence of a quiet lab. I applied for a summer program in biomedical engineering at the University of Minnesota, ready to be indoctrinated into the wild and woolly world of science. Research! Innovation! Cutting-edge science, here I come!

I was assigned to the lab of a brilliant professor working on the preservation of stem cells, which in the '90s were still mythical apparitions. I listened openmouthed as she told me of what they might one day do, embedded into a matrix to become a custom liver, or trachea. The possibilities were mind blowing.

The work, however, was mind numbing. Undergrad summer volunteers were not tasked with vital projects. In the early days of stem cell research, we were simply trying to keep the cells alive, so my job was to preserve them in various different solutions. I'd dip vials of cells into liquid nitrogen (OK, that part was cool), wait a day, then thaw them out and count how many survived the process. For eight hours a day, I peered into a microscope, scanning a grid for any pinpoints of light indicating a live cell as I clicked on a little device that recorded the number. Click, click, click. Click-click, click, clickety click.

If I finished early, I could wander down the hall and see what the other interns were up to. Most of them were mechanical engineers and were working on things like building prosthetic arms and artificial heart valves. It was much sexier, but I had chosen to minor in marine biology instead of engineering so I had no idea what they were talking about as they explained how they made their devices work.

One afternoon, I saw a group of scrubs-clad people marching purposefully down the hall toward another lab. "What are they doing?" I asked Chuck, the intern in that lab.

"They're implanting an artificial mitral valve in a pig," he said proudly. "Come by after work." He saw my face. "Don't worry, they live out their natural lives on the farm afterward. We *want* them to survive as long as possible."

By three p.m. I had tucked my pluripotent stem cells to bed, so I scurried over to Chuck's lab. The heart surgeons had just about finished, and they withdrew while a younger person stepped in.

"What is she doing?" I asked.

"Just closing up," Chuck said. "They let the veterinary students do that."

"Needle holders!" the student barked. Her colleague plunked them into her hand. "Two-aught PDS!" From a distance, I watched her sew the skin closed, intent on her goal.

Her hands flew. She placed ten stitches in the skin while her fellow students watched approvingly.

"Yesssss!" they said, giving her a high-five once she pulled off her gloves. High on the fumes of the successful stitch placement, they strode away discussing which bar they should hit up to celebrate.

Chuck, who had just helped engineer one of the most important artificial devices in modern medicine, was unimpressed. I, however, was mesmerized.

"I think I'm going to apply to veterinary school," I told him.

CHAPTER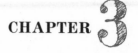

By the time I realized being a veterinarian was maybe my goal after all, I had missed the deadline to apply to vet school for the next fall. I graduated college with a year to kill before the following application round, which meant I had to find myself a job. The veterinary clinics I approached didn't want to hire someone with no work experience, so I went on Monster.com and hoped for the best.

Unable to escape the comfortable, familiar sight of a doctor's office, I wound up working as a clinical trial assistant for Dr. Nadim, a Beverly Hills urologist. The year was 1997. "We're completing a stage 4 trial for a drug that was initially intended for heart disease," he told me. "It didn't seem to do anything, so the manufacturer pulled the plug on the trial. But when they asked for the unused drug to be returned, none of the trial participants wanted to give it back. They asked why they wanted to hang on to a drug that didn't work, and . . . we got this."

The drug in question was an unassuming little diamond-shaped blue pill called Viagra. Word at the senior center was that this was the pill to end all pills. Before Viagra was approved in 1998, the only treatment available for impotence was an injection straight into the genitalia, which many men were understandably reluctant to try. In 1997, the only way to get your hands on Viagra was through an FDA-approved clinical trial.

No one ever says to themselves, *I bet talking to guys in their seventies about their erectile dysfunction will be a great way to learn to handle unusual conversations and get over my shyness. I should look for a job where I get to do that*, but I learned more than any twenty-one-year-old needed to know about the human condition. Most of my time on the job consisted of screening potential study candidates over the phone, but when the lines were quiet I attended to paperwork. Some of the studies required Polaroids, an early form of the X-rated selfie. It was here I developed my poker face.

Dr. Nadim loved being a doctor and reaped the benefits, handsomely. "Why don't you apply to medical school instead of rolling around the hay in the barn?" he asked, absently stroking his Rolex.

"If I don't get into vet school," I told him, "I'll apply to medical school. As long as you write my recommendation."

He smiled. "Yes! You can study female sexual dysfunction and we'll team up!" Yay?

There were two things that made me hesitate at the thought of leaving Southern California for four years of vet school. The first was the realization that I really had no idea what the average veterinarian actually did on a day-to-day basis. Kiss kittens and bask in the adulation of a grateful public? I volunteered at a local vet clinic in my spare time, but my experience was pretty minimal: Volunteers, they told me tersely, do laundry and clean litter boxes.

The other reason was my new boyfriend. The dating pool at Loyola Marymount had seemed as shallow as the personalities of the men who inhabited it, leaving me single and less than hopeful about romantic prospects after graduation, but my high school friend Mieko had been encouraging me for some time now to drive back to San Diego and go with her to her co-worker's legendary parties. "There's a ton of single guys in our IT department," she promised me. "They're good guys. And the parties are amazing." That year, since I had no Halloween plans, I promised Mieko I would accompany her to the Tower of London party.

Mieko tried her best to prepare me. "The Brotherhood spent the last month re-creating London in someone's backyard," she explained. "It's amazing."

"What's the Brotherhood?" I asked.

"Mostly, guys who throw parties," she explained. "They all met on a dial-up bulletin board service they started a few years ago. First it was talking online, then they started meeting at Fuddruckers, and then they all started working together and throwing real parties." She paused and furrowed her brow in concentration. "There may have been a Dungeons and Dragons league in there at some point too."

Mieko assured me this wouldn't be the type of party I was accustomed to in LA, where leering guys in deep V-necks would dismiss anyone who hadn't yet had their first plastic surgery. In Los Angeles, the average guy my age was getting his tips frosted and scanning Hermosa Beach for Pam Anderson look-alikes while blaring Smash Mouth on the radio. The Brotherhood was bound to be an improvement.

We pulled onto the street and parked in the first spot we could find along the sidewalk, making our way past twenty or so cars until we reached the party house. It was impossible to miss. If the guillotine in the front yard didn't give it away, the hordes of people in full-length Victorian finery would have tipped me off. Looking down at my hastily assembled wench costume, I realized I had already underestimated this group. Mieko grabbed my hand and dragged me in, scanning the crowd for people she knew. "Over there!" she said. "Follow me."

Mieko first introduced me to Kevin Workman, an imposing six-foot behemoth in a top hat and cape. Perhaps sensing that I was overwhelmed, Kevin gave me the grand tour, poking his friends out of the way with his cane. "Isn't this cool?" he cackled. "I built this scaffolding myself." He peeked behind a curtain stapled to a piece of drywall and pleasantly told whoever was inside to knock it off.

"This is my roommate Paul," he said, pointing to a guy with a long black braid. "What are you supposed to be, Paul? Jack the Ripper? Did they even have tat sleeves in 1888?" Paul rolled his eyes and walked away.

And as we circled back toward Mieko, another person popped up next to him. "This is my other roommate," Kevin said, gesturing to a fellow Victorian top-hat-wearing gentleman. "Brian. The mayor of London." Brian smiled and started to tip his hat before realizing he still had a beer in his hand. He was much better looking than my stereotype of the average computer geek, even with the ubiquitous '90s goatee. Kevin saw someone else he had to wave his cane at, and he excused himself, leaving me with the mayor.

The first words out of the mouth of the man I was going to marry were, "Can I get you a drink?"

Brian held out his elbow, and when I put my hand on his arm, I just knew.

Our relationship lacked any of the drama and uncertainty that had characterized my previous attempts at romance. We immediately started dating and became a couple within weeks, a comfort in each other's company that left me little doubt as to whether things would work out. I drove to San Diego every Friday after I was done with work, happy to leave Los Angeles behind. I'd sweep into the house Brian shared with Kevin and Paul, spray a little Bath & Body Works Vanilla Bean Noel mist around, ignore the less-than-savory magazines on the coffee table, and then head back to LA on Sunday for another week at work. Our little routine was working well so far, and the idea of moving even farther away for four years of veterinary school was suddenly a whole lot less appealing.

Brian knew I had applied to vet school. I had asked him very early on in the relationship if he liked animals. "Sure," he said. "My mother has, like, five cats." He neglected to mention at the time that he was allergic to every single one of them.

"Where do you think you'll go if you have your choice?" he asked one night as we hugged good-bye.

"Davis, if I get in," I said. It was the only veterinary school in California at the time. It was also the only one I could afford; out-of-state tuition at any of the other schools was out of the question. But it was also a six-hour drive away.

"What if you don't get in?" he asked, a little too hopefully.

"I'd probably move back to San Diego," I told him. "Apply to medical school instead. Dr. Nadim's been working on me to change my mind. If I don't get into vet school, it wasn't meant to be."

Brian rested his chin on the top of my head. "It wouldn't be the end of the world if you moved down here." I agreed. So we waited, wondering where we would end up.

When I'd submitted my applications in September, I'd directed all correspondence to my parents' home in San Diego. On April 1, my father called me to let me know a letter had arrived from UC Davis. "Do you want me to open it?" he asked.

"Is it a big envelope?" I asked. "Or a little one?"

"Uh..." I could sense him weighing it in his head. "Medium-size?"

There was no way I could wait until the weekend. "Open it, Dad."

"Dear Jessica," he read. He paused. "We...we are thrilled... to invite you to be a part of the incoming class at the UC Davis School of Veterinary MEDICINE! YEAHHHH!"

I frowned at the phone. "Dad."

"Yes?"

"I swear to God, Dad, if this is some sort of awful April Fool's Day joke I will never talk to you again."

"It's not a joke, Doctor. I promise." And the second he said that, it sealed the deal.

Brian tried his best to be enthusiastic on my behalf. "You know," he said, "if this isn't really what you want, you don't have to go. You can stay here. With me."

I looked at him, kindness and loving personified. Then I remembered a moment during college when my grandmother, iron-willed Babcia, had taken me by the shoulders. Like Dziadziu, she had weathered some awful moments during the war, but her spirit had somehow come through with more willingness to see the beauty in the world. She couldn't read or write English, but she was wiser than anyone I knew, could coax life from anything with an ounce of hope left in it. She was the earth. Though my grandparents' income was meager, she insisted on purchasing me a college ring. I tried to turn her down, but she was having none of it.

"You learn," she said, fixing me in the eye. She was a striking woman, raven-haired with ramrod-straight posture, who wore her pearls even when she was digging in the garden, her hair tucked into a babushka. "You are strong. What you have, your school...no one else can take from you." She kissed me on the forehead. "You can take care of yourself, no matter what. You are independent girl. This ring reminds you of that, always." She never used the word *dignity*, but that was part of the deal too.

I thought of her, and I weighed staying home with my boyfriend against leaving to become Doctor Me. "You know," I told Brian, "Southwest has pretty cheap flights to Sacramento." If we were meant to be, we were meant to be. So I left.

CHAPTER 4

Though I was thrilled to be going to Davis, to be honest I wasn't quite sure why they agreed to let me in. Surrounded by peers with an average of five thousand hours of experience working in veterinary practices, I found it hard to admit I had spent two months volunteering at a local clinic along with the local high schoolers who needed community service hours for school credit. The only thing I knew about veterinary medicine at that point was that it was smelly and generated a lot of poop (still true). I just hoped we would skip over the whole euthanasia thing and proceed straight to puppy cuddling class as quickly as possible.

My first clue that things were going to be a little less warm and fuzzy than that was our first classroom meeting. The entire incoming class sat nervously in a conference room while the dean hesitantly addressed the newest group of students at what was, until that very summer, the number one vet school in the country.

"So, you may have heard we are in danger of losing our accreditation," he said, clearing his throat as we all looked at him in disbelief. "Don't worry. It's actually great news. The quality of your education is top-notch, there was no doubt about that. It's just...well, our facilities are old. Really, really old. Falling-apart old. The medical schools—ha, yeah, they always seem to get all the new buildings, and it's finally our turn! So we'll have it fixed as soon as we get the money—right after you graduate, probably—and it'll be fine." He spread his arms expansively. "Welcome to vet school!" Not sure what else to do, we applauded our decrepit campus, which, as promised, would be beautifully renovated two years after we all graduated.

There were certain perks to taking classes in the rotting hulk of a decaying ancient building not up to even 1974 OSHA code. Bonding, for one. The freshman class took all of their courses as a unit, with 137 of us stuffed into what used to be the pathology lab back in the 1960s and was now retrofitted as a high-ceilinged, slightly creepy classroom. We huddled together like a herd of gazelle avoiding predatory professors shining laser pointers at their unfortunate victims. "You! What's this nerve called?" We would leave them to their fate, glad to be spared this day.

If you were bored enough to be staring at the ceiling, which was an unfortunately regular occurrence during neurology lectures, you could trace the old track on which heavy meat hooks would drag in livestock for necropsies. You couldn't get too distracted, however; if you weren't vigilant, cockroaches would still occasionally emerge from the long-rusted drains in the floor and skitter across your feet. At least once a day a small squeal would emanate from a corner of the darkened room from a complacent student who had let his or her Birkenstocked toes dangle a little too closely to the floor.

When they let us out of lectures, we would shuffle down the hall en masse to the anatomy lab and file in to our assigned tables. We were surrounded by Far Side cartoons, an upbeat contrast with the rows of dogs waiting to be dissected, three students to a dog.

As maintaining a herd of cows for student dissection was an impractical prospect, we were spared having to do that work ourselves. In the corner, a large dead cow hung with one side neatly peeled back like a sardine can, little flags stuck in various muscles and vessels. This was the prosection, a preserved cow that was already dissected and labeled with the day's assigned structures by Bob the Lab Guy before our arrival. We merely had to memorize it. At the end of lab, Frank the cow would be wheeled back into the refrigerated room to patiently await the next session.

Closing my nose off against the pungent reek of formaldehyde, I joined my tablemates at our assigned dog, all of us uncomfortable at the task before us. While the other people in the class focused on their tasks with laser-like precision, arguing over who got to tease out the nerves of the brachial plexus and who was stuck holding the anatomy book, my little trio of sensitive souls spent most of our time apologizing to the dog for the indignity we were putting it through. In order to understand anatomy, you have to get in there and really feel the body's structures and how they relate to one another, feel how each organ is not a free-floating bit in a bunch of empty space but wedged firmly with a bunch of other really important structures. Though we didn't enjoy it, we always thanked our dog for giving us the gift of knowledge.

We learned to work efficiently, because after an hour or two the formaldehyde would start to build up in our lungs and we'd have to leave the room for a breather so we didn't pass out. If I close my eyes, I can pull up the images in my head like it was yesterday: the rows of metal tables, the *Miller's Anatomy* book propped up in the corner with edges slightly brown and crinkly from one of us forgetting to wipe our gloves before thumbing through it, our furrowed brows as we tried to reconcile the images in the book with what was laid before us, the dust motes dancing under light just a shade too dim for our late-night work. The vet school brochure never mentioned this part. I still hadn't snuggled a single puppy.

The school promised to make up for our sad classrooms by repurposing the top floor of an old barn long abandoned by the upperclassmen into a lovely retreat for studying, relaxation, or the occasional nap. Determined to claim our space, my lab mate Carrie and I hiked our way to the top floor, trying not to choke on the dust or imagine what must be scurrying about in the dim light. After the first unexplained scratching noises in the wall we abandoned ship for the beautifully appointed library at the med school. I later learned that the only reason the top floor was deeded to the vet students was that the barn had a bat infestation and we were the only students at Davis guaranteed to have a rabies vaccination.

Those first few months felt like jumping on a treadmill cranked up to top speed, so I found myself desperately looking forward to the long holiday break. I spent it back at my parents' house, piping frosting on gingerbread and mainlining potato chips while my mother fretted over Taffy. Mom had a big neighborhood party planned for the evening, and she was worried the dog was going to bite someone. A legitimate concern, really. Despite her advanced age of twelve, she could still move like a viper when someone got in her way.

The years had taken their toll on Taffy. Her flea allergy still meant that every summer she needed a full shave, resulting in what my dad dubbed her "drowned rat" look. She'd been diagnosed with epilepsy at three years of age, resulting in blessedly rare but terrifying grand mal seizures. And to top it off, she developed cataracts in both eyes, one of which had to be removed when she was ten. Now she was bald, half blind, and decidedly less cute than she had been as a pup. I still found her charming in a grumpy sort of way, a cranky senior citizen.

It was rare that my father agreed to entertain more than two people at a time in the house, so having fifteen neighbors in all at the same time was a major event for my mother. She went all out with the decorations, wrapping yards of garland on the banister and hanging ornaments off every hook she could find. Every so often she would pause with a sigh to throw out some item of decor, commenting that it had been either chewed or peed on before glancing briefly at Taffy.

After my departure for college, Taffy had taken up residence in my parents' upstairs bedroom, but she spent the daylight hours downstairs. We debated where we should leave her for the party; in with the guests was out of the question. Mom was determined to sequester the house Grinch from the events downstairs.

Mom and I decided to just put a baby gate up at the top

of the stairs and give her free rein of the top floor. Before the first guests arrived, I lugged her up the stairs, her body melting like a noodle in limp passive resistance.

"Sorry, Taffy," I said, handing her a rawhide. "Them's the breaks."

She stared at me as she watched me attach the baby gate to the landing. She pushed at it, testing.

"No, Taffy," I said. As the guests arrived, she pouted and stood at the top of the stairs like a silent sentinel, daring any and all who entered to come upstairs and pet her. Our neighbors all knew her, so no one took the bait.

Taffy's sullen demeanor stood in stark contrast with the festivities swirling below. About halfway through the party, she started to whine.

"Can you check on her?" asked my mom. And then, a little hopefully: "Maybe give her some Benadryl to make her sleepy?"

I trudged back upstairs, grateful for a chance to get a break from the neighbors and their well-meaning but perplexed inquiries as to why my boyfriend was not yet my fiancé or their requests for free medical advice.

I rubbed Taffy's belly for a few minutes, ignored the suggestion about the Benadryl, then climbed back over the baby gate. Taffy protested.

"Sorry, girl," I said. "Trust me, you don't want to be down there." I walked downstairs, refusing to acknowledge Taffy's unhappy whimpers.

Several minutes later, there was a loud crash from the vicinity of the front entryway. We all rushed down the hallway, where we saw that the baby gate lay halfway down the stairs, overcome by the full weight of an angry Lhasa Apso. Taffy lay at the bottom of the stairs, convulsing in a full-blown epileptic seizure. I ran over to her and rubbed her head.

"Oh my God," someone said. "Is she dying?"

"No, she's just having a seizure."

And so we all stood in mute horror as Taffy reenacted *The Exorcist*. Mom tried to lure the guests back to the living room with promises of gingerbread cookies, but no one moved. A thin howl escaped from Taffy's mouth as she started to regain consciousness. She tried to stand, but kept flopping over. Finally, she got up and bumped to and fro among the guests like a baby seal on land, unable to bear any weight on her hind limbs. This is it, I thought to myself. She broke her pelvis and we have to put her to sleep and oh my God Christmas is ruined and I should have just given her the stupid Benadryl so it's all my fault. Some vet I'm going to make.

But just as quickly as it began, the seizure ended. Taffy lay on her side on the floor, staring at me. *You should have paid more attention to me when you had the chance*, her eyes accused. We tried to get her to stand up, but she refused.

"I think she hurt herself," I said to no one in particular. "I should bring her to the ER vet."

"You're much too upset to drive," my father said, grabbing the keys.

"No, Dad, I'm fine," I said, wiping away tears. I stood up. In the midst of her seizure, Taffy had peed on my wool trousers, which now clung to me in a soggy mess.

"No, really, I don't mind," he said. Then he saw my pants. "I'll wait while you change."

By the time we pulled into the ER parking lot, Taffy's post-seizure disorientation had worn off and she was sitting happily in the backseat, licking my palm.

"Maybe she just wanted to get out of the house," I offered. "Think we should go back?"

Dad raised his eyebrows in horror. "Why the rush?" he asked. "We're here. Might as well get her checked out."

So we sat in the waiting area with a dog who'd eaten a bag of holiday truffles, a cat whose foray into the world of gravy led to a raging case of pancreatitis, and a sobbing woman whose Jack Russell had apparently darted out the front door between the legs of the UPS man and met the front wheel of a Mustang. I watched her body heave for a moment before realizing she didn't have any tissues.

"Here you go," I said quietly, putting a box in her lap.

She looked up, her tears reflecting the red glow of her light-up Christmas sweater. "Thanks, sweetie." She patted my hand and pulled out a tissue, dabbing her eyes. I looked back at Taffy, who was now not only fine but the most cheerful she had been all night. The tech called us into the back room.

"I hope your dog is all right," I said to the woman, and carried Taffy into the room.

The ER vet examined Taffy, prodding at her back, bending her legs this way and that, flipping her foot knuckle-down on the table to test her reflexes, all of which were normal. She didn't protest once.

"What happened right before the seizure?" he asked.

"She fell down the stairs," I said.

"So she started having a seizure and fell down the stairs?" he said.

"No," Dad interjected. "Our neighbor was waving a sausage at her, so she jumped over a baby gate, then she fell down the stairs, *then* she had a seizure." He had hidden that crucial detail from me until now. Dad saw me glare at him and shrugged.

The vet nodded. "That happens a lot over the holidays," he said.

He popped the X-rays onto the viewing box while Taffy sat on my foot with her back to him, refusing to acknowledge his presence. "So that's her tail and that's—"

"I know," I said, taking in the sight of her bones. The soft glow of the backlight beckoned to me as I studied each inch, looking for cracks.

"It looks good," he said, smiling. "I don't think she broke anything. Just keep her calm tonight and if she's limping or anything unusual tomorrow, follow up with your regular vet."

"Can I look at this a little longer?" I asked. "I just want to see if I can identify the organs."

The doctor grinned, pointing out the heart, the intestines, the spleen. I peered at the black space defining her lungs, eyeing her trachea, marveling at her mastoid. "That's pretty cool."

In response to his quizzical look, I told him I was halfway through my first year of vet school. He spent the next several minutes quizzing me on structures, pleased with my answers.

Then a frowning technician knocked on the door and gestured him over with an urgent wave.

The doctor excused himself, and as he disappeared into the back I said, "Is that Jack Russell going to be OK?"

His smile disappeared. His head dropped. "I'm glad Taffy is all right, Future Doctor Jessica. Merry Christmas." Seeing another box of tissues on the bench, he picked them up and strode through the door.

I took Taffy home, grateful for her health, and wondering how many boxes of tissues the ER went through in an evening.

CHAPTER 5

One of the first things I learned in veterinary school is that people were unabashedly fascinated by my career path. This didn't take long to emerge, since like all newbie vet students, one of the first things I did was buy a sweatshirt emblazoned with my class logo and the big veterinary caduceus. I wore it everywhere for a good few months, forgetting that small talk with strangers had never been my forte.

The questions would start innocently enough. "You're at Davis?" he or she would begin, gesturing to my sweatshirt.

"Yes," I'd say with pride. "First year." Behold the future pet doctor!

"That's great," they would invariably say, and then just as invariably launch into a long description of every pet they had ever owned. That part was fine; I had nowhere to go, so it was fun just to hear people brag about their favorite pets. Years later, I still get a kick out of it—ministers, teachers, captains of industry, you name it, no one can resist the impulse to pull out their smartphone and show me their dog.

I spent a lot of time in airports during veterinary school. On Fridays, I'd shrug out of my coveralls, jump in the shower to steam the animal smell out of my pores, and race the tomato trucks up Highway 113 to be at the airport with time to spare. It was common for me to be in the terminal for an hour or two if a flight was delayed, so unless I remembered to bring class notes to flip through while I was waiting and signal I was otherwise occupied, I was fair game for bored passengers to engage.

I was sitting on the floor at the Sacramento Southwest terminal, back when you had to stake your place in the boarding line with your plastic A, B, or C pass as soon as you passed through security. Captive to that plot of real estate, I was stuck for the next hour. A smiling woman with a cat cardigan and a Carol Brady haircut rolled her bag up next to me and took a seat.

"Oh," she said, noticing my sweatshirt, "are you studying to be a veterinarian?"

"I am," I said proudly.

She smiled appreciatively. "My daughter wants to be a vet someday." I smiled. I got that a lot too.

"How old is she?"

"Twelve. I keep telling her she needs to study more math, is that true? That you need math?"

"You do," I nodded. "There's lots of drug calculations."

"That makes sense," she said. "Do you need to go to college?"

"Yes," I replied. "Four years of undergrad, then four years of veterinary school."

"Holy cow!" she said, impressed. "That's like...*medical* school."

"It is," I told her. "Animal medical school."

"I thought it was like a two-year program, like an associate's or something."

"Nope. Four years of undergrad, four years of vet school, plus more if you want to specialize."

She shook her head, her world rocked, unable to fathom why I'd put myself through all of that. "So," she ventured, cocking her head—here it came—"if you have to do the same amount of work and all...Why didn't you become a *real* doctor?"

From that day forward, I wore nothing that marked me as a vet student—unless I was on campus where no one would ask me for advice.

The first three years of vet school left us contained in classrooms for the vast majority of the time, so most of us sought outside opportunities to work with animals and hone our newly acquired diagnostic skills. After examining my options, I decided to volunteer one Saturday a month with Mercer Clinic, a student-run organization that provided veterinary care for pets belonging to the homeless population of Sacramento.

Dogs without a license could be impounded by Animal Control at any time. In order to get a license, they needed to have a rabies vaccine. The Mercer Clinic students provided that necessary shot, with the caveat that the dog needed to be spayed or neutered first. We worked with area veterinarians to get that taken care of, and grants covered our costs. It was a great arrangement.

New volunteers often wondered how likely the homeless

owners would be to actually keep the appointments we set up for them, but in all my life I have never met a group of clients more likely to show up. Everyone in the community knew which days the vet students would be there to take care of their pets, and by the time we arrived at the warehouse we used on Saturday morning we'd have a line stretched around the block. We were supervised in our work by clinicians from the vet school who generously donated their time year after year.

The care we provided was simple preventive medicine, mostly vaccines and dewormings and skin infections. We practiced basic things like how to hold a pet safely and how to quickly administer a vaccine with a minimum amount of sting. Those tricks you pick up quickly. My most valuable lesson, one that could never be conveyed in a classroom, was about giving every patient who walked in your door the same level of professional respect, no matter what.

One Saturday at Mercer Clinic, I encountered Dr. Lewis, who taught large animal surgery in the downstairs portion of the teaching hospital. He spent his time at Davis handing out shoulder-length plastic gloves and bottles of lube while explaining the proper way to palpate a cow's ovaries. For short people like me this resulted in your head being pressed right against the cow's tail while you were up to your rotator cuff in cow booty.

I was surprised to see him at the Mercer Clinic, and I told him so. "Why not?" he replied. With his pouf of gray hair and his easygoing smile, he reminded me a little bit of

Mr. Rogers, but in coveralls. "It's a nice change of pace." The clients clearly recognized him from past clinics, chatting him up about their dogs, their lives, perhaps sharing a favorite Bible verse with him.

"Before I got sober," one man told me, "Truck here would stand over me when I was out cold and keep my stuff from gettin' nabbed. Ain't never had no one stay by me like that before. Is his ear gonna be OK?" He nodded in relief when we said it would. "Good."

Another client hesitated when we explained her dog would have to be spayed before she could get a rabies vaccine. "Will she have to spend the night at the vet?" she asked.

"Yes," Dr. Lewis told her. "Just a night."

"Forget it," she said, and started to leave.

"Wait!" called Dr. Lewis. "Can I ask why? It's really for Diamond's safety to keep her overnight after surgery."

The woman shrank down into her big puffy coat, hiding behind her long hair. I looked more closely at her. She couldn't have been much older than me, mid- to late twenties, tops. She put her hand on her dog protectively.

"Diamond keeps *me* safe," she told him. "Before I got her..." She flushed and looked away, leaving the sentence unfinished. "I don't want to be without her."

Dr. Lewis nodded slowly. "If I promise you we'll keep you safe while Diamond is recovering, can we do this?" he asked her. "She'll have a longer, healthier life if we do."

The woman cocked her head. "Maybe."

He sent her off to speak with the clinic director Laura,

a fourth-year veterinary student currently organizing patient records in the lobby.

"How does that work?" I asked him.

"I have a trailer on my property," he said. "My wife's got it set up very nicely. She won't mind a guest for one night. Can't take care of the pet if you don't take care of the owner, sometimes." He took a sip of water and cracked his knuckles. "Would you like to bring in the next client?"

"OK, Dr. Lewis." I picked up the chart on the top of the pile and flipped it open. Two cats! We didn't see those nearly as often as dogs at the Mercer Clinic. I scanned for the client's name so I knew who to call for out front.

Hmm. This should be interesting.

I walked outside the warehouse entrance and looked down the sidewalk, which was lined with shopping carts and bags, dogs pulling at leashes tied to bicycles, and waiting clients huddled against the rapidly evaporating morning chill, clutching small Styrofoam cups of coffee Laura handed out after we arrived.

"Mr. Tanner?" I called, peering down the sidewalk. "Mr. Tanner?"

"What's his first name, hon?" said a woman sitting cross-legged on the sidewalk, holding a brindle puppy in her lap. A smile creased her sun-weathered face. "We don't use last names."

"Oh. Ummm…Randy. Randy Tanner. He has two cats."

"RANDY!" the woman belted out, her voice cutting through the murmurs of conversation. "This young lady's calling you!" A man looked up, stubbed out his cigarette, and picked up a plastic carrier. "Go on, *Mister Tanner*," she teased, chuckling.

"You watch it, Luann," he shot back with a grin, stuffing his pack of cigarettes into the pocket of his flannel shirt.

"Hi, Mr. Tanner," I said. "I'm Jessica. We're ready for your kitties."

"Yeah, they're ready for you too," he said. "They're full of it today." From the depths of the carrier, I heard a small plaintive meow.

I held the door for him as we entered the exam room. Dr. Lewis looked up through his thick black-rimmed glasses and smiled. "Hello!" he said, and, turning to me, "Who do we have here?"

Dr. Lewis had taught me that it was always proper form to use a pet's name as often as possible when talking to the client. "This is Mr. Tanner," I said, "and...his two kitties. They're here for their first set of vaccines and a dewormer. He thinks...the gray one has tapeworms."

Dr. Lewis frowned at me in mild disapproval as he took the chart from my hand. "OK, let's see who wants to go first." He flipped open the chart, blinked, and then cleared his throat.

I pulled out the first patient, a fluffy, orange tabby kitten with big green eyes. "Hello, uh...A-hole, is it?"

"His name's Asshole!" Randy bellowed gleefully. "He sure is, too. And the other one's Shithead. They're really something."

"Indeed," said Dr. Lewis. I watched his lips press together and his nostrils flare, his genteel sensibilities clashing with his professional obligation to recognize a patient by his or her name, regardless of his own feelings on the subject.

He took a deep breath. "Hello, Asshole," he said, rubbing the kitten behind his ears and managing to make the name sound actually halfway sweet. Dr. Lewis looked up. "Asshole has fleas, so he likely has tapeworms, Mr. Tanner. We'll treat both the kittens." He smiled as if it were the most comfortable conversation in the world, now that he'd committed to it. Neither this kitten nor his brother showed any signs of living up to their names, even when we gave them their vaccines. They purred the whole time. Dr. Lewis shook Randy's hand. "We'll see you in three weeks for boosters."

"Thanks so much!" said Randy, stopping to shake out another Marlboro before picking up the carrier. "Where's my manners? Want one?" he asked, offering the box to both of us, which we declined. After Randy left with his charges, Dr. Lewis again paused for another sip of water, followed by a Tic Tac.

"That's a new one," I said, just to say something.

"Actually," said Dr. Lewis as the slightest smirk quivered on his mouth, "it happens all the time."

CHAPTER 6

After four years of dating, Brian and I married in San Diego the July before my final year of veterinary school. I was too distracted to fully enjoy the planning process, which actually eliminated much of the anxiety known to plague modern brides. I planned most of it from up in Davis, crossing my fingers that the wedding coordinator knew what she was doing and telling my bridesmaids to pick out whatever black dress they felt like wearing from their various locations across the country. I found a random guitarist on Craigslist and asked him if he could learn the theme from *The Princess Bride* in a month; he said sure and the price was right, so I sent him a CD and prayed he would show up.

The weeks before the wedding were a flurry of envelopes and fittings and panic, but to my delight everything came together for one glorious afternoon. The guitarist showed up and nailed "Storybook Love" as I walked down the aisle. Babcia, alarmed we weren't getting married in a Catholic church, discreetly sprinkled the holy water she had smuggled in from the vestibule of her church as I passed her row of seats. Not one person asked me about their dog's strange rash. It was perfect.

In the weeks after our honeymoon I tried to forget Davis, spending as much time as possible with my new husband before I disappeared for another ten months. I dreaded the idea of a long-distance first year of marriage, but we didn't have much choice. Brian loved his job and his company was very good to him, so leaving San Diego wasn't an option. We'd tough it out.

To keep me company, I adopted a tiny kitten named Apollo, a little black bundle of teeth and luminous yellow eyes. It was right around this time that Brian finally confessed he was allergic to cats. "I'll get you some Claritin," I said. We were off to a great start.

When fall arrived, I locked my shiny new wedding rings safely away at home, far from the detritus of the hospital floor, and descended into the dark night of the soul known as vet school senior year. I'd read the manual, I'd watched someone else drive, and now, giddy with fear and excitement, I finally had the pedal under my foot.

This was a big change from the first three years of vet school spent sitting in a classroom. Sure, we had labs and the occasional foray into the sprawling teaching hospital where the world's leaders in specialty medicine plied their trade, but I'd spent most of my time trying to stuff an impossibly huge amount of data into my brain and keep it from falling out. All of this changed senior year, when they turned us loose full-time at the teaching hospital.

At the UC Davis Veterinary Medical Teaching Hospital, helpfully shortened to the VMTH, each specialty has its own "service": medicine, surgery, oncology, dermatology, and so on. During this final year of school, we were assigned to rotate through various services depending on our interests. There were a handful of services everyone had to experience, like pathology; that was actually interesting, doing postmortem exams on anything whose cause of death needed to be determined, be it hawk, dog, or horse. One group of students was astonished to come in and find they would be helping to examine an elephant, who was euthanized due to severe arthritis.

But before the final year, we'd selected a track—small animal, large animal, mixed animal, equine, or individual—and our chosen track dictated where we spent most of our long days and nights. Those in the small animal medicine track would work the majority of their weeks on the second floor, tending to dogs with lymphoma in the oncology ward or gasping cats in emergency. Those in the equine track would be in the barn most days, or out in the field. If they were really lucky they could help place a horse in the giant cave-like large animal MRI machine, a hulking, rattling beast that looked like it came out of the *Enterprise* engine room.

Being the indecisive type that I am, I had decided to create an independent track. It was the one track with no preset electives, so I had to propose my own.

"What do you want to do after you graduate?" asked my adviser, a goofy yet intense pharmacology professor with a rapid-fire delivery and a scary memory for drug interactions. My answer would determine whether or not he signed off on my track proposal: A month in the primate lab. A month in lab animal medicine. Six weeks at a research facility that conveniently happened to be in San Diego. And the rest of my time on the top floor of the VMTH where all the small animal services resided, hedging my bets just in case I decided to work in a clinic after all.

After almost four years in school, my mind went back to those students in Minnesota and their contributions to heart transplant surgery.

"I'd like to do research," I offered, and my adviser's eyes lit up as he checked me off. I still wasn't sure, but that seemed as good an idea as any. When he asked if I would consider staying on for a PhD, my mind returned to those years counting stem cells, and all I could squeak out was, "Maybe." I still had a lot to figure out.

I was hoping my first rotation would be something mellow like dermatology, to kind of ease me into the maelstrom, but I had no such luck. I was assigned to small animal internal medicine, one of the most grueling services in the hospital. Long hours, intense residents, and pets with really complicated illnesses such as necrotizing pancreatitis, or diabetic ketoacidosis, or maybe both at once. There were no simple fixes here.

On my first day, I walked in bright and early Monday morning with my clean lab coat and my shiny new Littmann stethoscope hanging around my neck. Stuffed in my coat pocket was a penlight and a Nerdbook. *The Small Animal Veterinary Nerdbook*, an invaluable pocket guide to all the facts a vet student might get called out on in rounds, was a classic text penned by a well-organized veterinarian in her final year of school, and my best friend for the next three years. I knew nothing, but the Nerdbook knew it all.

It was admittedly thin armor against the onslaught of things I didn't know, but it was all I had. I was so nervous I could barely squeak out a greeting to the collected people in the room.

"Good morning," said a tall woman in clipped tones. This was Dr. Manning, the senior internal medicine resident. She'd only been there a year and her penchant for withering glares was already the subject of teaching hospital legend. Perhaps it was merely a rumor, I thought, as she pushed a plate of scones at me.

"Here," she said. "I made scones." That was nice of her. It was all a ruse.

"Oh, thank you," I said. "I already ate this morning, but I'll have one later." She frowned.

One by one, the other students on the service trickled in, all on the South Beach Diet, already full, or otherwise inclined to pass. "Doesn't anyone want one?" she asked with irritation, despite the fact that she hadn't had one herself.

"I'll take one," said a voice from the doorway, and in loped Dr. Johnson, endocrinology god and acting head of the small animal teaching hospital. I was hoping for the vet school B-list on my first rotation, but for whatever reason I was to be making my maiden voyage into veterinary medicine under the direct scrutiny of the people I was hoping to avoid until I knew what I was doing.

About forty-five minutes into our day, Dr. Manning was leading the discussion, pinning us all with her steely gaze while Dr. Johnson examined his fingernails. I had purposefully sat in the middle so that whichever end of the table she started on, she wouldn't call on me first. She presented a case, a twelve-year-old diabetic cat who was dehydrated. I surreptitiously flipped to the diabetes section of the Nerdbook, squinting to read the tiny letters.

"So what IV fluids would you pick for this cat? Jennifer?"

Silence.

"Jennifer. I'm asking you." I looked up. She was looking at me.

"It's Jessica," offered the person next to me.

"OK, so, Jessica. What fluid would you pick?"

I squeaked out, "Saline?" My Nerdbook had suggested that it was a better choice than the standard Lactated Ringer's in this case, though it didn't say why. Dr. Manning's eyes twitched toward my hands hidden under the table and back to me. I had a sinking feeling this was all information I was supposed to know without a Nerdbook assist.

Dr. Manning cocked her head. "What kind of saline?"

There's more than one? I blanked. "Ummm...I don't know. The usual one."

"Just saline? Nothing else in it?"

I decided to commit to it, right or wrong. "Yes," I said, and in that moment it was decided that I was this rotation's village idiot.

Dr. Manning gave an exasperated sigh and moved on to

the person next to me. "LRS qs twenty millequivalents a liter of KCL?" she said, and Dr. Manning nodded that would do. Curses.

The days always followed the same routine. We started with morning rounds of the cases in the hospital, and discussed how we would handle each patient's care. Midday was set aside for appointments. If we admitted a pet to the hospital, we were also in charge of generating treatment plans, finding a cage in the appropriate ward, and passing the pet off to the technician in charge of implementing the whole process. In between appointments, we took care of our hospitalized charges, helping with treatments, running them from the radiology ward to the treatment ward, and keeping the owners updated. We spent a lot of time getting in the way of the ward techs, too. We gathered again for afternoon rounds, quads quivering from all the squatting in front of cages.

I was petrified of interacting with owners during appointment times. The student's job was to retrieve the owner and pet from the lobby, get the medical history to determine why they were there, perform a physical exam, and then find the doctor assigned to the case. Once we briefed the clinician using proper veterinary terminology and format, we would enter the room together and present a treatment plan to the owner. Being alone in the room with an owner was something I dreaded.

After three days, Dr. Johnson finally figured out that my constant eagerness to help in the treatment wards was a clever ploy to avoid seeing appointments. "I'm not sure I'm ready yet," I said.

He pushed the computer printout of the day's schedule at me. "Pick one," he said. "You need to get into an exam room and practice talking to people." I surveyed the appointments, looking for one that sounded relatively simple.

Bosco McIntosh seemed like a good choice: a four-year-old Yorkie who was seeing Dr. Johnson for vaccines. I didn't stop to ask myself why a healthy young dog would need to see a world-renowned endocrinology professor for vaccines and what that might say about the owner. I just saw a slam-dunk healthy dog in for preventive care, and put my initials next to his name. "Who has Bosco?" Dr. Johnson asked later, before we scattered to the wind after morning rounds. I raised my hand. He motioned me over.

"Mrs. McIntosh is an…interesting lady," he said in low tones. "She's been coming in ever since we treated her dog for a liver shunt when he was a puppy. The dog's fine now but she insists on seeing me for everything. She does…things. She might rearrange the exam room tables or refuse to talk to you. Just let her do what she wants, do your exam, and come get me." He handed me the chart and wandered off, searching for a coffee refill.

I patted my lab coat, smoothing it down and making sure my name tag was on straight. I took a deep breath, and pushed through the double doors leading into the waiting area.

The lobby of the small animal teaching hospital is large by necessity, as it is used for every service from surgery to oncology. People and carriers reclined on every chair; the beige tile of the floor was barely visible under all the dogs piled underfoot and squeezed under the seats. Tiptoeing gingerly through the mass of pets were students like me with clipboards pressed to their chests, calling out "Fluffy Snyderman?" "Mr. Tibbles Smith?" I joined them, snaking my way through the aisles calling for Bosco until I saw a head snap up.

"That's us," said Mrs. McIntosh, pushing herself to her feet while still holding the small fluffy pillow that had been in her lap. On it reclined a tiny silver dog, long fur pulled back from his face and tied with a red bow into a small ponytail atop his head. Bosco's fur was a near-perfect match for the silver crown on Mrs. McIntosh's head. Both were impeccably coiffed. She picked up her huge tapestry purse in her free hand and started picking her way over the dogs on the floor, heading for the exam rooms. "Are we in Room 4? I asked for Room 4."

"I'm sorry," I said, "we're in 7." She snorted. "Can I help you with Bosco?"

"No."

As we passed Room 4, she peered in the window and pursed her lips upon seeing a doctor in scrubs examining a dog in a cast, and then strode into Room 7, plopped her bag on the floor, and surveyed the room.

"I'm Jessica," I began, "and I'm going to—"

"I know, I know," she said, cutting me off while placing the pillow on the exam table. "You're the student. Just get to it." She started pushing chairs around.

I debated multitasking my chores, starting my physical exam while getting a history, but I was too afraid I would miss something. I began by asking Mrs. McIntosh questions about how Bosco was doing. He was fine, she told me. He was drinking fine and eating fine and could we please just get Dr. Johnson already?

"Almost," I assured her, and started my examination. Bosco was going to get a head-to-toe exam no matter what. I needed Dr. Johnson to know I was thorough. One by one, I went down the list. EENT: eyes, ears, nose, throat. A retained baby canine. I placed my stethoscope on his chest to hear the thump-thump-thump of a healthy heart, palpated his tiny tummy, and worked his back legs like a bicycle while I felt for the telltale snap of a kneecap sliding out of place.

Mrs. McIntosh was silent, her eyes huge and unblinking behind her bifocals as she stared at me. She had arranged her chair directly across from me so she could observe my thorough but slow approach, punctuated by breaks when I had to look down at my chart to prompt me as to what I needed to examine next. She strummed her fingers on the table as I wrapped up.

"I'll be right back," I said. "I'm going to go get Dr. Johnson." Mrs. McIntosh nodded curtly.

I strode down the hall, letting out a sigh of relief. I'd gotten through the exam. I didn't drop Bosco. I even got a temperature with a minimum of fuss on the part of the dog. Yes, Mrs. McIntosh was a little grumpy, but that couldn't be helped.

I found Dr. Johnson in the conference room, flipping through a *JAVMA* article about thyroid tumors. "Was she OK?" he asked.

"The owner? She seemed to be," I said, and launched into my presentation. Dr. Johnson's head bobbed as I went down the list of all the information I had gleaned, a ritual he'd been through day in and day out for the last couple of decades, ticking off numbers and data for my benefit more than his. "Bosco's just due for a DHPP and a rabies booster. She declined bordetella."

"All right," he said, snapping his journal shut. "Let's go." Dr. Johnson was very tall, and despite his slow gait his legs were so long I still had to scurry to keep up. He rapped on the door with a knuckle and pushed it open before getting an answer. "Hi, Mrs. McIntosh," he said to the frowning form perched expectantly across the room. "Hi, Bosco." He rubbed Bosco's chin, and the dog leaned in happily to his outstretched fingers. "Glad you're both well." Mrs. McIntosh grunted.

"So, did you take it easy on Jessica here?" he asked. "It's her first day."

"I could tell," said Mrs. McIntosh, turning to look at me. "I was going to wait until after she left the room, but since you asked, she was an abysmal example of your school."

I stood there in silence. There was nothing to say.

"She was slow," Mrs. McIntosh said, as Dr. Johnson stood there stoically nodding. "She didn't know what she was doing." She elaborated on each of my many inadequacies, ticking them off one by one with obvious relish, encouraged by his silence to continue in her evisceration. "I don't know what you people are thinking admitting such dippy young

70

blondes to your institution, but I'll tell you one thing"—she turned to me and pointed a sharp nail toward my face—"if you don't shape up soon, you're never going to make it as a veterinarian." Satisfied at the look on my face, she sank back into her chair and crossed her arms across her chest.

"OK," Dr. Johnson said, and then started his exam. He decreed Bosco healthy and agreed with the vaccine plan. "We'll be back in a minute." He left the room, me dogging his heels like a kicked puppy.

This was it. I was done. I was a total failure.

As we rounded the corner toward the pharmacy, Dr. Johnson gave me one brief pat on the shoulder. "You OK?" he asked.

"Y...yes," I lied, tears welling in my eyes. Oh no, God, please don't start crying. Now I'm not just a failure, I'm an overly emotional failure.

"You know," he said, rubbing his temples, "she chews her dog's food."

"I'm sorry?"

"She puts food in her mouth and chews it up for her dog," he said. "She's not all there. Ignore her. I do." He tapped the chart. "Do you want to add Lyme vaccine?"

"He's not a high risk," I said. "So...no?"

He nodded in agreement. "The pharmacy will give you the vaccines. Meet you back there in five." Oh God, I had to go back in?

Dr. Johnson watched dispassionately as I lifted Bosco and gave him his shots, one in the scruff, one in the hip, ignoring

Mrs. McIntosh's request that he do it instead. "Bad back," he told her, despite the fact that Bosco weighed about four pounds. "Thanks for coming in."

Mrs. McIntosh scooped up her dog and headed for the checkout desk. I didn't accompany her. I could barely look at her.

By the time I made it back to the conference room my eyes were puffy and red and I was sniffling. All of my worst fears and insecurities had been realized. I really didn't have what it took, Mrs. McIntosh was right, I never should have applied. I couldn't figure out which was worse, the things she said or my complete breakdown in response to it. My rotation mates grimaced in sympathy as I relayed the details in between hiccups. Dr. Manning wrinkled her nose in annoyance. Realizing I was in no shape to represent the future of veterinary medicine to clients, I was dismissed for an hour to marinate in my inadequacy and embarrassment.

Dr. Johnson was waiting outside the room as I exited, scribbling on a chart. I froze, waiting for him to quietly tell me to pack my bags and go back to San Diego.

"Did you always want to be a veterinarian?" he asked me.

"No," I admitted. "I thought I was going to become an MD."

"Why didn't you go to medical school?"

I said the first thing that popped into my head: "I thought it would be too hard to get through medical school."

He laughed. "Oh, this is harder, don't you think? Most people never even get in." He snapped the chart shut. "But you did."

It was as close to a pep talk as anyone ever got from Dr. Johnson.

I slunk down the hall looking for a quiet place to gather my thoughts, but quiet places are few and far between in a busy veterinary hospital. Eventually I wandered downstairs past the pharmacy, and out the back door leading to the barns. I settled on the concrete stairs, letting the sun dry my cheeks. It was much more peaceful out here, and as the breeze passed over my face I could catch the smell of alfalfa.

Over the course of the year, I often found classmates similarly resting with their heads on their knees on what I would eventually dub "the Crying Step." The hospital never stopped, never slept; the back steps were pretty much the only place on the grounds you could go to have a small meltdown in relative peace. In our first three years of school, we learned what drugs treat what conditions, where nerves and blood vessels lay in relation to one another, how to be technically proficient at the medical management of a biological process. But no one ever sat us down and told us that we would also be dealers of hard-core emotion: handing out diagnoses bringing on stress and fear, loss and anger, joy and relief, much of it absorbed and then redirected back at us. Until we learned the fine art of deliberate deflection and developed the confidence to reject the feedback we couldn't use to improve, it could be rough sailing.

That was the first and worst of my internal challenges that year, that crisis of "Can I really do this?" but it wasn't the only one. It is a strange irony of being in a healing profession that we often take as many wounds as we fix. Part of the unspoken learning curve, as I would soon find out, is looking heartache and tragedy in the face, and continuing on, coping the best we could. One by one as we had our moments, our puppies who faded or clients who cursed us or that heroic police dog who pulled through an eight-hour surgery only to die overnight, we crawled to the Crying Step, sobbed it out, shook it off, and went back in for the next round.

On that first day, I settled on the step and tried to decide what this whole debacle said about me. Was this the universe trying to give me a hint: Get out while I could? Was this a challenge to overcome and emerge from victoriously? Or was this simply a cranky old lady who pre-chewed her dog's food taking out her frustrations with the universe on me? I paused at that uninvited thought, surprising myself at the notion of being incredibly upset with someone while simultaneously feeling sorry for them. I had only two choices, really: Go on, or don't.

"We have more rooms waiting," said a voice from behind me. Into my periphery stepped a pair of neat Sperry Top-Siders. Dr. Manning, dispatched by Dr. Johnson to scrape me up off the cement. Break time was over.

"You're going to run into people like that all the time, you know," she said. "Fortunately for you, they're not the ones who decide if you graduate. I do. So go see another room and stop feeling sorry for yourself. If you're going to pity someone, pity that poor dog who has to live with that woman every day."

I pushed myself up with my hands on my knees, nodding.

"And eat a scone," she said. "They have chocolate chips." So I did, and I went on to see a perfectly lovely Cocker Spaniel with a thyroid condition who kissed me and told me, in his doggy way, that he loved me.

In a weird way, Mrs. McIntosh gave me a gift, the gift of knowing I've already encountered the worst client I'll ever have. Fortunately for me, for every one of her there were twenty lovely and kind pet owners who had faith that we were doing our best, aware that we spent many nights stuffed into a metal kennel with their pets so they wouldn't feel so lonely in a strange hospital. I'm sure I'm not the first or the last student Mrs. McIntosh sent to the Crying Step over the years, but if the lack of sun-bleached bones in the back field is any indication, we all learned to persevere despite her dire predictions.

There's something freeing in facing a fear and having it be every bit as awful as you had imagined. After you survive the experience, there's nothing more to be frightened of. Once I figured out that the clinicians were used to bumbling veterinary students with large knowledge gaps, I stopped worrying about what they thought of me and started concentrating on the patients. Things got a lot better after that, even when I accidentally lost a contact onto a dour surgeon's sterile gloves shortly before he banished me for the afternoon.

Toward the end of the year, I found myself back in the small animal internal medicine service for another two-week rotation, this time under the auspices of Dr. Lee, a white-haired urology specialist (I seemed destined to work with them) who had started practicing medicine shortly before the Vietnam War. He, like Dr. Johnson, was a legend in his field.

My patient Lucky was a ten-month-old Golden Retriever who presented with a mass in the bladder. In a theme that would continue to play out over the course of my career, I quickly learned that the easiest way to guarantee your pet an early demise from cancer, accidents, or other untoward tragedies was to bestow this most ironically unfortunate of names upon him or her. Lucky's owner, a human anesthesiologist, had a long list of questions I couldn't answer, so I went and got Dr. Lee and gave him the rundown. "My differentials are infection, polyp, cancer—"

"Not cancer," he interrupted. "Dogs that young don't get bladder cancer." He told the owner the same thing: "I've never, in forty years of medicine, seen a one-year-old dog with bladder cancer. My money's on polyp. We'll start with an ultrasound."

In the meantime, I wandered over to the oncology department and asked one of the residents about juvenile bladder cancer. "Rhabdomyosarcoma," she said without missing a beat. "Biopsy it." She was, unfortunately, correct. This puppy had cancer, and a bad one at that.

Dr. Lee was amazingly unperturbed by being completely, confidently wrong. "There's a first time for everything," he said. "How'd you know it might be cancer?"

"I asked the oncology residents," I said, but in fact the reason I even thought to ask them in the first place was because the Nerdbook had mentioned it. Saved once again.

"Are you going to do an internship after school?" he asked.

The thought of more training after graduation had crossed my mind, but by that point all I wanted to do was go home and hang out with my husband. "I wasn't planning on it."

"Well, let me know if you change your mind and want a letter of recommendation," he said. "You'd make a great small animal internist." If I hadn't been worried about breaking his hip, I would have given him a bear hug.

CHAPTER 7

On the day I graduated from vet school, my mother presented me with a beautiful blue silk scarf covered with little skipping dogs. "This can be your lucky scarf," she said, knotting it around my neck over the stethoscope we had all been presented with at graduation.

It was this scarf around which I constructed my interview outfit, a carefully chosen navy suit designed to say *put-together professional* and draw attention away from the reality: terrified, inexperienced newbie. At the last minute, I also added a pair of tortoiseshell glasses, which I normally only wore when I lost a contact but which I hoped added a certain level of intellectualism to my overall appearance. Young, yes, but very astute.

It had turned out that the life of a laboratory animal veterinarian was not in the cards for me. My weeks in the laboratory animal rotation were a bust: After the second day of vicious migraines, I realized I had a rat allergy, so that was out. I considered primate medicine, but I felt more like Josef Mengele than Jane Goodall: I did not feel good about what I was doing. Perhaps we were making lives better for future generations of people, but the animals certainly weren't getting anything positive out of the deal. Looking for reassurance that this work was worth it, I asked one of the residents what he liked most about this specialty. He scowled, "Nothing. I hate what I'm doing here and I'm quitting this month." Suddenly life inside a traditional dog and cat clinic started to look a lot more appealing.

So, for lack of a better plan compounded with a short window of time before student loans were going to be due, I decided to look for a job in small animal medicine. I sent my résumé to several clinics around San Diego, hoping to get a few bites.

My first interview was at a small hospital run by a solo practitioner, a man who was realizing he needed a little more time off than he had been getting. Dr. Peters strode in halfway out of his surgical gown, straightened his tie, then frowned in annoyance at the powdery fingerprints his latex gloves had left. He settled behind the desk, flipped over my résumé, then steepled his fingers.

"Are you pregnant?" he asked immediately.

"Oh...no," I said, self-consciously putting my hand on my stomach.

"Planning on getting pregnant?"

"Not anytime soon."

Brian and I had talked about having kids, but we wanted to wait a bit and enjoy spending time together before adding on another person. Nonetheless, I wanted them at some point. And wasn't that illegal to ask, anyway?

"Good," he said, eyeing the wedding ring on my left hand. "You young women always seem to do that right after you get hired."

As I tried to think of a response, Dr. Peters held up an index finger and turned to bark an order at a terrified staff member, who skittered by him like a nervous hamster in a plastic ball as he told her to mop up the treatment room. He sighed and turned back to me, fixing me with a sharp eye.

"Mid-twenties. You're not one of those lazy Gen Xers, are you?"

"Not to my knowledge, Doctor."

"Good," he said. "I can't stand those clock watchers who whine if they don't get out by seven or eight." According to the sign on the door, the clinic closed at six. "You're here till you're done, right?"

"Right." As I watched the afternoon sun slant through the window and illuminate the dust motes dancing around the doctor's head, the office slowly transformed into a Dickensian warehouse in my head. I don't mind hard work at all, but it's been my observation that those who perceive the world to be full of sloths always seem to find evidence to support their assertions. I began to understand why Dr. Peters had been searching for an associate for so long.

On my way out, the receptionist fixed me with a frozen grin. "So nice to meet you!" she said through her rictus. Her eyes said something different: *Run*.

My second interview was at a facility run by a veterinarian in her mid-forties, a no-nonsense sort of person with a perfectly straight blond bob and long fingers that she constantly drummed on surfaces: desks, exam room tables, the wall as she walked by. Her associate had recently moved to another state and she was too busy to run the clinic alone. Dr. Brown quizzed me on some medical problems—thank goodness I knew the answers—put my résumé down, and asked me, "How many cystotomies have you done?"

"Oh, well, one," I replied, resting my sweaty palms on my lap. On a cadaver in school.

"Gastrotomies?"

"One." Same deal.

"GDVs?"

I paused. Gastric dilatation volvulus, the bane of dog owners' existence, often referred to as bloat, was a difficult and nasty condition I hadn't gotten to see at all in school. "None."

She licked her lips. "We're very busy here," she said. "I'm willing to take on a new grad, but you have to be the sort of person who's OK with being very self-directed."

"Oh, I am," I said, "very self-directed." That being said, having a little mentorship would certainly be appreciated.

"Good," she said, standing up. "I've got some records to catch up on. How about we make this a working interview? I have a blocked cat in the back—can you do a PU?"

A male cat who cannot urinate is an emergency. If he's lucky, a catheter can dislodge the obstruction and he can go about his life with no further problems. Often, though, the cat reblocks, and then we look to surgery. A perineal urethrostomy, or PU as it's abbreviated, is a procedure performed on male cats that, in essence, turns them into girl cats. It is not a minor undertaking.

I had never done one. "That," I said, "I cannot do just yet."

Instead, I shadowed her in an exam room and said enough correct things to be offered a job for Thursdays through Sundays, on call two nights a week. I might finally be living with my husband, but if I worked every weekend, I still would never get to see him.

Which was how I found myself winding the back roads above La Costa on my way to my third and final interview; I was meeting Isaac, the medical recruiter for a group of practices. "It's corporate medicine," my classmates had whispered the year prior. "They're bad. They make you practice cookie-cutter medicine. They take anyone. They're ruining the field." None of them had actually worked in one yet to make that judgment call, but the message was clear: You don't want to be one of Those Vets.

I decided the least I could do was go for the initial interview and decide for myself.

But first I had to get there. The San Diego County Fair was in full swing, and the freeway was crawling along at about five miles per hour. I had planned plenty of extra travel time and it still wasn't going to be enough to arrive on the dot. Obsessive dedication to punctuality was one of the last New Englander habits I retained, so this sent me into full-blown panic mode. I felt my hair melting into a sweaty helmet on my head as I rubbed my hands on my pants. One minute before the interview, I was still several miles away.

I pulled into the parking lot exactly ten minutes late, smoothing my hands over my lapels as I strode up to the front door.

"Hello," I said to the girl at the reception desk. "I'm Dr. Vogelsang. I have an interview here."

"Oh hey!" she smiled, a wide grin splitting her freckled face. "I'm Mary-Kate. I'll let Isaac know you're here. He's in the back with Dr. Joff."

"I am so, so sorry I'm late," I said when I was installed in an empty exam room opposite a smiling man in a gray suit. "I really underestimated fair traffic." He gave an understanding grimace and waved his hand dismissively.

"Don't even worry about it," he said, extending his hand. "Southern California traffic stinks." Dr. Isaac Rathbun was the medical director for the region, in charge of managing all the CareClinic veterinarians in the county. "And call me Isaac." He smiled, and I found myself taken aback at how genuinely friendly everyone I encountered had been so far. "We're just so pleased you are considering a career with CareClinic."

So far, so good. I exhaled.

He flipped through a leather binder of paperwork, handing me a pile of glossy brochures featuring young doctors in lab coats cradling a variety of happy-looking puppies and kittens. "Working at CareClinic: A Wise Choice!" proclaimed one. "Starting Your Career Off Right: The CareClinic Environment" announced another.

"So what is it you're looking for in a job?" Isaac asked, fixing me an intent, interested look under his bushy eyebrows.

"Well, the main thing as a new grad would be mentorship—"

"Agreed!" he proclaimed triumphantly. "We here at Care-Clinic feel the same way. New grads need guidance and leadership to get you off on the right foot. I think you will really like Dr. Joff—he's the head vet here—and he's very excited about showing young vets the ropes."

I looked around the pristine exam room, neatly decorated with posters declaring the value of the CareClinic experience. A small plastic heart model with heartworms boiling out of the aorta sat on a shelf, appearing to float in space like a thought bubble over Isaac's head, one filled with spaghetti.

"How much of your medicine is directed by company policy?" I asked. "Are vets allowed to treat pets in whatever manner they deem appropriate?"

Isaac nodded seriously. "We are very proud of our Care-Clinic protocols," he said. "We have a high standard of care that we expect our doctors to maintain. Here, let me show you."

He jumped up and started tapping on a computer on the wall. "Here's a cat in the clinic right now who's just been diagnosed with acute gastritis," he said. "Dr. Joff entered the diagnosis, and the software provides the list of recommended items to help him come up with a thorough treatment plan." Bloodwork. Radiographs. IV fluids. Antibiotics. If I'd flipped open my Nerdbook at that moment, it would have recommended the same things. Isaac hit the PRINT button and picked up the estimate that slid out of the printer underneath the countertop. He paused long enough to frown at a bit of fluff on the shelf, then popped back up. "See? You just check off what you want to order, and your nurse will do the rest. This allows you to focus on the important work. Treating pets."

"Will I be by myself in the clinic?" I asked, voicing one of my biggest fears.

"Not at first," he said. "You have a three-month probation-

84

ary period that is considered the formal mentorship period. Most vets find that sufficient to feel confident manning the clinic on their own after that."

"What about being on call after hours?"

Isaac recoiled. "We refer to an emergency clinic after hours. When you're off, you're off." Evil corporate overlords or not, the idea of working in CareClinic was pretty appealing so far. Isaac stood up. "Shall we meet the staff?"

I trotted behind him into the treatment area, where two spotless steel tables shone under the fluorescent light. Rows of gauze, alcohol, and ear cones were lined neatly up in the center of each table. At the first table, I saw a woman with a long gray braid holding a Chihuahua to her chest while a shorter woman trimmed its nails. The dog was not happy.

"That's Rachelle," Isaac said, gesturing to the woman holding the dog. She looked up and nodded, grimacing as the dog strained in her arms. "She's one of our technicians."

"And I'm Susan," said the woman holding the nail clippers. She smiled before blowing her shoulder-length black hair out of her face. "I'd shake your hand but we just expressed Gretel's anal glands."

"I understand," I said. "Thank you." The dog took advantage of the momentary distraction to turn around and grab Rachelle's scrubs with her teeth. "Now, now," said Rachelle as the dog shook her head back and forth like a thresher shark. "That isn't nice."

"We're very proud of the team here at this location," Isaac said. "They work very well together. It's a very supportive environment." Out of the corner of my eye I saw Susan look at Rachelle and grin.

Isaac eyeballed Susan and pressed his lips together before turning to the other corner of the room. "Dr. Joff? This is Dr. Vogelsang. We just had a great conversation about her working here."

At the second table, a trim man stood with his back to us, the overhead light bouncing off his bald head like a spotlight, like a rock star about to reveal himself to the crowd. He stood with his legs split in a V, lowering himself like a tripod until his head was at the same level as the fluffy white cat he was facing. The cat was resting against a solid-looking younger man, who was murmuring quietly to the cat as he held him still on the table. Dr. Joff quickly slid a needle into the cat's jugular vein and withdrew a syringeful of blood with a flourish, handing it to the male technician. He turned to me, peering at me sharply through his glasses. He paused to drop a dollop of hand sanitizer in his hands before striding over, rubbing his hands together as he crossed the room.

"Barry Joff," he said. "Good to meet ya."

"Jessica Vogelsang," I replied, extending my hand. "Likewise."

He wiped his hands on his short-sleeved plaid shirt, took my hand in a firm grip, and pumped it up and down precisely two times. "A good handshake is key, you know," he said. "Remember that."

"I will."

"Well, I'll leave you guys for a few minutes and let you check the place out," said Isaac, beaming.

Dr. Joff turned back to the male technician, grabbing a Sharpie from his khaki trousers to scribble something on a glass tube. The man was still holding the cat, keeping pressure on the neck where Dr. Joff had drawn the blood. "Manny, tell the owner we'll call her in an hour with an update when we get the bloodwork back." He nodded and handed the cat off to Rachelle.

The cat, having suddenly decided he was done with being held, scrambled up Rachelle's shoulder and tried to claw down the back of her shirt. She detached him gently and placed him in a treatment cage, slipping her fingers into a fanny pack she had around her waist and removing a pinch of green leaves, which she sprinkled on the towel in the cage before shutting the door.

Rachelle saw my quizzical look and said knowingly, "Catnip calms them down."

Dr. Joff looked at me appraisingly. "Dr. Vogley-snag. Voglesnig? What was it?"

"Vogelsang."

"Married name?"

"Yes."

"What's your maiden name? Maybe you should have kept it, ha ha."

"Marzec."

"Oh, that's not any better. Bummer. I'll just call you Dr. Jennifer."

"Jessica."

He sighed. "Dr. V, then. Where did you go to school?"

"UC Davis," I said.

"Oh, you're one of those," he said, waving his hand away as he rolled his eyes at Rachelle. "Well, life in the real world is different from the ivory tower of vet school." He patted his chest proudly. "We'll teach you real medicine here."

"I'm really happy for the opportunity," I said, trying to puzzle out what he meant by "one of those."

"So do you want the tour?"

"Absolutely."

He gestured around the small room, spinning in place. "This is it, pretty much," he said. "This is the treatment area. We do everything here." Bright movable lights stood poised at the ready above both stainless-steel treatment tables. Manny was pointing a beam of light at a Poodle's leg like he was about to give it a thorough interrogation.

Cages lined the far wall, filled with wary cats and dogs surveying us with varying degrees of interest as they tried to ascertain whether we were friend or foe. Some of the feistier pets had a red card clipped to the cage: CAUTION. Rachelle was now busying herself by one such cage, hanging a towel over the front grate.

Dr. Joff saw me looking and put his hand on his hip. "Rachelle is our cat lady," he said. "She really likes cats. The crazier the better, right, Rachelle?"

"Not crazy," Rachelle admonished with a stern grimace. "Nervous. Poor Mitzi," she cooed, addressing a hissing cat behind the towel. "This is a stressful place for them, you know." She reached into her pocket and crumbled some more catnip into the front of the cage. "She needs a cardboard box to hide in." A minute later, she was rummaging through boxes of supplies to find an empty one.

Dr. Joff shrugged. "Radiology is in the corner over there—" He pointed to an X-ray table behind a jutting wall, where a row of heavy blue leaded aprons hung on hooks. "And this is the surgical suite." I followed him to the far side of the treatment area and looked into the brightly lit operating room, with two tables and anesthetic carts neatly lined up and tracheal tubes hanging on the wall, organized by size. From the number of surgical packs lined up, I guessed that he had a couple of spays to do.

"How many surgeries do you do a day?" I asked.

"Usually three, maybe five," he said. "Mostly spays and neuters. The techs—don't call 'em techs if Isaac's around, you have to call them nurses—do the dental cleanings and we do any extractions."

"Why do we have to call the techs nurses?"

"Someone thought it sounded better," he said, snorting.

We turned back into the treatment room. "Where's the office?" I asked.

He laughed. "You're looking at it. CareClinic rules. They don't want us hiding and goofing off." He pointed to two rolling stools. "We share those, because someone figured out the staff was more efficient standing up than sitting down. So every clinic has two regulation stools." He put his hand possessively on the one with slightly less stuffing poking out. "This one is mine."

"Do you have online access?"

"Just for email and the CareClinic website," he said. "You

don't need anything else." Right after the turn of the millennium, this was still acceptable, but barely. He popped open a can of Diet Coke and took a long swig. "So you think you're going to come to work here? I have a lot to teach you."

I swallowed. "I guess that's up to Isaac."

Dr. Joff waved carelessly. "He'll hire you. I can make up for whatever slack you create."

The next day, Isaac proved Dr. Joff correct with an offer letter $10,000 above the salary quoted by the angry solo practitioner who wanted me to remain childless, and with much more agreeable hours than the woman who was looking forward to having her own weekends off. I'd still have to work Saturdays, but this place was closed on Sunday. "It seems like a good enough clinic," I said to Brian. "And I really like that they have a formal mentorship program."

"Didn't everyone pooh-pooh CareClinic at school?" he asked. "Aren't you going to keep looking?"

"I liked them," I said. "They all seemed happy there. I think I should go for it."

And so it began.

One week later, I stood in front of the mirror, fiddling nervously with my outfit. Conservative camisole and sweater set, check. Machine-washable chinos, check. Sensible flats, check. I turned to Brian as he brushed his teeth. "Hair up or down?"

"Up," he said around a mouth full of toothpaste. He leaned over to spit. "It makes you look older."

I surveyed my appearance and decided I still looked like a kid in a vet costume. "How do I look?"

"Like you've been doing this forever," he lied. He leaned over and gave me a hug. "You'll be great."

I pulled into the parking lot and took a couple of deep breaths before entering the clinic. I hefted my backpack of necessary items over my shoulder: my Nerdbook, already well worn with notes and highlights from school; *Plumb's* book of drug dosages; *Emergency Medicine*; *Dermatology for Small Animals*; stethoscope; penlight; Altoids. Staggering slightly under the weight, I strode into the clinic.

"Hey!" beamed Mary-Kate, swinging her long brown hair over her shoulder. "We're glad you're here, Dr. Vo-Vogle-Vogligsnag." She pressed the intercom. "She's here, guys." She turned to me. "Go on into the back."

I turned the handle of the treatment room door and walked through a wall of streamers. The staff stood lined up beside the treatment table beside a vase of flowers. "Welcome!" beamed Susan, coming over and giving me a hug. "We're all so glad you're here."

I smiled back, taking in the people that, if all went well, I would be spending the next couple of years with. Susan, dark-haired and dimpled, rocking on her heels. Manny, grinning broadly. Rachelle picked up the vase and handed it to me. "I brought the flowers this morning," she said, looking down and realizing she had just dipped her gray braid in the water. What a sweet group.

"They're beautiful," I said sincerely. "Thank you all so much. I'm excited to be here."

"We can call you Dr. V, right?" asked Susan. "We kept messing it up."

"Sure." I was still getting used to my married name myself. In German, it translates to "birdsong," but in English it mostly stands for "hard to pronounce."

Towering over the rest of the assemblage was Manny, whom I had seen but not spoken with on my interview day. "I don't think we got to talk last week," I said. "Manny, right?"

"Yes, ma'am," he said, sticking his hand out. "I'm the one you call for all the big dogs."

Susan elbowed him. "Don't sell yourself short. You're our translator too." Manny grinned proudly. "*¿Sí, se habla español?*"

"*No, señor,*" I said regretfully.

"Good," he said approvingly. "Job security."

I liked this group even more. I put my backpack on the shelf, claiming my foot of counter space.

Susan spent the first hour with me in the storage closet that served as her office, going over paperwork. "We'll get you a name tag and your own lab coats in a week or so," she said. "I can also get you some official CareClinic scrubs." She gestured apologetically at her scrub top in the same garish print I saw everyone wearing at the interview. "Or not."

"Do they come in solid colors?" I asked.

"Soon, God willing," she said. "Dr. Joff refuses to wear them."

After I spent the morning fiddling with the ponderous CareClinic online record system, Susan asked me if I was ready to start seeing patients. "Might as well," I said. "Got any easy appointments to start me off while I figure out the computers?"

"How's a four-month puppy exam sound?"

"Great," I said.

"Hi, I'm Dr. Vogelsang," I said to the client in the exam room. A bouncing yellow Lab sat on her lap, nibbling her fingers. "Nice to meet you."

The client furrowed her brow and looked up at me. "Dr. What?"

"Jessica—Dr. V," I replied.

"Are you new?" she asked. Her eyes took in the HELLO MY NAME IS sticker Susan had dug out of the supply drawer for me. "I haven't seen you before. We've only seen Dr. Joff."

"I just started here," I told her, skimming over the fact that I just started, period. I leaned down and scratched the puppy behind the ears. His rear end wiggled appreciatively. "Ready for your last shot of the year, Dexter?"

Dexter took it like a champ, giving out the slightest of yelps that was quickly assuaged with a treat. He looked at his hip quizzically—how dare it pinch him like that—scratched the area with a hind leg, then gave me a kiss.

"Aw, he likes you," said his owner. "Just wait till he gets neutered."

The afternoon settled into the beginnings of a routine. When a pet arrived, Mary-Kate would get the pet's weight before putting him or her into an exam room. One of the technicians would go into the room, get a history and do a cursory exam, and then come in the back and give me the rundown. I'd do my exam on the pet, tell the client what I'd like to do, and have the technician present the estimate. Just like vet school.

For a newbie, this had many advantages. Having a technician go in before me gave me a hint of what I was dealing with, so I'd have a minute to get my thoughts together before walking into the exam room. Six-month-old retriever vomiting for a day? Probably ate something he shouldn't have. Sixteen-year-old cat vomiting for a year? Cancer, maybe kidney failure. Time to look things up.

I popped out of a room and looked on the counter where I had stashed my Nerdbook for quick reference. It wasn't there. How could I possibly manage? Before panic set in, Manny came around the corner, flipping through the pages and nodding. "You can get lung fungus?" he asked, impressed. I took back my red vinyl security blanket with a sigh of relief.

Dr. Joff swept by with a handful of syringes on his way into a roomful of kittens. He had lapped me two to one on appointments as I henpecked my way through the computer system, and when six o'clock rolled around, he threw his Members Only jacket over his shoulder and bid us adieu while I still had an hour left to go. "Time to pay your dues!" he cackled, and off he went.

My last appointment of the day was a pit bull with an ear infection. Slam dunk. Usually the hardest part was getting the dog to hold still enough for me to slide a cone deep into the ear canal and get a good peek. It was like spelunking—I never knew what surprises I might encounter, from ulcerated masses to grass awns to goobery pools of pus to a ruptured eardrum. If it looked like an uncomplicated infection, I'd swab some of the goop out of the ears. While the technician identified whether the problem was a bacteria, a yeast, or both, I would clean out the discharge and send the pet home with proper medications.

Susan came out of the exam room and handed me the chart with a slight grimace. "Earl definitely has an ear infection," she said. "His ears are super-smelly. It's been going on for a week, and the owner was cleaning them with vinegar."

"Is he a good dog?" I asked.

"He's great, just wiggly," she replied. "But Mr. Porter is in a crabby mood because he wanted to see Dr. Joff. I told him you were our new doctor and you were great, but he threw a little bit of a fit. Just thought I'd warn you."

I was prepared for resistance from clients who had gotten accustomed to seeing the same doctor for the last several years. But I was determined to win them over with my thoroughness, professionalism, and kindness to their pets. "I'll do my best," I said.

I straightened my lab coat and headed into the exam room. "Hi, Mr. Porter!" I said, sticking out my hand to the stone-faced man sitting on the bench with his arms crossed. He was about thirty, with spiky black hair, a goatee, and an old Def Leppard shirt. "I'm Dr. Vogelsang, and I just joined Dr. Joff here." His dog Earl came bounding over, leaving trails of slobber on my legs as he investigated.

"Where's Dr. Joff?" he asked. "I always see him. I'll wait."

"He's gone for the day," I said, wondering if I was supposed to fib and say he was "busy." Too late now.

Mr. Porter frowned. "Do you know what you're doing?"

In this case, yes. "I promise you, Mr. Porter," I said earnestly. "I know how to treat ear infections. And if I didn't, I'd tell you." He grunted.

I leaned down and scratched Earl's head. He plopped

down and groaned appreciatively, floppy ears wiggling. "Itchy, huh?" I flipped up his right ear and got a whiff of yeasty odor. "Well, that looks uncomfortable." I scooped out some of the rust-colored goo with a cotton swab and handed it to Susan, who took it into the back to examine it under the microscope.

Earl regarded me with his big brown eyes. His strong jawline gave him a rather serious demeanor, but his wagging butt was all play. He was as adorable as his owner was stony. I slid my otoscope into Earl's ear, noting the amount of inflammation, the absence of foreign bodies I would have to dig out with long alligator forceps. His foot pounded on the floor at the stimulus. "Sorry, kiddo," I said. "Just let me check the other ear."

"I tried cleaning his ears with vinegar and water," Mr. Porter said. "But it just keeps coming back."

"That can help with minor infections," I said, "but with something as severe as this you're going to need something stronger." Earl gamely let me check his other ear. Other than the infection, he was in good shape.

"I think we should clean his ears out here to get you a nice clean slate," I said, "and then we can send you home with some medicated drops. We'll have him better in no time."

"How much is this going to be?" Mr. Porter asked, resuming his arm cross.

"I'll have Susan get you the estimate," I said, leaning down once more to give Earl a pat for being so good just as he jumped up to give me an enthusiastic lick on my face. On the way back to the floor, his paws caught in my camisole, and I felt the gust of wind as the gravitational pull of his fifty-five-pound body brought it down. I'm pretty sure the shirt made it halfway down to my navel before I toppled over. We both fell on the floor in a heap, his paws still stuck in it.

I rolled onto my side, gently disentangled Earl from my bodice, and looked up in horror to see Mr. Porter sitting there expressionless.

"Well, Earl," I said while standing up, "that one was free but next time I have to charge you."

"OK," said Mr. Porter. "I mean... let me see the estimate."

I excused myself into the treatment area, feeling a flush creep up my cheeks. One day in and I'm already giving clients a peep show. Never let it be said I didn't go the extra mile.

"Are you OK?" Susan asked. "Was he mean to you? You look upset."

"Oh, I'm fine," I said, gulping some water. "Just give him the estimate."

He approved it all.

After he left with a bag of ear medications, flea preventives, and a bag of dental chews for good measure, Mary-Kate came into the back, shaking her head.

"What did you say to Mr. Porter?" she asked me.

"Huh?" I asked. "Nothing. Why?"

"Well, he was so mad when I said he'd be seeing you today that I was sure he was going to walk out. But when he left, I asked him how the appointment went and he said, 'The new chick's not bad.' He never likes anyone except Dr. Joff."

I collapsed onto a stool, mortified, and told them what had happened, hoping for sympathy. They all thought it was hysterical. Manny promised to bring his brothers in the next day. "Now we know how you win them over!" crowed Mary-Kate.

"This isn't my normal MO," I protested.

I walked in the front door at home right at seven, clutching my vase and balloon. "How was your first day?" asked Brian.

"I need to buy some button-down shirts," I told him.

CHAPTER 8

With Nerdbook in hand and Dr. Joff within shouting distance, I felt reasonably confident that I could muddle my way through most of the appointments that trotted through the door. I was much more intimidated by the row of dogs and cats who stared at me from the back wall of cages, mistrustful and hungry from being fasted all night. Those were the surgeries, and there was no Nerdbook for that—just you, a tray of metal tools, and your patient.

The two surgeries that are the bread and butter of most veterinary practices are the spay and the neuter. Sure, you get to pull socks out of stomachs and cut pendulous pink masses off legs as well, but from a day-to-day perspective, desexing dogs and cats is the main raison d'être of the veterinary OR.

A neuter is a relatively simple procedure, involving a small incision just above the scrotum through which the testicles are removed. You tie a couple of loops of suture around the mass of blood vessels, slip the stump back into your incision, and suture it shut. Done and done.

A spay, on the other hand, is a more complicated procedure that involves cutting into the abdominal cavity. Unlike people, dogs and cats have long, Y-shaped uteri that run the length of the abdomen from the ovaries (which are way up behind the kidneys) down to the cervix (which sits below the bladder). In order to remove both ovaries and uterus, you first need to feel your way up to the ovary, pushing aside the spleen, and tug at the ligament that holds it to the body wall until it tears just enough for you to pull it from the abdomen but not so much that you rip through the blood vessels feeding it. Those you need to tie suture around. You don't see the ovary while you're tugging on it, so you need to trust in your fingers that they have indeed found the right organ. Even when you get the hang of it, the process can be a little scary.

And bloody. While small puppies can be spayed with relative ease, spaying an obese Mastiff who's had five litters of puppies can look like the set of a horror movie. The blood vessels are embedded in layers of slippery fat, making it difficult to know whether you've tied the stump off securely enough until after you've cut it loose. If you haven't, all you get is one fleeting glimpse of a pulsating mass slipping back into the deep recesses of the abdomen before it disappears from sight entirely, oozing away from your slick, grasping fingers. You are allowed three seconds or so to curse before informing your technician that your routine spay is now an abdominal exploratory surgery.

It was during just such an event in vet school that my classmate, a jumpy man who already had stress management issues, passed out right over the body of the dog he was trying to spay. He avoided a face plant into the exposed abdomen only when a quick-thinking classmate body-checked him onto the floor instead, pulling the sterile tray of instruments down on top of him with a bang. It was the only time I've ever seen a person thank someone else for almost giving them a concussion. I believe he ended up going into radiology.

The more experienced and/or long-fingered veterinarians have their spays down to a science, managing to pull that entire long mass out of the body through miniature incisions an inch long. Diving through their opening with a curved spay hook like ice fishermen, they quickly nab the uterus and slide it out like a magician's handkerchief.

It took me a long time to get the hang of the spay hook, at first pulling out loop after loop of intestine without nabbing the uterus. It felt like one of those claw games at the carnival where you think you're so very close to your prize, only to have it slide away and leave you empty-handed again and again. In the beginning, it was faster and easier for me to simply make a bigger incision and find the uterus with my eyes. Our surgery instructor agreed. "Make the incision as large as you need to get good visualization. It won't heal any slower." This was true even if it meant a six-inch incision, as it usually did for the students.

On my third day of work, Dr. Joff decided it was time to have me perform my first spay. The patient I was assigned was Reeta, a small, nervous Bichon owned by a small, nervous woman. "Have you done many of these?" Mrs. Hayworth asked, since of course Dr. Joff had already made a habit of bragging to clients that he was mentoring a new graduate. She fidgeted with her blazer.

"Oh yes," I said. That seemed suitably vague, as long as you went with a generous definition of *many*.

When the CareClinic building was originally constructed, someone had the brilliant idea of putting a window in the door leading from the waiting area to the treatment room, through which a determined client could walk up and peer into our inner workings. This didn't work out very well for the clients or the staff. Not that we were embarrassed or trying to hide what we were doing, but it's not always pleasant to see a dog with a needle in her abdomen getting a cystocentesis, or a yowling cat stretched out on her side for a blood draw. It makes it hard to concentrate on your job when you're worried about how a stranger will interpret your restraint techniques, which, no matter how humane, might not always look that way.

Most of the time Susan worked around this problem by taping a bandanna to the window, thus cutting off the view, but she had removed it to clean the pane and hadn't yet replaced it. I realized this shortly after placing Reeta's catheter and starting to administer the injection of anesthestic induction, when a muffled gasp emanated from the far side of the window. I looked up and saw Mrs. Hayworth's face pressed to the pane, her breath fogging the glass, wide-eyed in her panic.

I heard Mary-Kate's voice from the other side of the door: "Can I help you?"

"Oh, she's just . . . Reeta just passed out. I got worried."

"Yes, Mrs. Hayworth, she does need to be put to sleep for the surgery."

"Put to sleep?"

"Not that kind of putting to sleep—I mean—just making her sleepy," Mary-Kate said reassuringly. "Please come away from the window, Mrs. Hayworth, you're just stressing yourself out. Right this way. Want a glass of water?" Their footsteps got fainter as Mary-Kate directed her charge back to the lobby.

Susan strode over to the window, muttering under her breath, and taped the bandanna back in place.

Ten minutes later, after we finished intubating, clipping, and prepping Reeta's skin, and putting on the surgical drapes, the intercom buzzed. "Mrs. Hayworth wants to know how Reeta is doing," she said.

"She's fine," said Rachelle. "We're just starting."

I heard a faint shout in the background. "Just starting?"

"Mary-Kate, tell Mrs. Hayworth that Reeta is doing just great and I will send Rachelle with an update as soon as we're done," I said. "Rachelle, please turn off the intercom."

Reeta's spay was uneventful. She came out of it with a two-inch incision, which was pretty good for me at the time. I closed the incision in three layers, finishing with the skin itself, with a neat row of X-shaped sutures. They were regulation UC Davis protocol, evenly spaced simple cruciates, with just the right amount of tension on the sutures. Very proud of my precision work, I dabbed her skin with gauze, poured a little peroxide to remove the blobs of blood from her pristine white fur, and handed her off to Rachelle for recovery while I snapped off my gloves.

I pulled my mask down under my chin and sat down to do my surgical notes after letting Mary-Kate know that all was fine. Thank goodness.

"Geez, Dr. V," said Dr. Joff, peering into the OR as Susan cleaned up. "Could you waste any more suture?"

"Huh? I only used two packs," I said.

"For a dog that's only ten pounds? One pack, max," he said. "The guy I used to work for used to charge me if I wasted any." He eyed my table meaningfully, catching the long tails of suture hanging off the needle.

"Well, I'd rather use too much suture than not enough and have a stump bleeding," I said. "I'll work on it."

He grunted.

"Can I watch you do a spay and see how you do it?" I asked. "To see your efficient techniques, I mean."

He rubbed his bald head. "Yes. That's a good idea."

Later that day, I watched him fly through a cat spay, tying each ovary and the uterus off with one solid loop of suture. "Aren't you worried about only having one ligature on each stump?" I asked. "We were taught to always place two."

"No."

"Ever drop a bleeding stump?"

"Yep. But it's not hard to find them." His hands were quick and efficient, muscle memory kicking in where I'd been stopping to think about every next step.

Instead of placing X-shaped sutures outside the skin, he

used ones under its surface that zipped the skin closed with nothing visible on the outside. "It looks better this way," he said.

"But isn't that more suture inside that the body has to deal with?" I asked.

He laughed and reminded me how many packs of suture I used compared with him. "When you're in school they teach you five levels of redundancy," he said. "I used half the amount you did. When you practice and become more efficient you'll see what I mean.

"In the meantime you have to convince these people you know what you're doing. All a client knows is what they see," he said, shaking a scalpel at me. "They have no idea what you did inside the dog. Your incision is all they judge you on. If it looks good, you did good."

Two hours later, Rachelle took Reeta out to the lobby, where Mrs. Hayworth had been camped out all day, to go home. Mrs. Hayworth shrieked.

"My dog looks like Frankenstein!" she sobbed. "What did you *do* to her?"

I ran out, Dr. Joff trailing on my heels, cackling.

"Is something wrong?" I asked. "Reeta did great."

"Yes, there's something wrong," she said. "You butchered my dog."

"I'm not sure what the problem—"

"My friend had her dog spayed and the incision was only this big." She held her fingers out a centimeter apart.

"Well, every surgeon has a different technique—"

"And it was a bikini line incision!"

That pulled me up short. "Bikini line? Are you sure?" While a human uterus can be accessed through a low horizontal cut, dog anatomy is very different and the opening is made much higher on the abdomen, closer to the belly button.

"Are you calling me a liar?"

"No, Mrs. Hayworth, that's just not something I've ever heard of," I said. "This was a standard spay procedure. We have to make a vertical incision higher up because of the way the uterus is shaped."

She was rubbing her face in Reeta's fur. "I'm so sorry baby, I never should have let the new person touch you." I glared at Dr. Joff, who refused to look at me. Mrs. Hayworth narrowed her eyes and turned to him. "You said she'd do fine!"

"She did do fine."

"She's got these huge Frankenstein stitches!"

"They'll be out in ten days."

She cradled Reeta on her back like an infant, exposing her belly with its little neat line of X's. "Really. You're OK with this?"

He shrugged. "Surgery went well. You won't even see the scar when the fur grows back."

Mrs. Hayworth slung her purse over her shoulder and walked out, refusing Mary-Kate's offer to help her to the car. "You've all helped enough," she grumbled.

"Thanks for your...backup," I said to Dr. Joff. "Couldn't you at least have told her you don't do bikini line incisions either?"

He rubbed his chin. "That's a new one for me, too." He

poked his finger at the door. "You see? That is why you do intradermal sutures. You'll figure it out soon enough, newbie."

Chuckling, he went into the back. I felt my eyelid twitching. Nonetheless, I started using his technique instead of the one I'd learned the year prior, and that was the end of the Frankendog complaints.

CHAPTER 9

Two months in, my work was finally beginning to feel routine. Dr. Joff had recently stopped calling the office hourly on his days off to make sure I didn't kill any of his patients, and I was even starting to accumulate a few clients of my own. My inherited clientele were often the elderly people; I always took the time to sit down and chat with them for a few minutes instead of jumping right into the exam, and they in turn were patient with me while I took my time working through a diagnosis.

But aside from the reprieve of the occasional low-stress visit from a favorite client, I still had plenty to learn. Having focused so heavily on dogs and cats in school, I broke out in a cold sweat when faced with any species outside that narrow confine. A few weeks into our respective careers, a classmate had emailed me a horror story about a parakeet whose beak fell off when they were attempting to treat him, and from that day I decided, "No birds." The staff already knew to send any bird appointment requests off to the exotics clinic, along with lizards, snakes, and tarantulas.

But hamsters, guinea pigs, and rats—affectionately known as pocket pets—came in quite a bit, and those were fun to work with, once I got the hang of things. Guinea pigs were sweet and easily frightened; you had to treat them like tiny, terrified glass ornaments to avoid injury. Hamsters were fighters, at least the ones I always saw, and I learned very quickly that if you didn't carefully collect the vast quantities of skin around their scruff before picking them up, they could turn a full 180 degrees and sink their teeth into the fleshy part of your thumb. And rats, contrary to what many people think, were affectionate, good with kids, and surprisingly sturdy. On the rare occasion we needed to anesthetize one of those little guys, we'd putter around the hospital constructing miniature anesthesia masks out of syringe cases. It was fun.

Ferrets, however, were another story.

Ferrets were an enigma to me, a sort of mischievous weasel-like creature I had heard of but never seen in person. The California Department of Fish and Game has long declared it illegal to keep them as pets. (Along with sugar gliders, hedgehogs, and gerbils.) As the official veterinary school in California, the curriculum department at Davis decided that "they're illegal" was good enough reason to skip teaching those species in the general ed curriculum, which was all well and good except for the inconvenient fact that many people owned these contraband pets anyway.

Fortunately veterinarians are under no obligation to report them to the state as if they were common criminals, should one present for veterinary care. As purveyors of health and not law enforcement agents, most veterinarians don't have any interest in reporting ferret ownership at the cost of the pet not receiving care, so on the rare occasion that one would be brought into the clinic we would enter him or her in the computer and do whatever we had to do.

Since the system did not allow for "ferret" as a species entry and the program would freeze if you tried to leave it blank, the staff's workaround was to just enter the closest thing we had: "cat." That was fine, as long as they remembered to tell you that the patient was actually a ferret in witness protection, but that didn't always happen.

This is how I found myself staring in surprise at the unblinking red eyes of the skinniest white cat I had ever seen while Manny said, "Oh yeah, Iggy's a ferret. Sorry."

"They said you saw ferrets here," said Iggy's owner dubiously. "All he needs is a rabies vaccine."

"Sure thing," I said, eyeing Iggy with distrust. He was perfectly cylindrical, oozing through my fingers every time I tried to hold him still so I could listen to his heart. "Do you have any health concerns?"

"No," said the owner. "He does disappear into the wall a couple times a week, but he always comes back. I don't really know where he goes."

"Huh," I said. I regarded Iggy for another moment before deciding to skip the temperature taking. "I'll go get the vaccine."

Manny dutifully followed me into the treatment area, where I was flipping through all the clinic protocols to try and figure out exactly where I was supposed to stick Iggy with the needle for the vaccine.

"That's a sketchy-looking weasel," Manny said. "I don't trust him. Plus he smells like my old man. Musty."

I shrugged and took the vaccine back into the room. "Ferrets do that, I think. Just hold him the best you can."

"Do you see a lot of ferrets?" Iggy's owner asked as Manny tried to hold our slippery patient by the shoulders and then the pelvis. His torso was so long he just twisted it back and forth, alligator rolling between Manny's palms.

"Not really," he replied. Our window to get this done was closing rapidly, so I figured I better just go for it before Iggy escaped entirely.

I uncapped the needle, lifted a little piece of skin to give the needle a place to slide, and popped in the vaccine. As expected, Iggy protested mightily. As I withdrew the needle, he broke free of Manny's grasp and in a split second sank his oversize yellowing canines right into the webbing between my thumb and index finger.

"Augh!" I screamed, yanking my hand back. Because Iggy had yet to let go, he came right along with it, pausing to give my hand one more good chomp for good measure before letting go and dropping onto the floor.

"Oh great," Iggy's owner said as we watched his little white butt disappearing into the small cutout in the cabinet that the computer wires passed through.

Pressing a paper towel to my bleeding hand, I watched Manny try to squeeze into the computer cabinet to extract Iggy, eventually flushing him out by shooting him with cold air from one of those canisters we used to clean dust out of the keyboard. Out he ran, clambering up his owner's leg and allowing her to put him back into a little harness.

"He had a *harness*?" I asked Manny when we got out of the room. "Why'd she take it off in the first place?"

"I have no idea," he said. "Maybe she wanted to test us or something?"

Regardless of her reasoning, we never saw Iggy again. I was OK with that.

The rest of the afternoon proceeded without incident. All that was left was a Collie with a flea allergy and one patient who was waiting to be discharged after surgery. Rachelle called for me as I was about to head into my last room of the night. "Dr. V, Chloe's owners are here to pick her up, but her incision is still oozing."

I went over to the table where Chloe, a sedate Basset with velvety, pendulous ears, was wagging her tail. A small amount of blood was pooled on the floor. I walked over and gently moved her onto her back.

I dabbed at her incision. Blood was bubbling up through the sutures. "Was she moving around a lot in her cage?"

"No, she was sleeping most of the afternoon."

Blood and surgery go hand in hand. Even when you have performed the procedure perfectly, the blood vessels you've sliced through on the way to your destination are going to protest. With time and rest, the clotting mechanisms kick in and all is well. The trick, when you're just getting started, is figuring out what is normal and what is a potential problem. A seemingly tiny little vessel can pump out horrifying amounts of blood in a short time if you haven't properly closed it off, and for whatever reason "it seemed OK at the time" is generally not an explanation owners care for if things go south once they get home.

I prodded Chloe's abdomen. It didn't feel distended. I checked her gums. Nice and pink. Dr. Joff continued to roll his eyes at the amount of suture I used attacking every pedicle and stump like a mortal enemy to be obliterated, but I'd still rather be the slow wasteful surgeon than the one who let a pet bleed out. Chloe seemed fine, but I hadn't seen enough cases of dogs who *weren't* fine to know what that really meant.

I scrubbed a patch of skin on her stomach and did a quick check for internal bleeding, sliding a needle into her belly and pulling the plunger back. Nothing. I frowned. There was nothing to indicate that she was having a complication, nothing that gave me trouble during the surgery earlier that day. I had tied all the vessels off with my usual overzealous attention to tightness, but who was to say she hadn't slipped a ligature?

I sighed. It's times like these that I really wished there was at least one more veterinarian around to run things by. Dr. Joff left promptly at six, as had been his custom since my second day of work, departing with a chipper "Hope there's no broken legs! Har har!" before slipping out the door. I called Isaac to see what he thought of Chloe, and after listening to my explanation he said, "I think she's fine, but offer the owner the option of having her stay at the ER for observation."

The last client in Room 3 was still waiting to be seen. I popped my head into the lobby and explained to Chloe's owner that she was bleeding a little more than I would like, and even though I wasn't particularly concerned, it might be best if she went to the ER overnight for observation, just to be safe.

"Is she all right?" asked Mrs. Langston, eyes wide with worry.

"Yes," I said, internally wincing. "They'll be able to keep her quiet and watch to make sure everything's fine."

"OK," she said. "Can you write down the address?"

I ducked back into the treatment area where Chloe and Rachelle were waiting. Drops of blood hung off Chloe's abdomen, plopping onto the floor and splashing little red splatters onto her inner thighs. That just looked bad.

"Can you clean her up and get a belly bandage on her?" I asked Rachelle. "I still need to finish in Room 3." Rachelle nodded. "Then send her off to the ER. I'll let them know she's on her way."

I went home and fretted about Chloe until about eleven p.m. before breaking down and calling the ER to check on her. The doctor came on the phone.

"Hey Dr. Vogelsang, it's Dr. Troy," said the male voice on the other end in clipped tones. "Chloe's doing fine."

"Oh, good," I exhaled. "I haven't seen a dog ooze like that before and it just freaked me out a little."

"Well, we ran a quick clotting time on her just to be safe," he said. "She's got a real oozy incision but everything else looks good. It happens. Usually if you put a good belly bandage on them and check them in the morning you can save the owner the ER bill."

"OK," I said, "I just figured better safe than sorry."

"Yes, well, her owner was a little freaked out by the time

she got here so even though I said she could go home, she wanted to leave Chloe here overnight. Which is fine, that's why we're here."

"Thanks, Dr. Troy. I appreciate it."

"Dr. Vogelsang—I don't think we've talked before," said Dr. Troy. "Are you new?"

"Yes."

"New grad?"

"Yes."

Dr. Troy grunted and mumbled to himself, "Every September." He cleared his throat. "Good to meet you. Come over and tour our place sometime. We're always happy to meet our referring vets." Pause. "You work with Dr. Joff, right?"

"Yes."

In the background, I heard a female voice chuckling. Dr. Troy cleared his throat. "You call me if you ever need advice on something, OK?"

"Thanks, Dr. Troy. I might take you up on that."

"Please do." More chuckling, cut off by a hiss. "Thanks for the referral, Dr. Vogelsang. We're taking good care of Chloe. You take care now."

Assured Chloe was going to be all right, I headed to bed, but I still couldn't fall asleep. If things are this stressful when the pet's fine, I wondered, how am I going to handle it when they aren't?

CHAPTER 10

On Dr. Joff's days off, I was sometimes joined by Dr. Garcia, a relief veterinarian. A graduate of UNAM, the veterinary school in Mexico, he had recently completed the process to get a license in California. He had bided his time during the long bureaucratic process working as an exceptionally well-qualified technician in various clinics, and now that he held his license he was splitting his time between several locations while he decided where he wanted to settle.

On the first day I met Dr. Garcia, I found him in the back hallway filling a mop bucket. "Do you want me to bring that out to Rachelle?" I asked, extending my hand.

"No, she's busy running bloodwork," he said, drying his hands off on his blue scrubs before rolling the bucket out into the treatment room and attacking the smelly mess deposited on the floor by a dog with an anal gland impaction. I trailed behind him, wondering when was the last time I had seen a vet with a mop in his hands.

"We all help with what needs to be done, right?" he said, winking at Rachelle, who was perched in front of a microscope. She tilted her chin into her shoulder and smiled.

When he had an interesting case, Dr. Garcia would bring

the pet into the back and find me. "Look at this acute uveitis," he'd say, holding the cat on the table and handing me an oph- thalmoscope. The little black cat blinked up at me, squinting her left eye. Dr. Garcia bunched up his bushy eyebrows and looked at the cat in concern. "She's five months old."

"Are you running a FIP titer?" I asked. Feline infectious peritonitis is among the most dreaded viral diseases in cats, one for which there is no cure.

"That's a good idea. What else would you suggest?"

Dr. Garcia was everything I had wished for in a mentor. I watched him explain a diabetes diagnosis to an elderly owner, sitting down next to her on the bench in the lobby and writ- ing down information with one hand while handing her a tissue with the other. The sound of crying children would lure him out to the source, where he'd lop fifteen minutes off his lunch break to blow up gloves into little animal balloons or let a toddler listen with rapt amazement to the sound of their own heart. Like a fairy vetfather, he glided in to pick my dejected butt off the floor when I found myself having a crisis of confidence and transform me with a swoop of his slightly cologned hand into someone who might actually have an idea of what they were doing.

"I really appreciate your help, Dr. Garcia," I said at the end of our first morning working together.

"Call me Luis," he smiled. "Please don't hesitate to ask me any questions." The opportunity presented itself sooner than either of us anticipated.

One hour into the afternoon, Mary-Kate came running full speed into the back with a tiny kitten meowing in her arms. "A delivery man ran over him in the parking lot next door!" she cried, handing him to me.

"Pull up some buprenorphine," I said to Susan as I gently placed the kitten on a towel. "Who brought him in?"

"The driver did," Mary-Kate responded. "There's a family of stray cats that live over there. The driver's really upset."

It was easy to ascertain that the kitten had a badly broken leg. It was very likely he had other internal injuries as well. Dr. Garcia came over while I was talking to Susan.

"The store manager said he'd pay for us to take an X-ray," I told Dr. Garcia. "How much can we do?"

"This is a stray?" he asked.

"Yes," said Mary-Kate. "So can we take the X-ray? The driver says he has $100 too."

Dr. Garcia hesitated. "You could," he said, "take the X-ray." He turned to me. "Neurologic function?"

I pinched the kitten's toes to see if he could pull the leg back, one of the reflexes we use to determine spinal cord injury. It didn't budge. I looked at Dr. Garcia, who was gently, with his fingertips, doing an exam.

"He likely has a shattered pelvis," he said, facing Mary-Kate but directing his words to me. "We could spend several hundred dollars to determine this, and ask who wants to take over the $1,000 bill to see if maybe a surgeon can put his pelvis back together. This is assuming he doesn't have other internal injuries or a broken back, which he probably does." He rubbed the kitten's chin. The kitten, breathing heavily, didn't respond.

"He is a stray, so you could ask Animal Control to take

over. When they return your call in a few hours, during which this kitty will be in a cage and in pain, they will tell us to euthanize him." He held the earpieces of his stethoscope out to me, holding the bell over the part of the chest he wanted me to hear. The lungs were rattling. "If he were an owned cat, I would recommend the same thing."

"So we don't try to save him?" asked Mary-Kate, wiping her eyes.

"We cannot save his life," said Dr. Garcia. "But we can save him from suffering." He met my eyes. "I leave the final decision to you, Doctor."

One of the most dreaded moments in a new graduate's career is their first euthanasia. Up to this point, we've been observers, or helpers, but in school the final decision had always belonged to someone else higher up the totem pole. There is something vast and terrible about being the one to make the call and then push the plunger on an injection that is taking the life of another living thing. It's not a task anyone takes lightly, but it's some consolation that we are helping families say good-bye to a terminally ill pet in the gentlest way possible.

In those cases, at least we have the benefit of an owner to help us make that call, but in this case there was no one. It was just the kitten, who had barely had a chance to start his life, and me.

"I'm not ready to kill him," I said to Dr. Garcia.

Dr. Garcia frowned and put his hands down on the table across from me. "You are not killing him. This accident killed him. You must always remember that." He was right, but it was still one of the hardest things I've ever had to do.

My time in the clinic was gradually getting me accustomed to the concept of death, but I had yet to experience it in my own family circle. I can't explain why I felt so shocked when I finally got the call from my mother about Taffy: She was sixteen, after all. Half blind and mostly sedentary, Taffy had spent the majority of her retirement years sleeping on whatever soft surface had the greatest access to sunlight angling in through the windows.

Age had mellowed her considerably, a fact my father was pleased with until a team of burglars broke in during broad daylight one weekday and cleaned the place out. By that point, Taffy had become a Zen master of complacency, choosing to rest on her well-deserved reputation as a man-eater rather than actually do anything to reinforce it. She observed the criminals remove electronics, jewelry, and even a safe from the bedroom with a disinterested scowl, watching only, I imagine, to make sure they left the Milk-Bones behind.

"You have a dog?" the policeman had asked incredulously. "Never seen a place get hit so bad with a dog in it."

As far as we knew, she was in decent health for a pet so elderly, until one day she wasn't. Mom had taken her in to our longtime family vet to get a cough checked out, thinking it was something simple like a touch of kennel cough. The vet, suspecting something else, took an X-ray and determined she was in advanced heart failure. By the time my mother called to tell me the news, Taffy was already gone. I drove up to my parents' house later that afternoon.

"I'm sorry," she said in response to my accusatory stare.

"Why didn't you tell me before you put her to sleep?" I said, hurt.

She sighed. "I had to do it. Right then, when they told me the diagnosis. They asked if I wanted a minute to think about it, but I said no, just get it over with. I didn't think I should drive after that, so I walked home."

I put my hand to my mouth. "How could you do that?" I asked, devastated. "Didn't you even want to talk to me? Ask my opinion?" Or, I silently added, let me be there with her? My mind started running through all the what-ifs: We could have done an ultrasound. Diuretics. Pimobendan. We could have held it off, at least for a little bit. I felt so many things at that moment: Why didn't she trust me enough to ask my opinion? Why didn't I go spend more time with Taffy once I moved back to San Diego? Why didn't she try harder to keep her alive? I was so overwhelmed with grief and guilt and anger I couldn't figure out where one emotion ended and the other one began, so I just sat there with Taffy's collar in my hands and tears on my cheeks.

"If I waited," she said, "if I had talked to you, or your father, I would never have been able to go through with it. I would have taken her home and never gone back and she would have drowned in her own lungs. I couldn't let her suffer like that."

I thought of Mom, my sweet and loving mother, with her big purse and her ever-present sun visor, sitting in the lobby with a book waiting for the X-rays to come back. As a nurse, she would have known it was bad the second she saw the X-ray with the grapefruit-size heart.

Dog the First: TAFFY

I had been so upset that my mother didn't consult me, so focused on my own ownership of the dog that it didn't occur to me to think about how hard this had been for her. She was the woman who had taken care of Taffy day after day, long after I left for college, taking only memories. She cleaned her bed, tolerated her puddles and eyeball surgeries, and loved her even when she was bald, toothless, one-eyed, and useless against criminal elements.

"It was the right thing to do," Mom said. "But I had to do it right then. I only had a minute of strength in me." I looked at the way her brow furrowed as she relived the experience, her jaw set. My mother, having seen so many people linger and wither away in her time as a nurse, couldn't bring herself to go through the same with our dog. It's very easy to say, *Why didn't you do x/y/z?* when you're not the one who actually has to do all of it: Give a sick pet a pill three times a day and clean up their matted fur and help them outside to the bathroom while they slowly worsen despite your best efforts. I am pretty sure that when she was sitting in the exam room making that painful decision, the last thing on her mind was whether I would be offended I wasn't allowed a chance to offer a second opinion.

It had nothing to do with me. I wasn't angry after that.

As that feeling dissipated, I discovered grief hiding just beneath it. I'd made it all the way to adulthood without ever having to experience a death; it was the very first time I had lost someone I was close to, and I didn't know how to handle it. I told myself, Well, she was old, so it's fine. I'm fine. For a day or so, I actually believed that. Then reality set in. One minute I would be protesting that I was well, the next I'd dissolve into a puddle of tears walking through the grocery store when I spotted a box of Meaty Bones out of the corner of my eye. My husband stood there with a box of Cheerios in his hand as I wept next to the croissants in the bakery department. He was perplexed at the depth of my mourning.

"I'm not sure what to do about this," Brian said to me one night as I stared at the wall after finding Taffy's Christmas ornaments while we decorated the house. It was a month after her death, and I had allowed Bing Crosby to croon me away from my worries and start to pull me back to a smile here and there—until I found that Taffy ornament I had forgotten about. Brian, like most people, had a hard time understanding just how brutal this felt to someone like me. She was just a dog, I could tell he was thinking. You haven't even lived with her in years.

In vet school, I had spent several evenings a month volunteering for the Pet Loss Support Hotline. Most of the people who called were experiencing a perfectly normal state of grief, but had no one to talk to about it. After a day or two following a pet's passing, bringing up their sadness to friends and family would be met with ambivalence or even guilt for not "getting over it" quickly enough. They just needed someone to listen. I learned from that experience how isolating pet loss can feel. Now it was my turn.

I looked at the little ornament in my hand, a plastic picture frame with a yellowing photo of Taffy looking apprehensively at the camera. Dad had probably caught her pooping on the carpet just before snapping it. Under the photo was printed: BEST FRIENDS 1988. The year of Mouth Breather Dan and the skateboard face-plant. Despite myself, I smiled at the memory and planted a little fingertip kiss on the photo.

"There's nothing to do," I said to Brian, hanging the ornament on a low branch. "I just have to wade through it, I think. Did I ever tell you about Mouth Breather Dan?"

Dog the Second: EMMETT

"Guess what?" Kevin asked the assorted group of us who slouched on his leather couch eating pizza and reviewing the upcoming Comic-Con catalog. We all looked up expectantly. There was no point in guessing, with him. Maybe it would be, *I'm going to officiate a wedding on a Starship* Enterprise *replica next weekend*. Or, *I'm taking my roommate to Hawaii to see the submarine his father served on in World War II*. His daily agenda read like a magnanimous bucket list of everyone else's wishes or desires; it had no cohesion or common theme except for the idea of making someone else happy.

Kevin had an addiction to taking care of others, no strings attached. With no pets of his own and marriage still a faraway concept, he adopted the world. The week before, his phone had rung at midnight. It was an ex-girlfriend.

"I ran out of gas," she said. "And my daughter and I are kind of lost."

"Where are you?"

Long pause. "Tijuana."

"I'm in LA, Karen. I can't help you." Once she started crying, he said, "Hang on," and proceeded to coordinate a rescue endeavor with one friend who moonlighted as a chauffeur and a third friend who rode shotgun to try to find her car somewhere on Avenida Revolución. They drove around for two hours, dodging drunk nineteen-year-old kids and assault-rifle-toting federales until they spotted Karen in an alley, hunched up with her kid in the front of her SUV. Kevin didn't ask how she managed to get down there, or why she was there. He just fixed it.

With this recent rescue fresh in our minds, no one had a good guess as to what he might have up his sleeve today.

"You're going to Antarctica," one suggested.

"You met Axl Rose in the bathroom at Denny's," ventured another.

Kevin waved his hands dismissively. "Jessica. You're gonna love this one." I looked at him apprehensively.

He tapped his steepled his fingers together and cackled. "I got my parents a dog!" Kevin was exceptionally close to his parents, Betty and Ron. Since he was an only child, I guess he felt the need to give them something else to dote on once he had moved out of the house.

"What kind of dog?" asked Kevin's roommate Paul, leaning back and folding his arms behind his head.

Kevin's grin widened, splitting his face in half. "A Jack Russell puppy!"

We all groaned.

"What?" he asked. "My parents love watching *Frasier.* They're going to name him Niles."

"Your parents are almost retired," Paul reminded him. "Have you ever met a Jack Russell? They're nuts!"

Kevin waved his hand dismissively. "Meeeeeeaaaah. They'll be fine."

They were both correct, as it turned out. As Paul predicted, Niles was a terrible match for Betty and Ron, tearing up the furniture, terrorizing the neighborhood children, and quickly asserting himself as the king of the household.

But as Kevin predicted, Ron also fell in love with little Niles, psychoses and all, and soon they were inseparable. It was Ron who diligently administered Niles's twice-daily insulin shots when he developed diabetes, who made sure he never missed a walk to help keep his weight in check. When Ron began showing the early signs of Alzheimer's disease, his routine with Niles was the one task he could remember to focus on, long after many other memories had disappeared behind the veil of disease. Some of us just thrive best when we are working in service of others.

CHAPTER 11

With Taffy gone, my one link to the dog-owning population I now served was severed, and every day that disconnect bothered me a little more. I'd been pestering Brian about adopting a dog, but we hadn't gotten around to doing it. "In a few months," he had said. That was last year. In the meantime I contented myself with my little black cat Apollo, a love bug who would fetch balls and knead on my chest until he started drooling in happiness. I loved him to pieces, but I still longed for a big goofy dog I could wrestle with and take for a run. I would just have to make do with getting my dog fix via my clientele until I could get Brian to come around.

"I'm giving you Room 1," said Susan one morning, dropping the chart on the counter with a bang. "It's a Golden Retriever."

I grinned. What a perfect start to my Wednesday. Nothing made my day better than getting kisses from a Golden. There was something about their happy faces, their long, soft fur, and their willingness to get right in there and nuzzle whatever their nose happened to touch that I found irresistible.

Susan grimaced. "This poor dog. Emmett has a flea allergy, but the owner refuses to buy Advantage. He comes in every couple of months with a nasty skin infection and gets a flea bath. He's a mess."

I cocked my head. "Doesn't a bad pyoderma a few times a year end up costing more than Advantage?"

Susan shrugged. "Welcome to vet med." Well, at least I could make the dog feel better for now. I squared my shoulders and went into the room.

On the floor, a big rust-colored mop blinked up at me with huge chocolate-brown eyes. He rested his head on his front paws and raised his eyebrows at me, left-right-left.

"Hi, Emmett," I said.

His tail thumped on the floor as I took in the sad sight of his raw, angry-looking hindquarters. He looked like his rear end had been fed through a woodchopper.

"So, Ms. Francis," I started, "Emmett is having a flare-up of his flea allergies again?" I parted what remained of his fur. The skin over his hips was beet red and sticky with infection, dotted with little black spots of itchy fleas going to town. "It's infected for sure, but we can fix him up. I think you know the drill—"

"I want to put him to sleep," she said.

My jaw dropped.

"How old is Emmett, Ms. Francis?"

"Two."

"Why would you want to euthanize him? Flea allergies are very treatable. We can solve this."

Ms. Francis drew in a quivering breath, her permed platinum curls shaking with the effort. "I just can't do it anymore," she said. "Ever since my divorce, I can't even afford flea meds."

She dabbed at her eyes, smearing mascara on her cheek, then reached into her Louis Vuitton handbag for a tissue.

"Have you thought about taking him to the shelter instead? At least he'd have a chance that way."

Ms. Francis gestured to Emmett. "Look at him. Who'd want him, all messed up like that? I don't want him to die alone in a shelter. He doesn't stand a chance. I want him to die here, with me. I owe him that."

It was an argument I'd heard before, but usually people were talking about older, less adoptable dogs with serious medical conditions. Emmett didn't seem particularly unadoptable to me.

As Ms. Francis tearfully discussed ending his life because her own negligence had ruined him for anyone else, Emmett sensed her distress. Trying to comfort her, he wiggled over and tried to lick her hand. She moved her hand away. I tapped the floor so Emmett would come over, and he sat on the floor with his head in my lap. He looked at me with his soulful eyes, trusting and forgiving. There was no chance I was going to agree to euthanize this young and beautiful dog.

Ms. Francis edged away from Emmett's sticky skin, which he was trying to rub on her jeans to get some relief. I pulled him back and rubbed what few non-raw spots remained on his tail. Even with his hindquarters an open, weeping mess, he didn't complain while I prodded at his tender skin. When I finished, he licked my wrist.

I knew at that moment that my pledge to take care of animals meant more than just sending them home with antibiotics. The owner Emmett trusted his life with wanted to end it over a dermatologic issue, but I could fix his skin. I could fix everything. My mind raced, overcome with the feeling that it couldn't possibly be a coincidence this dog wound up in my exam room.

"I think you should take him to a shelter," I said. "At least give him a chance. I bet someone will take him." And then, I thought to myself, I can rush over there after work and put a hold on him.

"I want you to put him to sleep."

Emmett had his head on my knee, eyebrows raised as he calmly watched the exchange. "I can't."

"I told you, I don't want him to die alone and scared at the shelter. No one wants him."

"Ms. Francis," I said, as the image of Emmett's head perched at the foot of my bed intrusively popped into my brain, "someone will adopt Emmett. I promise. We can find him a home. I know someone at a Golden Retriever rescue and I bet they would take him in a heartbeat."

She thought about it for a long and silent minute while Emmett licked her drumming fingers. "Well....OK," she finally said. "Call her. That rescue person."

"Oh," I said, "I meant that you could call—"

Ms. Francis put her hands on her thighs. "I'm not leaving with the dog. I can't. Either you put him to sleep or you take him. I don't care which but I. Am. Done." And that was that. Susan, who had been listening with her ear pressed to the door, handed me the papers to officially take custody of Emmett.

"Are we allowed to just take a dog in here?" I asked her. "What do we do with him?"

"No idea," Susan said.

"Is Dr. Joff going to be mad?" I asked.

"Maybe, but who cares?" Susan said.

Fifteen minutes later, relinquishment papers in hand, the staff descended en masse onto Emmett to give him a beauty treatment. His entire back end needed to be shaved. He moaned in relief as the dead fleas washed off his skin. A little ointment, some antibiotics, and a touch of steroids later, he was half bald, comfortable, and sweet as sugar. Exhausted but in heaven after finally getting some relief from his awful itching, he sank into a deep slumber in his kennel.

"Can I keep him here until I get ahold of the rescue?" I asked Susan.

She frowned. "Depends on whether Isaac is coming by this week." Isaac, a by-the-books sort of manager, would definitely frown upon the free boarding. Susan looked at Emmett sleeping contentedly. "We'll figure it out. Dr. Joff would have just agreed to put him to sleep, you know. Maybe this happened for a reason."

I got ahold of the local retriever rescue that afternoon and pled Emmett's case. The volunteer agreed to take him in that weekend, so we arranged to meet up in three days so I could hand him off.

The next morning, I couldn't wait to get into work and check on my charge. Emmett met us at the treatment room door, mouth clenching a plushie that Rachelle had bought on her lunch break the day before. *Squeak, squeak, squeak*, it protested as his entire rear end wiggled with joy at seeing his new friends again. His skin had already started to dry up and lose its angry red hue.

"Hello, handsome," I said, leaning down for a lick. He jumped up and put his paws on my hips, knocking me into the wall. I leaned in and gave him a hug. Susan came around the corner and braced herself as Emmett barreled toward her like a linebacker. "Ha ha!" Susan said, patting his shoulder, careful to avoid the raw patches of skin. "Gotcha!" She lunged left and right, getting Emmett to bark excitedly as he flung himself down into the play position, forelimbs on the ground and tail wagging, butt high in the air. Yeah, he was hard to love all right.

"I'm going to bring him home," I told Susan at the end of the day. "Just for the night. I feel bad leaving him here at the clinic alone. And then Isaac can't complain about boarding him."

"OK," she said with a sideways smile.

Emmett gamely jumped into my car, trundling back and forth in the backseat, leaving little smears of antibiotic goo on the upholstery that I'd forgotten to cover in a towel. Whoops. He needed two attempts to get through the doorway of our house, repeatedly banging his huge satellite dish e-collar into the door frame. Brian, coming over to see what all the commotion was about, rolled his eyes and looked on with a dubious closed-lipped smile as Emmett crashed to and fro throughout the house checking out the new digs, knocking over a wedding picture, a candle, and Brian's guitar. He investigated Apollo's litter box and smeared little bits of ick on the newly painted walls when he scratched his rear on the corner.

Brian appeared apprehensive. "Nice dog," he said, looking at the half-bald fuzzy tank barreling through the kitchen, where he located Apollo's food bowl and cleared it out in one gulp. "He's leaving Saturday?"

"Calm down," I said, as Emmett's tail took out the remote control. "It's just for a couple nights." Brian grabbed the remote as it skittered across the floor.

"Come here, dog," he said. "Do you know 'sit'?" Emmett trotted over readily and sat on his foot. "You're a mess." He scratched Emmett's ears, and when he stopped, Emmett picked up Brian's hand gently with his muzzle. Emmett tipped his head backward until Brian's hand was back behind his fluffy doggy ears once again. Whenever Brian paused, Emmett would lift one eyebrow, then the other, back and forth in mock astonishment until Brian, laughing, petted him again.

After an hour or so, Apollo ventured out from behind the washing machine to investigate the interloper. Emmett caught a peek from the corner of his eye and took off like a bullet, leaving Brian's hand hovering over a small puff of dog fur floating lazily in the air. I found Emmett pacing back and forth in front of our bedroom dresser, where Apollo was perched in wide-eyed alarm. "Come on, buddy," I said, leading him out of the bedroom and away from his prize. As I left, Brian came in behind me to drop off Apollo's litter box and dishes before closing the door behind him.

When I went to bed that night, Emmett was plopped beneath Brian's feet, enjoying a massage as Brian kicked his legs back and forth, scratching his belly. Brian likes him, I thought, but he hasn't said a peep about keeping him .... yet. I made sure to relay the long sordid story of his life, spending extra time focusing on his sorry state of abandonment. If I'd had a Sarah McLachlan CD readily available, I would have popped it in for ambience. I ended with a heavy sigh. "So yes…at least now there is a *chance* he *might* end up with an *OK* home." Emmett played along, making sad noises at all the appropriate moments and settling down to lick Brian's toes from end to end.

On Friday, Emmett came home with me again to enjoy his last night of foster care before going to the rescue in search of a new home. At seven thirty that night, the front door opened, and in walked Brian, lugging an XL sheepskin dog bed and a box of Milk-Bones. I looked up from where I sat on the floor, rubbing ointment onto Emmett's bare red rear.

"Well, you wanted to keep him, right?" he said as I jumped up and gave him a hug. "You weren't exactly subtle." Then he gave Emmett a rawhide. "You're all right, dog." Just another confirmation that I got lucky in the husband department.

Early the next morning, I called the rescue to cancel the handoff. The coordinator laughed. "I figured that would happen," she said. "Yet another foster failure. Glad to hear he has a good home."

He did have a good home. And I, though I didn't know it at the time, had just adopted the best dog I would ever have.

CHAPTER 12

Though Emmett was in fact the best dog in the world, it took me a while to realize it.

One of the hardest things to convince people of when they bring a new pet home, be it a puppy or a senior from the shelter, is that there is an adjustment period. Pets aren't factory-direct, ready-to-wear, perfectly calibrated machines. They have quirks and foibles and bad habits that have to be worked on, just like us. It's like having a new roommate: It'll take some time to figure out that your housemate really can't handle you leaving socks on the floor, or how to ask them to please not cook smoked oysters in the house, but with a little communication everyone can make it through the adjustment period just fine.

We were no more immune to this rough patch than any other new pet parent. Emmett seemed to view himself as a Dickensian ragamuffin, a street urchin who needed to rely on his street smarts for survival. Independent and resourceful when it came to locating calories of any sort, he soon took to browsing the trash can for scraps at every opportunity.

"Emmett," I said, surveying the shredded Baggies and banana peels on the floor, "I fed you this morning. You can't be that insecure about your next meal." He just wagged his tail happily, unperturbed. Given his trash-can diving and one side effect of the antibiotics he was taking for his skin, Emmett was also gleefully, fearlessly flatulent, greeting friends new and old with a jump on the chest and an olfactory blast. "This isn't permanent, right?" Brian asked on the third day as he opened the windows. "Can't you give him some yogurt or something?"

The jumping was his other big problem. The first time he met my tiny mother, he was so excited to meet her he pushed her straight out the front doorway by her clavicles.

"Hi, Emmett," she said, chuckling, sprawled out on the patio. "He's very strong."

"He's a little bit of a fixer-upper," I conceded, "but he's got potential."

"Don't we all," my mom agreed, waiting for him to sit before handing him a bone.

No two ways about it, Emmett was a wild man. He jumped. He bolted. Our relationship needed some work.

"Down," I said, and he would cock his head to the side and most decidedly remain standing.

"Come," I said, shortly before he turned heel and peeled off after the cat, dust motes swirling in the air in his wake. The day after Thanksgiving was the last straw, when he dragged a day-old Thanksgiving turkey carcass, redolent and dripping with grease, across the kitchen and up the stairs before I could catch him and pry it from his mouth.

My meager veterinary experience with basic commands

was a drizzle poured on a forest fire, useless in the face of Emmett's boisterous temperament. I heard the behaviorists lecturing in my head: He needs training. You need training. I looked at it like language lessons: a way for us to better communicate across the vast species divide.

The first trainer I met with promised excellent results in a short period of time. "It doesn't take much," he said. "Once they get used to this"—he held up a large black collar—"the training goes fast."

"Is that a shock collar?" I asked.

"We don't call them shock collars," he said. "It's a static corrective training apparatus." Next.

The next trainer I tried walked Emmett around the block for an evaluation of his pulling tendencies and determined that he was a dominant dog who needed firm rules.

"OK," I said.

"And this," she said, holding up a prong collar. Next.

The third time, after I'd finally done my research and located a trainer whose positive reinforcement philosophies were more in line with my own, was the charm. Emmett was headstrong, yes, but as pliable as a lump of clay when treats were involved. A basic training course under our belt was all it took for Emmett and I to become fluent in Each Other, a singular language predicated on trust, affection, and little slivers of hot dog. We never looked back.

I wish I could say all my problems were so easily solved.

"When did you say this happened, Miss Fremont?" I asked, trying to get a glimpse at the Rottweiler hunched across the room. Betty Lou had her left leg folded under her, ears pinned back whenever I looked in her direction, clearly wishing she were anywhere but this scary place. The poor thing had a towel under her pelvis that was speckled with dried and fresh blood.

"Yesterday, I think," said Miss Fremont. "She was running around on our property, maybe she caught her leg on a nail or something. It's kind of torn."

A syringeful of pain medications and sedatives later, Betty Lou had relaxed enough for me to get a look at the tear Miss Fremont had described, which was actually a six-inch flap of skin that had peeled back from Betty Lou's inner thigh. The edges were dry and rubbery, a sign this injury was somewhat aged.

"This might best be handled by a surgeon," I said. "I don't think I'm going to be able to fix that."

"Well you're going to try," she said, and even though I had learned how to say no to Emmett, I hadn't yet gotten the hang of saying it to clients.

"It's going to be really hard to close at this point," I said. "The edges of the flap are starting to contract. It might be best if we let it scar over—"

"No. I want it fixed."

I said many things to her, things about skin flaps and wound tension, bed rest and granulation beds, and even the risk of the entire thing falling apart, but I sensed that all she heard was the trumpeting *waaah waah wahh* of the adults in the Charlie Brown specials. I had a bad feeling about this one.

I did what I could, but my repair had at best a fifty-fifty shot of actually holding together. Even with all the warnings and admonitions I could muster about the likely outcome of sewing this desiccated flap back on like it was a rip in a bedsheet, Miss Fremont still read us the riot act a week later when the wound repair did exactly what I predicted it would do and fell apart. The specialist who saw Betty Lou afterward recommended the same course of treatment I had pushed for on day one: the ugly but perfectly utilitarian let-it-scar approach, which she once again declined. After another failed skin flap attempt, this time performed by a board-certified soft tissue surgeon, the owner finally gave in. None of us ever did figure out how Betty Lou had gotten injured in the first place. Miss Fremont left that clinic disappointed that I couldn't solve her problems the way she wanted me to, but she wasn't the only person who needed help beyond my skill set.

My sister Kris had just arrived from Las Vegas for an extended visit. She was in the process of a divorce and needed some time away from her home and the memories it held, so she packed her bags, liquidated her accumulated vacation time, and headed to my house for some R&R. My sister, the gregarious extrovert who usually looked at all strangers as future friends, arrived transformed by the weight of that terrible breakup: hollow, deflated, and distressingly quiet. In our family, we dealt with pain, conflict, and grief in one way: pretending it didn't exist. It was all we knew how to do.

I am many things, but a born hostess is not one of them. I'll make sure you have towels in your bathroom and will probably remember to check that the toilet paper roll is not empty, but that's about it. The hospitality gene flew right on over my head when I was a zygote. So when my sister rolled her luggage through the door, I pointed out the air bed, the bathroom, and mentioned I remembered she liked tuna fish so I'd put a few cans in the pantry. She did not seem as pleased as I had expected she would be that I remembered the tuna thing. In retrospect I could have done a lot more.

Emmett watched this exchange with great interest. He approached my sister carefully, tail quivering with barely contained excitement at seeing a new person in the house. Encouraged by her enthusiastic pat on the head, he wiggled his rear end backward like a puma about to pounce.

"Emmett," I said with a warning in my voice. He paused, rear half an inch above the ground, and looked to Kris, then back to me. He settled for pawing her leg a few times. It was progress.

"Aw, he's a good boy," said Kris, scratching him behind the ears. He leaned into her, tongue extended in a joy-pant. He leaned into her so far she fell over into a chair, which put her exactly where he wanted her so he could plop in her lap.

Emmett was delighted when Kris opened her suitcase, a clear hint she was going to be staying for a while. "I hope you don't mind," I said as she unpacked her things, "but he's probably going to follow you around a lot."

"No," she said, "I don't mind."

Most days, distracted by my own busy work schedule, I ran out of the house before Kris was awake. It wasn't until a week in that I realized I hadn't fed Emmett breakfast since she arrived. Usually, I'd see his head popped up at the base of the bed as soon as he heard me stirring, making a beeline for his food bowl the moment my feet hit the floor. These days I had the kitchen gloriously to myself, making and enjoying my coffee without a wet nose nudging me ever so persistently toward the cabinet in which the dog food was stored. He was nowhere to be found.

I found out why that Sunday, when Kris strolled into the kitchen with Emmett trotting along happily behind her. Through the open door, I could see the bed with two distinct depressions in the sheets: one human-size, one smaller and edged with fur.

"Oh!" I said. "I'm so sorry."

"For what?" Kris asked, pouring a glass of water.

"I see Emmett's been inviting himself up on your bed," I said. "You can tell him to get down."

She looked down at Emmett in confusion. "Why would I do that?" She went to open the dog food container.

Kris was fine with the fact that we were gone most of the day, as her preferred method of decompression was reading, catching up on old episodes of *Buffy the Vampire Slayer*, and watching movies. In Emmett, she had the perfect companion for these mostly solitary activities: present, but unobtrusive. He intuitively attached himself to her like a magnetic charge, filling in all the gaps I realized I wasn't prepared to fill. He probably knew more about the ins and outs of Kris's relationship than I ever did. I'm certain he's seen more episodes of *Buffy*.

Dog the Second: EMMETT

"You're a good boyfriend," she said affectionately as Emmett put his paws on her shoulders to plant a big slurp on her face.

It was good for Brian to see Emmett being so useful. Up to that point he seemed to view the dog like a super-annoying college roommate always running late with the rent and eating all your snacks: tolerated, but barely.

Emmett answered to two names: "Emmett" and "Damn Dog." Brian used the latter even when he wasn't annoyed, a crusty term of endearment. "Want a bone, Damn Dog? Are you taking the Damn Dog for a walk?" Emmett didn't care.

One morning I woke up to a long, low, AUUUUUGG GGGGHHHHHHH from the downstairs office. I heard the back door open, then slam shut, followed by a moderately blue cloud of cursing. Despite the voice in my head telling me to remain upstairs, I went down to see what the fuss was about.

I smelled it before I saw it, and I knew. Emmett had had some sort of GI distress overnight. Guiltily I remembered him nosing me sometime around two a.m., but in my vague half-awake state I rolled over and went back to sleep. Clearly Emmett went downstairs to try to find a way out, but finding no suitable exit to the backyard he retreated to the office— *Brian's* office—and let loose. I appreciated the effort, but desperately wished he hadn't gone to the one room in the house with beige carpeting.

Brian stood with his hands on his hips, apoplectic. It would appear that after experiencing explosive diarrhea, Emmett attempted to bury the evidence in the rug.

"Just go," I said, sighing and waving my hand.

"You...hrm...don't you have any friends who could take him or something?"

I paused from my place on the floor with a handful of paper towels. "What did you just say?"

"There has to be a co-worker or something who wants that fleabag. Isn't there?" I just glared.

"Do you remember the day you got food poisoning at Morton's?" I asked. He nodded. "Remember how sick you were? Emmett slept on the bathroom floor next to you and I went into the guest room because I didn't want to hear you throwing up all night. He's the most sympathetic one in the house."

Brian paused, perhaps realizing his mistake. "I was just kidding."

"No you weren't." I threw a fouled paper towel toward him, just close enough to gross him out. "Why did you marry a vet if you didn't like dogs?"

"I like some dogs," he admitted. "Emmett's all right."

He went to the back door and whistled. "Emmett? Come in." Without asking, he made the dog a bowl of cottage cheese and rice. Later, after I had finished cleaning up the mess, my sister confided that she had seen Brian give Emmett half a salami sandwich with cheese the night before. As payback, I waited a full week before calling in a professional rug cleaner to erase the last stench of dog poop from the office.

When Kris had sufficiently recovered her bearings to the point she felt ready to return home, she was crestfallen to say good-bye to Emmett. They were inseparable. His face hadn't graced the foot of my bed in a month. As she stood at the door, Emmett watched with tail wagging, assuming they were about to head out on another walk. But as he took in the sight of her suitcase, his tail slowed down; dropping, as she wheeled it to her car, to a slow twitch. Emmett had healed Kris's heart, but had his own broken just a little in the process.

CHAPTER 13

They say that people and their pets often bear more than a passing resemblance to one another, and Emmett and I were no exception. We shared both a shock of unruly hair as well as a tendency to leave toys and household items scattered all around the house. It drove Brian, by far the most organized creature in the house, nuts.

I heard Brian fall before I heard him cursing, and rounded the corner to find him holding his ankle with a grimace on his face. The offending ball was rolling down the hall in a futile attempt to escape his wrath. He limped over and threw it in the backyard.

"I don't think we need to buy any more dog toys anytime soon," he said, hobbling around pushing all of them into a pile.

Emmett and I stood to the side and watched the pile grow—squeaky toys with busted squeakers poking out, slobbery fleece teddy bears, a couple of Kongs licked clean of peanut butter. One by one Brian tossed them all into a basket and left the living room.

I followed after him, catching Emmett out of the corner of my eye as he pulled a bone back out of the basket and settled down onto his orthopedic foam bed.

Dog the Second: EMMETT

"Seriously," Brian said. "Enough toys. He has more toys than a dog could chew in a lifetime." Which was true, but the one thing he did *not* have was a squeaky toy shaped like a piece of candy corn. But I decided now wasn't the time to let my husband know I had one in the trunk of the car.

My maternal instincts had been running amok for some time now. Emmett was a dog on whom I bestowed dog-like things (bones, leashes, walks, brushes), but also one on whom I imposed a little anthropomorphic child substituting: Halloween costumes, a holiday turtleneck sweater, excessive gifts. We also had pictures with Santa, a two-foot-long rawhide, and a growing photo album.

While any and all sorts of people participate in what I might call "elective pet overspoiling," it does seem to occur disproportionately more often in young couples with no kids. It makes sense; it's only human to want to care for something, and in the absence of a small human, who better than a compliant French Bulldog? Or perhaps a Pug, otherwise known as "the breed everyone sticks in a costume"? Go to any pet store close to Halloween and you'll see row after row of Pug-size Yoda, bumblebee, and ladybug outfits. Though there's not a whole lot of XXL dog costumes, I'm never one to let societal norms be a deterrent. I stuck a white tank top, long blond wig, and bandanna on Emmett and declared him the first-ever canine Bret Michaels.

But I'm not going to lie, all this willful overindulgence and attraction to hand-sewn dog collars on Etsy was the symptom of something larger. I wanted a kid. A human one. Fussing over Emmett was fulfilling in and of itself, but he was never going to have first-day-of-kindergarten pictures, or get married (I've seen people hold intracanine wedding ceremonies, but I have my limits), or keep me out of a nursing home in my dotage. For his part, I'm sure Emmett would be happy to be relieved of human substitute duty and never have to see another dog sweater.

It was an uneasy path traveled to get to this realization, as I had never thought of myself as much of a kid person. It's not that I disliked children, but I didn't really get them, with their sticky fingers and their insistence on asking the same question fifteen times and their love of the overshare. How was it possible to want a kid of your own even while feeling ambivalent about everyone else's? Dogs I could swoop in on with certainty and ease, instinctually knowing where to scratch to get them to melt into my palm, so I felt conflicted, almost treasonous, to want a kid even though I wasn't sure I was going to be naturally good at having one.

Things had settled into a groove at work. I made it through my probationary period without killing anything—including Dr. Joff, who was as perfectly content to be relieved of official mentor duties as I was to be free of his tutelage. Released from whatever pressure he had felt to mold me into his image, or perhaps just resigned to the fact that was never going to happen, we coexisted in peace, much to everyone's relief. When he finally introduced me as "Dr. V" while leaving off "the new grad" part, I was strangely touched. The first time Susan peeled a chart from Dr. Joff's hands with a satisfied, "They requested Dr. V," he wrinkled his brow in puzzlement, but now he just shrugged and went on to the next room.

The clients were gaining confidence in me, and better yet, so was I. I'd go days at a time without pulling out my trusty Nerdbook, an advancement that did not go unnoticed by the techs who no longer had to run and fetch it for me on an hourly basis. Now that I could reliably help whoever walked, limped, or staggered through the door without needing constant backup, I announced to Brian that I was ready to take the next step in our life.

"The next step?" Brian asked. "You want to go back and do a residency?"

"No," I said with an involuntary shudder. "I think we should start talking about a family." With my Type-A personality, I assumed this meant sheer force of will and pure grit would result in a pregnancy three weeks later, but that was not to be the case. As all seasoned medical professionals eventually realize, we are all but warm lumps of flesh and mucus that manage to superficially appear to follow the laws of physics, but in truth just replicate, disintegrate, or implode with a disturbing lack of predictability.

For the first six months of Project Baby, nothing happened. In an overabundance of caution, I was staying on the far side of the anesthesia machine and avoiding Brie and all the things maybe-pregnant women should do, but to no avail. I rolled an ultrasound probe around a Doberman's distended abdomen counting heartbeats, wondering why she got ten when all I wanted was one. Too much time wasted online had convinced me something was wrong, that I must have at some point in school been exposed to an exotic camelid influenza that rendered me infertile, but my doctor insisted everything was perfectly normal and that I should have a glass of wine—maybe two—and think about other things. But there was nothing else to think about.

A week later, exhausted by the anxiety of limbo, I was finishing lunch in the comfy rolling chair I brought in to get around the "two stools per hospital" rule, and the next thing I knew I was passed out with my head on my elbow. Susan let me catch a ten-minute nap before nudging me awake.

"You OK?" she asked.

"Yeah," I yawned, rubbing my eyes. "That was weird. I'm just really tired today."

"Late night?"

"Not really."

"Maybe you're getting sick," she said.

"Maybe," I agreed. "I have been a little queasy the last few days." I paused, my hand on my stomach. When I looked up, a smile was quivering at the corner of Susan's mouth as a realization dawned on me.

A few hours later, Brian and I stood staring at the little blue cross signifying that our lives were about to change. Emmett was concerned by our whooping and hollering, but overall he was unimpressed.

I contained my excitement for exactly two days before pulling Susan into an empty exam room. She was thrilled for me as I knew she would be, throwing her arms around me and squealing, "I am SOOOO happy for you!" She promised not to tell anyone, and she didn't, but her constant hovering over me with lollipops and ginger ale pretty much ruined the secret within the week. "Oh. My. God," said Mary-Kate as I popped open my water bottle. "You're preggo. You're pregnant!"

"How did you know?" I asked, leaning on the counter. No point in denying it.

"In all the time you've been here, I have never," she said, "seen you drink water when there's a Diet Pepsi in the fridge." She was right. Busted.

The rest of the staff accepted this news with the requisite polite cheer, including Dr. Joff, who had but one piece of advice. "Do not," he instructed, "barf after you're scrubbed in. Saw it once. Took forever to resterilize everything."

"I won't," I promised, but part of me wondered if this was a promise I was actually able to keep. Over the course of the week, the exhaustion had dialed back a smidge, only to be replaced with rolling ninja-attacks of nausea. They weren't enough to actually make me throw up, but enough to make me worried that I might.

Susan, herself a veteran of the highs and lows of pregnancy, started staying with me in the exam room to watch for signs of impending morning sickness. When I would feel a wave coming on, I quickly learned to contort my face into an expression of intense concern for whatever the client was telling me.

"I think my dog has skin cancer," said the lady sitting across from me with a small Pomeranian in her arms. The dog's head and tail ends were currently impossible to differentiate in its massive swirl of red fur.

"OK," I said, puffing my cheeks as I felt a small swirl of unpleasantness in the pit of my stomach. "What's going on that makes you believe that?" I looked at Romeo, wondering how Mrs. Cranston could possibly see anything on him at all.

"I felt something," she said assuredly. "I'm certain of it." I briefly debated examining Romeo on Mrs. Cranston's lap, then thought better of it. Instead, I asked her to put Romeo on the exam table so I could see which end she directed toward the top of the table.

Now I had some orientation. At the bottom of the ball of fur I could just make out four paws, toes pointing in the direction of the head. From the front end, a small growl emanated, confirming both the location of the head and the temperament of its owner.

"Did you get a temperature yet?" I asked Susan, more to amuse myself than out of any expectation she'd have been able to find the dog's rear end.

"Not yet," she said. "I was waiting for you."

"Where did you feel the mass?" I asked Mrs. Cranston, silently pleading *onthebackontheback*. That way I could get a good look while he remained standing. From the way Romeo was wriggling, I knew he had zero interest in being rolled onto his back so I could see his belly.

"On his stomach," she said. "Right about, oh, I don't know, here," she said, pointing at her own belly button.

As I performed my physical exam on an increasingly

unhappy Romeo, I found several things of interest—some dental disease, a mildly unstable kneecap that slipped from side to side, but no mass. As the acid in my stomach roiled, the room seemed to shrink around me, becoming toastier by the minute. Mrs. Cranston held Romeo up by his armpits while I ran my fingers up and down his stomach, but I couldn't find anything out of place.

"I know it's there, I just felt it yesterday," Mrs. Cranston told me. "I'm just so worried."

"OK, why don't we shave his belly and get a better look," I offered. Mrs. Cranston looked dubious. "It's the best way to be sure there's nothing there." Plus, I could hand him off once we got in the back so I could go get a Tums.

"All right," she replied unhappily. Susan reached for the leash, which Mrs. Cranston grasped to her chest like my grandmother pulling her purse away from a suspicious-looking character on the bus. "You can't take him! You have to do it here! He gets very anxious when he's by himself."

"I'll get the clippers," I said, and when Susan started to protest that she could do it, she saw the look on my face and just nodded.

In the back, I popped a Tums, a saltine, and a swig of water before grabbing the clippers and heading back inside the exam room. Shortly thereafter, Romeo was thrashing on the floor like an angry miniature crocodile, kicking at me while I tried to shave him gently.

"Where was this mass again?" I asked Mrs. Cranston, trying to minimize the amount of fur I had to remove.

"Here," she said. "No. There. Well, I'm not sure. Keep

going." As she hovered over me, I could feel sweat starting to bead on my eyebrow. I was not feeling good, at all.

The room lurched, the poop deck tilting under my feet. I took a deep breath, my hypersensitive sinuses filling with the smell of freshly expressed anal glands and eau de Parvosol. This was not good. I needed to get out, stat.

"The clippers are out of juice," I said curtly, flipping them to the off position. "I'll grab another pair." Susan looked at me strangely. We kept them in the charger at all times, so she knew they worked just fine, but she couldn't have missed the green cast to my skin as I pushed myself up to my knees and jogged out of the room. "I appreciate the thoroughness!" Mrs. Cranston called as I bolted to the back to find the nearest trash can. Rachelle scurried over with a wet paper towel as I started to realize the next nine months might not be as easy as I'd anticipated.

Rachelle and Susan completed the shave job while I caught my breath and brushed my teeth. I felt much better, at least for the moment. Susan emerged from the exam room shortly thereafter, pulling clumps of Pom-fur off her scrubs. "We found it," she said, rubbing a lint roller down her stomach.

"Is it big?"

"Come in and see for yourself," she said, opening the door.

"We found it!" said Mrs. Cranston triumphantly. "Right here." She placed her finger on his abdomen and poked.

I followed her eyes and rubbed Romeo's newly shorn abdomen, trying to feel what she wanted me to diagnose. "I still don't feel it."

"Right there!" she exclaimed. "Your finger is right on top of it!"

I looked down and removed my finger from his perfectly normal left nipple.

In the aftermath of this discovery, Mrs. Cranston sighed in great relief. Susan opened the door to the lobby and exited the room, leaving me typing in a few extra notes on the computer.

Mrs. Cranston cleared her throat. I looked up.

"Have you tried ginger ale with real ginger?" she asked. "It's much better than that Canada Dry stuff."

I squinted at her. "How did you know?"

She grinned. "Just a guess. My husband said I turned green as the Grinch when I was expecting. Congratulations."

As the pregnancy progressed, I found myself observing mothers like a *National Geographic* documentarian, looking for clues as to what awaited me. Exhausted moms rolling into the clinic were nothing new to us. Most of the time they came in the early afternoon, trying to get in after the baby's morning nap and before they had to pick up the grade schooler from elementary school.

Dr. Joff didn't like those rooms. "Will you please go in there and tell that kid to get his fingers out of the drawers?" he'd snap at Manny, who then had to go in and try to convince the toddler to put down the syringes, or the gauze. If he had time, Manny preferred to distract them by blowing up an exam glove and drawing a face on it with a Sharpie instead, a trick he picked up from Dr. Garcia.

"I wish they would leave the two-year-olds at home,"

Dr. Joff grumbled, and as someone who was never a natural with kids either, I got where he was coming from. It was hard to listen with the stethoscope while a little hand banged on the side of the dog, and the average mom was usually only halfway paying attention to what we were trying to tell her about her dog: that he was overweight, that he needed a dental, that his toenails were badly in need of a trim. On the other hand, I finally started to see the reality of having a child—the umbilical cord doesn't go away once you give birth; many parents don't have the luxury of readily available babysitters on short notice.

My expanding belly marked me as one of them, the one who let the kids try on the stethoscope instead of giving them the stink eye when I thought the parent wasn't looking. From these ranks, I started to build my own list of clientele, people who asked to see me and not "the bald guy," a request Mary-Kate was always happy to pass on to me. Dr. Joff had nothing to fear, of course, since he still retained his die-hard contingent of men with mustaches and people who resisted the use of muzzles. It was a good balance. Something for everyone.

One otherwise quiet Tuesday afternoon, my discussion of the next day's schedule up at the front desk with Mary-Kate was interrupted by the arrival of Mrs. DeWitt and her small army. A minute or two before they arrived at the door, we heard doors slamming, a muffled "Stop, Nathan! Wait for Mommy!" and a high-pitched squeal or two. The front doors slid open as Nathan's feet hit the welcome mat, and in he pounced to announce their arrival, the grand marshal of the incoming parade. Stomp, stomp, stomping in, swinging his sippy cup back and forth like a baton.

The parade float lumbered in behind him, a double stroller approximately the size and weight of a small golf cart. Small stuffed animals dangled on clips from the edges, presided over by a pair of bald twins sucking thoughtfully on binkies as they decided whether this new environment was to their liking.

To the side, the dog serving as their cleanup crew wandered about on a long leash, licking up Gerber puffs the twins had magnanimously tossed like confetti over the sides. He was one of the largest Beagles I had seen in my life, huffing and puffing to keep up with the parade. His stubby legs looked way too spindly to handle the round jiggly mass of flesh on top of them, but somehow he remained upright.

And behind this whole machine was the engine, a frazzled looking woman in sweats and flip-flops, with her hair gathered into a messy ponytail. The procession continued to the front desk and came to a halt, looking expectantly at Mary-Kate.

"I'm sorry I'm late," Mrs. DeWitt said, stuffing her glasses into a diaper bag that could easily double as a storm shelter. "Bacon's here for his vaccines."

Mary-Kate consulted the appointment book. Her brow furrowed. "I don't see...hmmm..." She shuffled the pages. "Oh." She looked up with a pained expression on her face. "We have you down for tomorrow at two."

Mrs. DeWitt's face fell. "Really? I don't know how that could have happened. I..." She turned and took in the scene before her, where Nathan was now attempting to dip his fingers in the fish tank while Bacon casually lifted a leg to pee on the corner of the front desk. "Is there any way you could fit us in? It's so hard to get them all out of the house, and I don't think we can come tomorrow."

I looked over Mary-Kate's shoulder at the appointment book. Dr. Joff, who was scheduled to see Bacon tomorrow, was still in surgery. I was technically still at lunch and my afternoon was fully booked, but when I saw Mrs. DeWitt's crestfallen face, I gave Mary-Kate a nod and smiled at the client. "We can get you in." She sighed in relief.

"That is one big dog," said Manny a little while later as he came out of the room, looking shell-shocked. "Just to warn you, it's kind of loud in there too." Manny always seemed rattled by young kids—his wife was expecting their first child and he was a little nervous as to what lay ahead.

"As long as you're not having triplets it won't be like that," I assured him, as if I had any clue. "OK, so just annual check, due for rabies, heartworm test, got it. You coming in?"

He shook his head. "I can't fit."

As I went into the exam room I could see what he meant. The stroller took up the entire far side of the room, leaving me a couple of square feet in which to navigate. The rest of the floor space had turned into a kid zone. The diaper bag lay upended on the floor, where Nathan was busily sorting through the contents in search of more food. In his left hand he clutched a soggy Milk-Bone from our treat jar, which was also sitting on the floor with the lid off. Investigating the contents of the jar was Bacon, the world's biggest Beagle.

"Hey, Bacon," I said, plucking the jar off the floor. He looked up at me resignedly, then waddled over to Nathan and plucked the bone out of his hand. Nathan began to scream. "No, that's MY BONE MINE!"

Mrs. DeWitt, who had been dangling a rattle in front of the twins, looked over. "Nathan, you have puffs. Please don't yell like that." The twins started to fuss.

I lifted Bacon to the exam table, mentally groaning under his size. My back was going to pay for that one. He hung there in my arms, deadweight, as I placed him down and began my exam.

I flipped through the notes on his record to see what they indicated about his weight gain. He had steadily gained two or three pounds each year. Dr. Joff's notes were the same visit after visit: *OVERWEIGHT. OBESE. TOLD OWNER PATIENT NEEDS TO LOSE WEIGHT. RISK OF DEATH/ JOINT DISEASE.* Bacon's thyroid, which we tested at his last visit, was fine. Apparently he just ate way too much.

I excused myself to go get Bacon's vaccines. Mrs. DeWitt, now bouncing a crying baby in her arms, scarcely noticed.

Dr. Joff, in the middle of prepping for his next surgery, saw the name on the chart and snorted. "That dog? Did he lose any weight?"

"No. He gained two pounds, actually."

He shook his head. "She shouldn't even have a dog if she can't take care of it. He's going to blow a cruciate by next year, mark my words." Now he was on a roll. "I don't get it. I've told her over and over and she just doesn't care that her fat dog is dying right in front of her." And while he had a point, I couldn't help wondering if there might be a more constructive approach to the situation.

I took the tray of vaccines and headed back to the room. The noise was now spilling out from beneath the door, three small voices bellowing, crying, and shrieking. Manny handed me the rabies certificate. "Just run in and get it over with, Doc. Get 'em out of here before someone blows."

My Lean Cuisine was congealing in the microwave. If I got in and out in five minutes I'd still have time to wolf it down before my afternoon appointments started. If I could speak with her while Manny took the dog in the back to get his treatments done, it would go even faster. I looked at the break area, then through the window into the exam room, where Mrs. DeWitt was being repeatedly smacked in the face with a stuffed bear while one of the babies screamed with delight.

"Manny."

"Yeah, Doc?"

"Come with me, please."

I opened the door and went into the room, Manny squeezing in behind me.

"Would it be OK if Manny took the kids to the waiting area? He's expecting a baby next month and needs the practice." Manny shot me a panicked look. I smiled at him.

"Um, sure. That would be fine." Manny navigated the double stroller slowly, clumsily out of the narrow door frame, while Nathan trailed behind, lured by the promise of crayons in the lobby.

I turned to Mrs. DeWitt, who looked surprised to be sitting in a quiet room. "I have Bacon's vaccines and dewormer here. I did want to talk about his weight—"

"I know," she interjected.

"It's just," I hedged, trying to be delicate, "it's still going up, and—"

"I know," she said. "Dr. Joff tells me the same thing every year."

"Did he tell you what to do about it?"

"He said to put him on a diet. It's hard to do in our house with everyone running around. I'm trying. Really." She waved her hand, *Get on with it.*

So now I had a choice. Should I give Bacon his shots and get her out of here? It seemed like she's heard it all before and it wasn't going anywhere. Should I list for her all the health problems Bacon was going to have and try to guilt her into being more proactive? Would that even work?

"It's just with his weight where it is right now, his joints are going to—" I looked up, and Mrs. DeWitt was looking at the floor with glazed eyes. I knew that expression.

I put down the vaccines and sat next to her.

"Mrs. DeWitt," I asked, "are you OK?"

"Yes," she hedged, in that voice that said *I am most definitely not OK.*

"Is there something I can do to help?"

"Come and babysit?" she asked ruefully. "I'm trying with Bacon, but my dad just keeps feeding him."

"Ah, you have a Spoiling Grandpa in the house," I said. "Have you explained to him—"

"Over and over," she said. "He has dementia."

"Oh. I'm so sorry."

"We got him Bacon when my mom died," she said, patting Bacon on the head. "He loves that dog. To death, I know." She sighed. "We thought about giving Bacon to a friend, but he's the reason Dad gets up in the morning. I hate that Bacon's so big, but I don't know how to get Dad to stop feeding him."

I poked my head out the door. Manny was in the lobby, surrounded by sticky fingers. He gave me a wave. He was fine. I sat next to Mrs. DeWitt and took a piece of paper out of the printer. "My dog needs to lose a few too," I said.

"Really?"

"Yes. But we're working on it, slowly," I said. "So tell me again how you feed Bacon." The Lean Cuisine could wait.

Now I knew the real problem. I can tell people what they should be doing until they're blue in the face, but what good does that do when our suggestions just aren't working? It's the definition of insanity. We vets can be pretty hard on clients sometimes, telling them what problem needs fixing while neglecting to give them a realistic way to get there. But what's the point of being a know-it-all if the end result is a guilt-ridden client and pet who doesn't get better?

My brain started to whirl. How could this person sitting in front of me, this busy woman with a hundred other priorities she was juggling, help Bacon lose weight?

Mrs. DeWitt asked for a written plan she could post by

his food bin, which we turned into a chart her father could cross off when he fed the dog. Dog treats were replaced with carrots. With some cooperation from a home health care aide who happened to like dogs and who used Bacon's weight as a reason to get both dog and the elder DeWitt outside for a walk, Bacon eventually ended up losing fifteen pounds. A few months later, Mrs. DeWitt joined a stroller exercise group with Bacon, and she lost ten.

CHAPTER

Over the next few months, it became evident to even my most oblivious clients and colleagues that I was pregnant. The nausea toned down, fortunately, but my expanding midsection, no longer confined by the buttons on my lab coat, gave me away. Used to bellying up to the exam room table to get close to my patient, I found myself trying to work awkwardly from a distance, folding over the belly that was now standing between myself and my charge. I suspect I resembled the robot from *Lost in Space* as I flailed with an otoscope in the general direction of the animal's ear.

It wasn't so hard in the exam rooms, as I had both technicians and the owners to help me improvise ways to manage. In the beginning I could gracelessly squat down and wedge my stomach under the table. Sitting on the ground was sometimes helpful, especially with large dogs. Getting up, not always so easy, but I managed with a helping hand and a few solid "oh, that's my back" grunts. I felt less like a fecund earth goddess and more like a prize steer, herded and roped and prodded into position in the chute.

Surgery was the biggest challenge. Our office, ever vigilant in OSHA compliance, furnished me with a gas mask suitable for chemical warfare to wear during surgery so my fetus wouldn't develop a third arm under the influence of errant sevoflurane fumes. The mask was stifling, exacerbating the light-headedness I already felt when I stood for long periods.

"Do I have to wear the mask at work?" I asked my silver-haired obstetrician, who scoffed before launching into another story beginning with "In my day…" Neither anesthesia fumes, which were well contained by the technology we used, nor other pregnant lady concerns like cat litter and toxoplasmosis, concerned him.

I knew on an intellectual level that toxoplasma was unlikely to be a problem for me, and I had no intention of getting rid of Apollo. Regardless, I was a paranoid first timer and asked the OB to order a toxoplasma titer anyway, just to see if I had been exposed.

"I'm sure you've been exposed already," he told me airily. "Stop reading the Internet. Change the litter. Eat some Brie. Have an occasional glass of wine in the third trimester." I relayed all of this dutifully to Brian, all except the cat litter part, which I let him change the entire ten months and a few months after. Can't be too careful.

"What are you doing?" asked Dr. Joff the first time he saw me doing a spay in a normal surgical mask. "Where's your fumigator mask?"

"My OB said I didn't need to wear it," I said, tying a knot.

"Well, our policies say you do," he asserted.

"I can't breathe in it!" I pleaded. "Try it on. You'll see."

He wouldn't budge. Rules were rules, he said. "You don't really want a two-headed kid anyway, right? Heh heh."

The number of minutes in which I could complete a surgery, which had been steadily shrinking since my first days in practice, was now creeping back up as I had to stop for frequent breathing breaks. Susan stood to my side, pulling the wretched mask up and positioning it on my forehead. She'd squirt water into my mouth, pat down my brow, and slip the mask back on. It worked for a while.

"My God," said Dr. Joff, watching from the corner while we went through our now common Pregnancy Surgery Ritual during my seventh month. "It can't be all that bad."

Later that afternoon, he decided to prove to me how much of a wuss I was being. He put the mask on and walked around for about five minutes, making strangled Darth Vader noises, before ripping it off. "How do you breathe in that thing? Ugh!" Shortly thereafter, Dr. Joff assumed all surgical duties for the duration of my pregnancy.

I had hoped that cutting back on surgeries would mean I could work all the way up to my due date, but my body had other plans. Clients would stare in a combination of amazement and horror at my puffy feet before asking, "Wow, are you having twins?" I felt like a Peep someone had put in the microwave, an ever-expanding mass of squish due to blow any second. My joints, melting under the influence of hormones, left me prone to ankle twists and a horrific crunchy noise as I walked across the room. The staff pretended not to notice, but I caught the way they would leap off their seats when I entered the treatment area and pretend they didn't need a place to sit. Rachelle, ever the nurturer, would slink up behind me and slide a cold-water bottle into my peripheral vision before disappearing again wordlessly, like a ghost.

Not everyone was so sympathetic. "Your blood pressure is getting up there," said my OB at my eight-month visit. Being one of those people who always panicked themselves into hypertension at the doctor's office—much like the stressed but otherwise perfectly healthy cats who would run a temperature of 103 at the vet—I wasn't surprised. "Are you still working?"

"Yes," I said, "but trying to take it easy. Am I going to get pre-eclampsia?"

"I don't think this is related to your pregnancy," the doctor said. "It's because you gained too much weight. Feet in the stirrups, please." I had become Bacon the Beagle, apparently.

And because we were just starting the appointment, I then had to sit there, half naked and humiliated, while the person who just said that to me jabbed around in my nether regions and lectured me about the value of exercise. "Have you ever tried walking?" Yes, I thought, I know what walking is.

Since my blood pressure was unsurprisingly just as elevated at the end of the visit when it was repeated, I was declared "at-risk" and told it was time to go on leave. That gave me plenty of time to hang out with Emmett at home and get the house ready. The mattress in the spare bedroom made way for a crib, Emmett watching in apprehension as I lumbered around placing pictures of baby giraffes on the wall. An hour into it, I was ready for a nap.

I eased myself onto the couch, the bowling ball of a baby in my stomach threatening to send me off balance again. I put my feet up, staring in horror at the inflated pale sausages they had become. Emmett, used to crawling up next to me on the couch, started to scramble up alongside.

"No, Emmett," I said. There was no way he would fit next to me now, not with my stomach poking out the way it was.

He wiggled up and tried to shove in next to me, his rear hanging off the edge of the couch as his paws scrabbled for traction on the cushion.

"No room, buddy."

As his back half slid slowly off the seat, I could see his eyebrows knitting together while he tried to figure out an alternative. At my feet, maybe. He heaved himself back up on the couch and settled on top of them.

Already stretched to the breaking point, the skin on my feet couldn't handle the pressure of an eighty-pound furball. "Get off, Emmett," I said.

He pretended not to hear me.

"I said, GET DOWN." I slid back, pulling my feet out from under him, and pushed at him with my swollen toes until he finally crawled off the couch. He turned back, gave me one sullen and confused look, and headed into the corner, where he dropped with a dramatic sigh and turned his butt to face me.

I sighed in annoyance, then immediately felt bad. Is this how it begins? I thought. I'd seen what happened when clients brought home their new baby. First the dog gets pushed off the couch, then he's pushed out of your lap. The dog bed

169

gets moved from the bedroom to the hallway, and long walks go from once a day to once a month. You're too distracted with feeding schedules to remember to apply Advantage, and before you know it you're at the vet asking them to put your flea-infested dog to sleep.

I looked at Emmett sulking in the corner and wondered if this was how it started for him in his other home as well. The golden child, the light at the center of the universe, wondering who changed the rules without consulting him about it first before knocking him to the outer orbits of the family solar system. Each new change in the house a subtle indicator of the changes about to come. He knew it. He slunk around nervously as we installed the crib, eyeing it with great distrust.

I had no way to ask him if he knew what was going on, but his body language told me all I needed to know. *It was good while it lasted*, his tail said with a resigned drop.

I took a breath and pushed myself up.

Emmett glanced up in surprise as I waddled over, throw pillows in hand. "I'm not sure how much longer I can do this," I said, easing myself down onto the ground and propping my feet up on the pillows. "But we'll figure it out, OK?" I leaned my head onto his back as I had so many times before, and lay there listening to him breathe.

We should both, I thought, enjoy the quiet while it lasts.

CHAPTER 15

The bright midday sun pounding down on my back seemed absurdly cheerful given the circumstances. It was almost mundane in its beauty, in stark contrast with the scene transpiring below.

I made it around the corner of the house, running from the creature that was chasing me, but my feet had become heavy, like I was slogging through quicksand. I looked up, and saw my sister's face in the window above on the second floor. She was turned to the side, talking to someone on the other side of the room. I reached out to the weathered yellow siding, opening my mouth to scream, to plead for help, but nothing came out.

My feet were getting slower and slower, stuck into the ground like cement. I felt the dark thing behind me, its dank breath on my neck, the rush of air as it reached for me. Above, the sun shone on, oblivious.

That's always when I woke up, as the sun faded from view.

When my eyes snapped open out of the nightmare, I was back in bed, my hands clenched on the sweaty sheets. The Chasing Thing nightmare was not new to me—in fact, I'd been having the same nasty one since I was five—but it had been so very long since the last time I'd almost forgotten how awful it was.

A first-time pregnancy was stressful, so I wasn't overly surprised that my subconscious was acting out. Over the last few weeks, Brian had started sleepwalking for the first time since I'd known him, jumping out of bed and running randomly toward imagined emergencies. The last time it happened he tripped over a box he had accidentally left on the floor and woke up, confused, by the impact of his head going through the drywall. Right now, though, he was fast asleep.

My heart was still racing, the baby starting to roll and kick in response to the adrenaline. Three a.m. I still needed more rest; she was due any day, and I needed to store up my energy while I could. I dropped my hand over the side of the bed and, like a genie sensing its summons, Emmett materialized and licked my hand, gently and calmly, until I fell back asleep.

The first emotion that went through my head when my daughter Zoe was born was sheer, utter elation. That lasted about two seconds, to be replaced by a gnawing terror telling me I had no idea what I was doing but was now in charge of a completely helpless human. I quickly discovered they were nothing like puppies.

I had done as much as I could in the previous ten months to prepare, reading all the parenting books, accumulating mountains of diapers and creams and little blankets in myriad sizes and colors, certain that this pile of stuff would somehow insulate me from the fact that I was driving this boat blind. My parenting class, which I entered thinking it would somehow bestow upon me the Mysteries of the Universe, only served to make me more paranoid that my child would suffocate in my bed, die of smoke inhalation (despite the fact that none of us smoke), or worst of all, shrivel up into a tiny, withered, illness-prone prune if I failed to breast-feed for a minimum of one year.

"Your baby is very jaundiced," said the nurse crisply on day two of my daughter's life. "Is she drinking enough?"

"I don't know," I admitted. Nursing was not going as intuitively as I had hoped. She watched me skeptically as I tried to get my daughter to latch on. A few minutes later, the nurse popped a bottle into her mouth and I watched my daughter relax as she actually got something to eat. "Your body," she told me, "doesn't want to cooperate. I'll get you some formula samples."

I was already a failure at day two. In desperation, I called in a lactation consultant, who prodded at my chest and hrmmmed alarmingly while she tried to determine how to coax my body into a state of production. By the time we were discharged, I had a rented medical-grade pump complete with a depressingly utilitarian-looking pair of suction cones, a diary in which I was to inscribe every in and out, and an every-other-hour round-the-clock pumping schedule under which I was transformed into a dairy heifer. And since it had become clear that Zoe's liver would need a little help catching up with the bilirubin accumulated in her blood, I was discharged with a fiberoptic biliblanket and strict instructions to keep her wrapped up in it for twenty-three hours a day.

Somewhere in the midst of all of this I also had to actually attend to the baby.

Dog the Second: EMMETT

Once we came home, Emmett was confounded at the transformation. For the first two weeks, I didn't leave the bedroom. In one corner of the room, Zoe was snuggled in her bassinet, wrapped in the soft blue light of the biliblanket, looking like a Glow Worm. In the other corner, I sat in a rocking chair with my diary and a bunch of plastic bags, listening to the mechanical whirring of the breast pump when all I wanted to hear was my baby breathing in and out. I slept in ten-minute increments while Emmett kept my feet warm.

Eventually I was able to get my daughter to nurse, but had I been a dairy cow, I would have been sent off to the hamburger plant long ago. In the meantime, Zoe had developed colic. If she was not nursing or bundled up in her swing under the heavy influence of a nuclear swaddle, she was crying. A lot. Nonstop.

As was I. To hear other women tell it, parenthood is the culmination of all that being a human was about. Joy. Exultation. Pride. I had none of this. I had a mechanical torture device sucking my chest inside out, a stomach like a deflated basketball, and a baby who, I was convinced, hated me. I hated me too. "She's so beautiful," visitors would coo. "You must be so happy." What else could I do but agree? I had a beautiful, healthy daughter and I was also miserable. It made no sense. Unnoticed by everyone, sliding in through a window or under a cracked door, an uninvited guest had just let itself in.

For the first two weeks at home, I'd had help as both my husband and my mother stayed with me, but when Mom went back home and Brian went back to work, I felt my throat constrict with panic as the reality set in that now I was really on my own. *Don't go!* I shouted in my head, but all that came out was "Have a good day."

It would be another year before Brooke Shields published her memoir about postpartum depression and shed a much-needed spotlight on the turmoil it creates. I was vaguely aware that such a thing existed for some people, but completely oblivious to the fact that it was already rooted in my own brain, wrapping it in a gray fog punctuated by shrapnel shards of anxiety.

My idyllic visions of sunny strolls every morning and afternoon followed by some baby yoga quickly evaporated under a crushing sense of paralysis. The energy required to simply roll out of bed and tend to my daughter was by itself enough to consume my day. I felt guilty about this too, thinking that every other decent woman on the planet could pull it together to at least go for a walk.

Instead of bringing me rushing to the rescue with a cheerful demeanor and a clean stack of wipes, Zoe's cries drilled into my head like a hammer. Why do I dread my baby waking up so much? I wondered.

"Because you suck," depression replied. "You probably should have stuck to dogs. Too late now, though—you have a baby and you're going to be awful at raising her."

These conversations played out in my head around the clock, snuffing out any capacity for enjoying the wonder of a new baby. Over the next month, it just got worse.

Depression, as so many who have suffered from it will tell you, messes with the rational portion of your brain that questions unreasonable lines of thought. The red flags are gone.

Dog the Second: EMMETT

There is nothing in your brain that says, *Hey, maybe it's not normal to casually wonder if getting hit by a Greyhound bus would be super painful, or just quick and painless.* Nothing to pat you on the back and say, *You are actually not the vilest human to crawl out of the muck.* So you stew in it, full of despair and self-loathing, acutely distressed that this child was cursed to have a creature as unworthy as yourself for a parent and unable to remember what happiness feels like: a silent asphyxiation of the spirit. There is no forgiveness in there. Over time, you regress to a detached state of numbness, because feeling nothing is better than feeling everything. My brain, the only thing I always felt I could rely on, was failing me.

Life's circumstances have nothing to do with postpartum depression; it happens to people from all walks of life and circumstances. I had everything I needed: a healthy child and a loving family. Unfortunately, my awareness of my luck and the feeling that I had no justification for being depressed led me to conclude I was a horrible whiny sort of person whom no one could ever sympathize with, and that guilt made me even more depressed and ashamed of myself. It's a long slow spiral of shame, throwing a pall over what I'd hoped would be a glorious time of bonding, and I couldn't imagine sharing that thought with anyone.

I can reason my way out of this, I thought. I just have to keep reminding myself how good I have it. My grandparents survived the Holocaust, surely I can make it through a fussy baby. Most people accepted me at face value when I said "Everything's fine," because that's what people are conditioned to do. "Every new parent feels tired," said my family and friends the few times I mentioned feeling exhausted. "It'll get better." I would smile and nod, and as soon as they left I would slump back onto the couch and stare listlessly at the ceiling. The message: Don't complain.

Humans are fairly awful at picking up on the emotional distress radiating from their fellow humans, or at least we are conditioned to politely ignore it. Dogs, on the other hand, figure it out pretty quickly. Emmett had a habit, as do many Goldens, of being somewhat pushy when it came to getting attention. If he was looking at you waiting to be petted and you did not comply, he'd lean into you, which given his eighty-pound frame was impossible to ignore. If you still didn't pet him, he would physically lift your hand with his muzzle, tip his head back so your hand fell onto the top of it, and wait expectantly, his eyebrows working up and down, up and down. How *you* doin', they seemed to say.

Usually, this made me laugh and turn my attention to him. But lately, all I could give him was a halfhearted pat on the head, if anything at all. He'd stare at my hand as it slid back onto the couch, and try again. "Stop," I told him over and over, wiping slobber off my hand, and eventually, he did.

Many new moms are familiar with the nursing pillow, a U-shaped bolster that sits around your waist and gives the baby a place to rest while nursing. I had become fond of the My Brest Friend, a rigid Styrofoam version that had a little strap that would belt it to your waist so you could wear it around without having to hold on. I could stuff the pockets with binkies, a dog treat or two, the TV remote, and leave it on all day.

Dog the Second: EMMETT

Constant motion was the only thing that kept Zoe from crying in her colicky phase, so around and around we'd go in laps around the house, baby in arms, Brest Friend strapped on like a flannel life preserver, and trailing behind, Emmett, trying to understand what was going on. For a time, that was his main source of exercise.

Emmett had his own anxiety to work through after the baby arrived. For the last two years he had been the big cheese of the household, the one doted upon, attended to by dog walkers, and given a daily massage. The change was abrupt. These days my main goal for him was remembering to feed him. That was also my main goal for myself.

I knew once life evened out I would have more time for Emmett, but he didn't know that, and he began to exhibit behaviors I had never seen from him before. The box the stroller came in, suddenly spattered with dog urine by a dog who had never once had a housebreaking incident. The leg of the changing table, chewed up by a mouth long past the teething phase. And the little teal pacifiers we wielded like anti-fuss talismans? If one of them ever fell onto the floor, Emmett would pounce upon it like a shark on a fat seal, taking out all his aggression on the blameless binky. Three chomps, and it was dead. For months I found little bits of blue rubber under the couch, wedged in corners.

He was never punished for this; one, because I was too tired to care, and two, because I knew why he was doing it. I also knew that he would make a play for any dirty diapers, given the chance.

Victims of the unending onslaught of products marketed to

new parents, Brian and I had bought into the idea that a simple trash can would never suffice for used Pampers and that we must instead purchase a demonic plastic device called a Nappy Nanny. It was supposed to effortlessly whisk diapers away to a magical stink-free land never to be seen or smelled again, but all it really did was stuff them like a stinky haggis into the receptacle, resulting in a long, slithering sausage you had to then wrestle out of the bin and transfer to the trash can. I'm not sure what about this was supposed to make my life easier, as it was by orders of magnitude more complicated than, for example, just throwing the diaper in the trash can.

The process of emptying the Nappy Nanny was not unlike performing a minor intestinal surgery: You had to undo the front hatch and excise the offending bits with a razor before putting the whole thing back together. As time consuming as it was I tried to limit the process to once a day or so. One typical morning when I put Zoe down for a nap, I collapsed on the couch to try and catch some Z's myself while I could, vaguely aware that Emmett had plopped down next to me. I fell asleep with my hand on his chest, comforted by his body heat.

The sound that woke me up was not the baby crying, but rather the rhythmic gurgling of someone about to vomit. Bluurp, bluurp, bluurp. In my half-awake state I wondered if my husband had come home and was plunging the toilet next to my head, but then I realized what I was hearing and snapped my eyes open. There was Emmett, still on the couch next to me, hunched over, stomach heaving.

"Get down!" I yelled, and he only had time to turn his face to the side before going full Exorcist all over the sofa.

Dog the Second: EMMETT

I could only stare. My leather couch was now covered in what appeared to be chocolate pudding, sliding down the back to pool into the cracks between the seat cushions. And then the stench hit me.

I'd been a veterinarian for a couple of years by that point. Between work, vet school rotations through the pathology lab, and my time at the coroner's office, I'd seen some bad things. Smelled some bad things. Rotting things, things pulled from rivers, things with weird gas producing gangrenous diseases. This topped them all.

So heavy and onerous was the smell that it took a minute to reach me, a gooey mass of invisible stink rolling slowly across the leather to invade my nostrils. Fans of the 1986 Jim Henson movie *Labyrinth* will remember the expression on the characters' faces when they are upended into the Bog of Eternal Stench, the wail of pain that comes with a direct assault on the olfactory nerves. I had always wondered what that place might smell like, and now I knew. I recognized the stench immediately: vomit and dirty diaper, somehow combining and amplifying the yuck factor.

I spun around to take in the sight of a disemboweled Nanny. In my two-second crime scene investigation I realized that I hadn't closed the latch all the way, leaving just enough space for someone to nose the door open and feast on the cornucopia within while I was passed out. Scattered casings of plastic lay strewn on the floor, all that remained of the contents of the Nappy Nanny. The rest of it, of course, had found its way to the couch.

As Zoe swung back and forth in her little electronic Fisher-

Price aquarium swing like a pendulum, the minutes stretched into hours while I tried to decontaminate the furniture. And there it was, my experience of early motherhood in a nutshell. What was supposed to be the ultimate experience of womanhood, Zen-level fulfillment, amounted to three hours of scrubbing half-digested poop out of the upholstery while Barney sang in the background about kindness and love, a nasally finger-wagging dinosaur reminding me that above all, remain cheerful.

As if on cue, that purple beast launched into a peppy rendition of "Clean Up," and that was it. I felt my last tenuous grip on sanity snap deep in my viscera. The floodgates were open, the net holding my head together evaporated, and down I fell.

I passed the afternoon in a haze. I don't remember what I said to Emmett but I'm sure it wasn't very nice. He spent the entirety of the afternoon in the corner, watching me nervously. Sob, scrub, sob, scrub. My husband texted me: *How's it going?* I replied: *Dandy.* If he had called instead and heard my voice, he would have gotten in the car immediately and come home, but with no hint that I was off a ledge, he simply told me he was working late.

And just like that, the demon from my dreams caught me. It reminded me that this entire hellish afternoon was my fault, and even if it weren't, a good mother would have been fine with it and gotten on with life, not taking breaks every five minutes to feel sorry for herself and cry some more; the kind of deep, body-shaking cries that leave you feeling like your sternum has split in two and your heart melted out of your chest. The abscess of guilt that had been festering for weeks finally ruptured, oozing guilt and anger and awfulness and confusion about where it all was coming from but certain of one thing: Wherever it originated, it was the result of my own inadequacy.

Recently Emmett had started avoiding me when I was upset, giving me time to clear my head before he approached. But this time, my distress went on and on. I was out of commission for the afternoon, my mind gone to some other place I can't even recall, wandering on autopilot with the baby in a Björn sling, powered by an endless stream of crying jags. It was during this later period that Emmett appeared at my side, following me from room to room, regarding me. I couldn't quite check out entirely as he would be there, nudging me back to awareness each time I paused for too long.

After a brief pause to eat, Zoe had gone back into her swing for a bit. I collapsed on the floor with my head on my knees, beyond crying at this point, blank, quiet. Then there he was, square in front of me, Emmett nose-to-nose with me.

"What?" I snapped. "What is it? What's wrong?"

There, in his unblinking eyes, I saw the question reflected right back at me.

I saw it before it could hide behind its customary wall of rationalization, the shadow behind me. I was not OK. This was beyond something I could overcome with smarts or strength or determination. This was not me.

"Oh my God," I whispered to myself, taking a breath and trying to focus through the fog in my head. "This is depression, isn't it?" I paused, suddenly certain that it was. For one brief, hopeful moment I thought that simply recognizing it for what it was might be enough, but I knew in my heart that acknowledgment was just the first step down a long road. Still, at least there was a road I could follow, instead of just sitting there with my head in my hands.

It was and is still extremely hard to stand up straight and admit there's a problem here you just can't fix, but I'm really glad I did. As much as I wanted to just sink back into the couch cushions and forget this whole day, week, month, I had to do something—beginning with swallowing my pride and my ego, which clearly hadn't been doing the trick on their own.

"I think I need to go to the doctor," I said to Brian later that evening.

"Everything OK?" he asked.

"Yes, fine," I said, not wanting him to worry. He started to turn back to the computer before I finally worked up the nerve to say out loud, "Well, actually, not really."

The next day, I called my doctor—not the OB with the horrible bedside manner, I switched to someone much better now—and said, "I need help." She booked me an appointment for that afternoon. I slouched in with my ratty hair and droopy sweats and the first wrinkly T-shirt I could dig out of the pile of clean laundry, hoping to remain anonymous behind my sunglasses. I hope none of my clients are here, I thought as I scanned the room. All clear.

As I waited in the exam room, sitting on the exam table listening to the paper crackle underneath me, my relief at being at the doctor's office was replaced by panic at the idea that she might not believe me, or worse yet, tell me there was nothing she could do until I actually planned to hurt someone. You got this, I said to myself. Explain to her, doctor to doctor, that you think this is more than just a little baby blues.

Dr. Whitman knocked on the door and poked her head in. "Hi," she said.

I burst into tears.

And she smiled, not a condescending smirk or a placating grin, but the sad yet relieved expression of someone who knows exactly what she is looking at. As she talked, I began to feel for the first time as though things might actually get better.

Dr. Whitman immediately pish-poshed my wondering if this was due to not eating enough vitamin C or lack of exercise or any of those other self-fixes I'd read about over the Internet. "Diabetics will benefit from a good diet," she said, "but they still need insulin, don't they? This is the same thing. You need medication." She paused and looked me in the eye. "I am so glad you came in."

Salvation came in a bottle, delivered to me by a Golden Retriever. You can fool yourself, you can fool your friends and family, but you can't fool a dog who knows only what he sees. And thank goodness for that.

CHAPTER 16

Life improved dramatically once the depression eased up, allowing me to evaluate my feelings about motherhood with a more objective eye. I loved my daughter deeply, but I wasn't as enamored of the day-to-day rituals of stay-at-home motherhood. Though I'd planned an extended maternity leave, I found myself making regular excursions to work just to get out of the house a little. I missed talking to other adults, this office filled with colleagues I also considered friends. While some of my mom-friends viewed their return to work with dread, I was looking forward to it.

I returned to work a much different person than the one who'd left a few months prior, weathered, battered, yet stronger for it. The mental demands of keeping up with a young baby took away from the emotional reserves I had to donate to my clients. I thought this process of letting go of obsessing over every detail of my work would make me a worse, less focused doctor, but it actually had the opposite effect. Being forced to prioritize where I spent my limited stress currency made me better at focusing on true concerns and able to let go of things I couldn't control. It also let me really start to enjoy the work instead of living under the constant fear of imperfect practice.

When people bring you a sick pet, they arrive with the expectation that you are going to make that pet better. You do your best. Some are easy (a minor skin infection), some are challenging (necrotizing pancreatitis) and some are just about impossible (metastasized hemangiosarcoma). I'd like to say that I found my greatest satisfaction in shepherding a pet through some of the more challenging conditions: pulling a dog through a bad uterine infection with a combination of surgery and medicine, or bringing a blocked cat with a ruptured bladder back from the brink of death. This may be true. It is tremendously rewarding to look back—especially if it's a condition you haven't dealt with before—and say to yourself, Man, that was tough, thank God I paid attention to that lecture on hyperkalemia.

Clients may or may not be as impressed. Sure, they know you just pulled off a complicated save, but they often assume—and how flattering of them—that *of course* you would, no matter how bad the case may be. Then they get the bill for the four days in the hospital, a bill they had approved in advance at the start of all of it, but suddenly they like you just a tad bit less when it hits them that your altruism is not all-encompassing.

And that's for the cases that end well. When a case goes poorly, when a pet dies despite your best attempt to put them back together after a coyote attack or a diabetic crisis that had gone on just a bit too long, they find themselves flipping through their paperwork for a nonexistent *Satisfaction Guaranteed Or Your Money Back!* claim.

But it bothered me a little less than it had before. I still felt badly when people couldn't afford the treatments their pet needed, especially when we were dealing with a pet who was seriously injured, but I no longer took it personally when I got blamed. I could offer a credit plan, a suggestion to consider pet insurance for the future, and the best treatment I had for what they could afford. The staff spent hours on the phone with groups that helped with veterinary bills, and it wasn't uncommon for Rachelle to slip an owner something she purchased with her own meager salary. (Only if the patient was a cat, though. Dogs were on their own.)

In an attempt to make veterinary care more accessible, we toyed with the idea of offering payment plans. Each person we offered one to promised, with tears and words of thanks, to pay us every month in return for their pet's necessary surgery or treatments. They'd sign the promise to pay, pat Mary-Kate on the back, and happily agree to whatever treatment was necessary once they realized they wouldn't have to pay for it up front. And 75 percent of the time, as soon as their pet left the building, we never saw or heard from them again. When I asked Isaac why we cut the program off so quickly, he pulled up a computer screen showing the number of people who skipped out on the arrangement. "That's thousands of dollars we'll never get back. We can't afford it anymore," he said. "I wish we could."

Shortly thereafter, Animal Control brought in a dog who

had been hit by a car. The poor thing was in bad shape, and we did what we could to stabilize him and provide pain relief while attempting to contact the owners.

A man arrived an hour later, screwing his eyes together as he took in the sight of his pup. "Broken back, you said?"

"I think so," I told him. I was holding in my hand an estimate for the various things we could do, X-rays and fluids and possible transfers to the ER clinic. The owner told me he had $10 to his name.

"How much is it to put him to sleep?" he asked. "I can't afford to treat him but I don't want him to suffer." I told him. It was more than $10.

"Well, I guess I'll take him home, then." I looked at him in confusion. "I'll take care of it somehow." He made a gun motion with his fingers, bang bang.

"I got this one," I told him. Regardless of the owner's ability to pay, I never denied a pet a peaceful passing when they were so very sick or injured. Small comfort in those situations, but it was what I had to give. The owners were always grateful, but we were doing it for the pets.

"You can take it out of my paycheck," I told Isaac that afternoon.

"That won't be necessary," he said. "We're a business, but we're not heartless."

Those kinds of days left me weary, and I found myself perfectly content with what others might call "horribly boring" days filled with simple problems and easy fixes, preventive care and teeth cleanings. Like the Wizard of Oz, there were a few tricks I could pull out from behind the curtains that had a high return on investment, leaving a happy client with a miraculously improved dog and a relatively small bill. I liked those visits, the ones that fortify the family unit. They were low-stress and satisfying for everyone involved.

"Room 4!" called Susan, pulling me away from rounds to rush into a room of sniffling children huddled around a tiny Chihuahua. The mother looked up with panicked eyes.

"I can barely wake him up," she told me, rubbing the puppy worriedly.

"How old is he?" I asked.

"Six weeks," she said.

"Is he still nursing?"

"No," she said. "We got him two weeks ago from a friend."

Susan grimaced—this was a pet removed from his mother several weeks too early.

"When did he last eat?" I asked.

"Oh," the owner said, checking her watch. "I don't know, maybe this morning? Six hours ago?"

I bundled the puppy up and put him in the owner's lap. "Keep him warm. I'll be right back."

The pharmacy filled the back hall behind our treatment area. I strode past the crash cart pushed to the side wall, skimmed past the ultrasound machine, moved my fingers past the bottles of antibiotics and steroids. I pulled out a tall bottle of dextrose, a thick sugary syrup, and poured some into a small syringe. A few seconds later, I was back in the room, sugar water in hand.

"Watch," I said, waving the syringe like a magic wand. I gently squirted a little of the sweet liquid onto the dog's gums. We waited. Then the magic happened.

Shazam! The dog opened his eyes. He wagged his tail, lifting his head. We gave him a little more dextrose. Within a couple of minutes, he was prancing around on the table.

The children, their tears now dried, looked at me in wonder as they mused aloud about the miraculous veterinarian who saved their dog with some sort of wonder drug. I took a minute to bask in the glory of the moment—might as well take it where you can—and then pulled the curtain back and let them know the main problem was that their little dog was hypoglycemic and needed to eat more frequently. Once they put the puppy on a more appropriate feeding schedule, he did just fine.

Later that day, a scraggly three-month-old pit bull puppy waited in an exam room, where Mary-Kate had put him in case he was contagious. The owners were scared to touch him because he looked like an earthworm, hairless and pink, and they worried he might pass something on to them.

"Is he itchy?" I asked, which is one of the classic signs of scabies—which can indeed be infectious to people.

He wasn't, they told me. That was promising.

The little pittie, whose name was Terrence, licked Susan's fingers as I gently took a scalpel blade to his skin. Holding it at an angle, I raked it along his hairless belly, scraping parallel to his skin instead of pushing in to cut. We scraped a few spots on his body, getting a nice waxy sample of skin cells and perhaps something more to look at under the microscope.

We handed the slide off to Rachelle, who mushed the goo on the scalpel blade into a drop of mineral oil sitting on a microscope slide. When she found what she wanted, she gestured to me to come take a look in the microscope eyepiece. The yellow blur under the lens wobbled in and out of focus as she rotated the knob, scanning the slide to see what was hiding in Terrence's skin. Dead skin cells. Old bits of broken-off hair. And there, lumbering into view like the Starship *Enterprise*, the wiggling, alien form of a demodex mite.

Segmented and conical, an unrolled cornucopia with legs, demodex mites are fairly ubiquitous in canines. Most dogs can have one or two without a problem, but in some pets, they stage a mass takeover of the hair follicles, resulting in a profoundly bald, pathetic-looking dog. Sometimes it's genetics. Sometimes it's just the immature immune system of the pup. The good news was, I could fix it.

To add to the drama of the event and increase the owners' likelihood of sticking with the sometimes arduous treatment schedule, we brought them into the back to show them the mites, happily writhing away under the microscope. They were appalled. They would not forget the meds.

Abracadabra! A few weeks later, after using the ivermectin and the antibiotics we sent home for the secondary bacterial infection, Terrence bounded in, happily on the mend. It turned out he had gray fur. After his full course of treatment, he was calendar-ready. I was rewarded with a slobbery kiss from Terrence and a firm handshake from a thrilled owner. Some payments can't be measured in cash.

By my fifth year of practice, my life had reached that

all-too-elusive steady state. My daughter Zoe had been joined by my son Zachary, a blond, blue-eyed boy with apple cheeks and an endless supply of affection. Aware of the likelihood of a relapse of my postpartum depression, I managed that pregnancy and postpartum period much more carefully and found this time around so much easier on my emotional health. Zach was a jolly baby, full of smiles, and Zoe was now a sweet and thoughtful toddler with a wave of strawberry-blond hair and, like her mother, an innate interest in animals. Her first word, in fact, was "Doggy."

Life was good. But it wasn't exactly simple, not with a newborn and a two-year-old. I had navigated my life into a happy balance, and realized that maintaining that was going to require constant attention and care. Next on the agenda: Minimize work stress. I was working part-time at this point, an option I was fortunate to have. I went to work with a single-minded determination to make it a positive experience, a task made easier by being surrounded by a staff I loved to bits. By this time they knew me well enough to know which kinds of appointments to throw my way.

There are some people who really need constant challenges in order to find career satisfaction, and those people often end up as specialists, unraveling the problems the general practitioners just can't decode. If not, they wind up in general practice twiddling their thumbs, waiting for the next big surgery to come in. Sometimes doctors would fight over who got the "fun" appointments like the broken leg that needed splinting, or the splenic tumor removal. I didn't mind the simple stuff, the ear infections and lipomas. Things that others found repetitive, I found comfortingly routine. When clients were happy, I was happy, and the easier the solution was for all of us, the more likely that was to happen.

Gratitude, while not required or even expected, was always happily accepted. There were those clients who never failed to bring in cookies or brownies for the chronically hungry staff, and I'd be lying if I didn't say everyone looked forward to their visits. Not only for the cookies themselves, but for the warm fuzzies that such kindness spread to us all. It helped make up for the occasional angry online review.

It was easy to identify the writers of these reviews, since they always provided a detailed rundown of the visit that caused such offense. Much of the time it's fair to say their perception of the visit did not coincide with our own impressions of what transpired, but such is life. All we could do was fix what we could and move forward. Fortunately, happy clients also posted reviews, and usually those endorsements outweighed the bad ones in both impact and number.

Mrs. Adams had been coming to the hospital for at least a year before I started working there. She had three Miniature Pinschers, all in states of obesity she was managing with varying degrees of success. It was very important to her that each dog receive the veterinarian's full and undivided attention without the distraction of its siblings, so despite our protests that we really didn't mind seeing all three at once, she brought each in on his or her own whenever they were in need of a visit. We saw her a lot.

Mr. Adams was in the military and traveled quite a bit. Having followed him to the States from her native Japan, his wife spent her spare time taking English classes. She was getting there, but it was a slow process. She would patiently sit in the waiting area with a leash in one hand and an instructional English textbook in the other until it was her turn to be seen, then she'd spend the first few minutes of every visit updating me on her latest English lesson. Sometimes she practiced by reading tabloids. "What is this word?" she would ask, scribbling notes furiously in the margins as I translated *back to rehab* or *baby bump watch*. She'd ask me if I liked Charlize Theron's Oscar dress as her perpetually starving dog nibbled contentedly on my ankle.

I know some of the other doctors got frustrated with her visits because they always involved so much chitchat, but I liked Mrs. Adams. I thought of my friends who are military wives and how lonely they got in foreign countries while staying with their spouses on deployment, and I really respected her dedication to learning English. It couldn't be easy, but she was always smiling and cheerful. In a lot of ways, she reminded me of a younger version of my grandmother.

"I brought you my Shiba Inu," she said on one such visit.

I looked at her, confused. "I thought they were Miniature Pinschers?" The two breeds look nothing alike.

She laughed, never really explaining the joke, and on we went. From that day forward she always called her Miniature Pinschers Shiba Inus, and I always just went with it.

One day, Susan took me into the office and said she wanted me to see the latest online review. I sighed. "Is it bad?"

"Just look," she said, clicking on the screen.

"The doctors here are so nice. Dr. V is my most favored.

She take all the time to tell me my fat dog needs diet and helps me with English too. Some day I can teach her Japanese. 'Shibo inu' mean fat dog in Japanese."

I pictured her tapping away on the keyboard, working her way meticulously through all the words as she translated them in her head. It probably took a while. It was, and I include both the cookies and the holiday soaps in this assessment, the nicest thank-you I've ever gotten.

CHAPTER 17

When you're in vet school, you picture a career filled with adrenaline rushes and lifesaving CPR exercises, bloat surgeries and yelling "EPI STAT!" That holds for those intrepid souls who venture into ER work, but for the rest of us general practitioners, the reality is we spend a disproportionate amount of our day with poop. Talking about it, looking at it, examining it, mushing it around. It's not a line of work for the squeamish.

Poop is also notable for containing all sorts of strange items ingested by dogs, usually Labradors, for whom the tongue seems to be as important a sensory organ as the eyes and ears. Some of the larger items require surgery to extract, causing no small amount of regret for the owner who didn't realize he or she had a dog with such strange tastes. When they're lucky, the GI tract manages to move everything along and take care of the problem without my assistance.

When veterinarians get together, "What weird items did your patients eat this week?" is just as much standard dinner conversation as "Seen any good movies lately?" Rubber duckies, golf balls, piles of rocks, fishhooks, jewelry, serrated knives—just when you think you've seen it all, some dog out there manages to top it, performing some form of esophageal voodoo in order to choke down an entire (deflated) soccer ball.

Anyone who has worked with dogs for any length of time knows that some dogs just can't turn away a good pair of underpants. Taffy had been one of those dogs. Because she was small and dainty, she'd just chew out the middle and leave the waistband crumpled in the corner of the bathroom. Larger dogs with such distasteful proclivities tend to just gulp them whole.

One afternoon, on my way into an exam room, I heard Manny on the phone, counseling a worried client who said her dog had something sticking out of his rear end.

"Purple?" he said. "Like purple flesh or purple something he ate?...That's OK, you don't have to poke it...No, don't pull on it...Just come on in." Half an hour later, Charlie was sitting contentedly in the treatment area as I snapped on a pair of gloves. He was a big brown shepherd mixed with, you guessed it, Labrador, and so far he seemed to be in a great mood.

This was only the second time we had seen Charlie in the clinic. Kallie Wilson, Charlie's owner, had brought him in for vaccines one month earlier when she was moving in with her boyfriend. "I just want to make sure he's perfectly healthy," she said at the time. She had no concerns other than his occasional tendency to eat random socks and toys on the floor.

Dog the Second: EMMETT

Today, Ms. Wilson elected to leave Charlie with us for a couple of hours while she went shopping. We promised to call her with an update.

I lifted Charlie's tail, and as promised, a small piece of purple cloth protruded from his rear end. It's important not to yank on items of indeterminate length; long items such as pantyhose can be tangled farther up in the intestines, and if so, pulling can be damaging. But smaller items, with a little professional coaxing, are usually simpler to remove. I asked Manny for the lube for a rectal exam.

Charlie eyed me nervously and decided to save me the effort. Rather than wait for us to poke him anymore, he went ahead and produced for us a small purple G-string, turning around to examine the result and seeming rather surprised himself at what he was looking at.

"Well, that was easy," I said. "Ms. Wilson will be happy, I'm sure—no bill! Stick it in a plastic bag for her in case she wants to see it." Normally clients don't feel the need to inspect such things themselves, but you never know. Sure enough, when she returned an hour later Ms. Wilson asked to see the plastic bag. Manny dutifully trotted it out to her. Shortly thereafter I heard her raised voice, high-pitched and angry, and Manny responding in placating tones.

He came into the back area a minute later, rubbing his temples.

"Do I need to go out there?" I asked. "What's wrong?"

"I showed her the bag," he said. "And she said, 'These aren't mine.'"

"Uh-oh," I said.

"So I said, I don't know, maybe they were in his GI tract for a while or something, before she and her boyfriend got together?"

"If you say so, Manny."

"She didn't buy it either, Doc. They've been dating for eight months."

"Good effort, though." I poked my head out the door to see if there was anything I could do.

Ms. Wilson was already gone. After she spoke to Manny, she had grabbed Charlie's leash and hustled out without another word, jabbing her fingers at her smartphone as she texted (we assumed) her soon-to-be-ex-boyfriend. Mary-Kate and the other client in the waiting area exhaled in unison. A minute after the door shut behind her, Ms. Wilson ran back in, silently snatched the bag of purple evidence off the counter, and ran back out while we all stared at the ceiling, the floor, and the countertops.

Needless to say we did not see the Wilsons again after that.

I have long held the opinion that crummy medicine is most often a by-product of crummy communication. While some veterinarians may simply be poor at the task of diagnosing disease, the vast majority of veterinarians I've known are excellent clinicians, regardless of their personality. More often than not we are failing not in our medicine but in relaying to our clients, in clear and concise terms, the benefit of what it is we are recommending. Or even what we are recommending, period.

Muffy was a patient I hadn't seen before, a one-year-old Shih Tzu who presented to the clinic for sneezing spasms. They had started suddenly, according to the client, Mrs. Townsend.

"So he doesn't have a history of these episodes?" I asked.

"I don't know," she replied. "I'm just dog-sitting for my daughter."

As we spoke, Muffy began sneezing again—achoo achoo aCHOO! Seven times in a row. She paused, shaking her fuzzy little white head, and pawed at her snout.

"Was she outside before this happened?" I asked.

"Yes," Mrs. Townsend said. "She was out with me for a couple of hours this morning while I was weeding the garden."

Immediately my mind jumped to foxtails, a particularly pervasive type of grass awn found in our region. During the summer months, they have a nasty habit of embedding themselves in all sorts of locations on a dog: ears, feet, eyelids, gums, and yes, up the nose. Working like a one-way spearhead, these barbed plant materials are known for puncturing skin and wreaking havoc inside the body. It's best to get them out as quickly as possible.

Unfortunately, due to the nature of the little barbs on the seed, foxtails don't fall out on their own—you have to remove them. Sometimes, if you're lucky, you can pull one out of the ear canal while a pet is awake, but noses are a different story. Unsurprisingly, the average dog has no interest in holding still while you slide a well-lubricated pair of alligator forceps up his or her nose to go fishing for foxtails in their sensitive sinuses. And it's dangerous—if they jerk at the wrong moment, you are holding a piece of sharp metal one layer of bone away from their brain. The standard nose treasure hunt in our clinic involved general anesthesia, an otoscope cone functioning as a speculum to hold the nares open, and a smidgen of prayer.

I explained all of this as best I could to Mrs. Townsend, who eyed me distrustfully from behind her cat-eye glasses, blinking as I told her about the anesthesia.

"Can't you just try without the anesthesia?" she asked.

"Unfortunately, no," I said. "It would be impossible to get this long piece of metal up her nose safely without it. Her nostrils are very small and it would be very uncomfortable for her, so she wouldn't hold still."

"I need to talk to my daughter before we do that," she said.

"I understand. Before we anesthetize her, we do need your daughter's consent."

Muffy left with Mrs. Townsend and a copy of the estimate. I was hoping to have them back in that afternoon so we could help the dog as quickly as possible, but they didn't return.

The next day, Mary-Kate scurried into the back and came trotting toward me, loud voices pouring into the treatment area as the door swung shut behind her.

"Muffy's owner is here," she said. "And she's MAAAAAD."

I sighed. "Put her in Room 2."

Like a game of telephone, trying to communicate what's going on with a dog who can't talk to owners who weren't there via a pet-sitter who misheard you is bound to cause one or two misunderstandings. When Mrs. Townsend relayed her interpretation of my diagnosis to her daughter, the daughter rushed home from work and took Muffy to her regular veterinarian, who promptly anesthetized the dog and removed the foxtail.

Dog the Second: EMMETT

"My vet said you are terrible," said Muffy's owner without preamble. "Didn't you know foxtails can go into the *brain*? You nearly killed her!" Her voice reached a crescendo.

"I think there might be a misunderstanding here. I wanted to remove it," I told her. "The pet-sitter—it was your mother, correct? She said she needed to talk to you before approving the estimate."

"That's not what *she* said," replied the owner. "She said that you said there was no way a foxtail would fit up there and we should put her to sleep. Well there *was* one up there! You were wrong and you almost put her to sleep because of it!"

I took a slow inhale and reminded myself not to sigh. "What I told your mother," I said, "was that I thought Muffy had a foxtail, but there was no way I was going to be able to remove it without anesthesia. So I gave her an estimate for all of that."

"Are you calling my mother a liar?" she demanded. This was not going well.

"No," I said, "I just think that she may have misheard me."

"OK, so now you're saying she's stupid." I silently prayed for a fire alarm to go off, or an earthquake to rumble though. The waves of indignant anger pulsing from this woman were pressing me farther and farther into the corner and there was no escape.

"No, absolutely not," I said. "I think maybe I just didn't explain myself well enough." I pulled the record up on the computer and showed her. "See? She declined the anesthesia."

She thought about it for a minute and decided she still wanted to be mad. "You suck and I want a refund for the visit." We provided it gladly.

Shortly after the client left the waiting area, I had the pleasure of taking a phone call from Muffy's veterinarian himself.

"How can you not know about foxtails?" he asked. "Those kill dogs! Are you not from around here? I know that Care-Clinic always hires foreign vets but someone has to teach you people how to practice medicine."

"I'm from San Diego," I said. "And I went to Davis, just like you." I decided not to add that all of the foreign vets I occasionally worked with were all exceptional.

"Even worse!" he said. "I can't believe what you told that owner."

My patience was exhausted by that point. "Well, I can't either," I shot back. "You actually think I'd tell someone to euthanize a dog for sneezing? Can I tell you what really happened now, or do you have more to tell me about my clinical skills first?"

He listened silently as I explained that I had offered the exact same diagnosis and treatment as he, the self-proclaimed good veterinarian, had. "I can send you the record," I offered. "I could have done that yesterday too, had you called and asked for it."

There was a long pause while he thought about all the rotten things he seemed to have told Muffy's owners about my skills. "Oh, you should have said that sooner, then." Click.

From that day forward, whenever a client tells me about some bizarre-sounding misdiagnosis or strange recommendation from their previous vet, I always request the records before forming any opinion about how the case was handled. It's astonishing how often muddy explanatory skills can work like a carnival mirror, distorting correct information into seeming malpractice.

I made two big changes after the Muffy Incident. First, I end every exam with a printed summary. Second, I replaced "put to sleep" with "euthanasia" or "anesthesia" in all conversations. It's made visits a lot less stressful for everyone involved.

CHAPTER 18

We speak of pets in the possessive: my dog, my cat, my rabbit. This is *my* ball of fur, not yours. Who else could ever understand the way you blink your wide brown eyes, not quickly like we humans do, worried we're going to miss something important—but languidly, without a care in the world. No one else but me can kiss your brow and rest my cheek in the angle of your fuzzy snout, chin to muzzle together like puzzle pieces as we breathe in and listen to the wind rustle the leaves. These moments are mine.

But while we can attach ourselves to our pets all we want, we're deluding ourselves if we think that our sense of possessiveness actually means we own them. We simply borrow them for an indeterminate period, and we're never happy when the void comes knocking to tell us our lease has expired.

Sometimes we get an early notification that our time together is coming to an end, leaving us to fret for weeks or months. Other times we have no warning. I don't know which one is worse.

One Saturday morning while out running errands, I dug my buzzing phone out of my purse, annoyed that yet again, my office was bugging me about something or another. I paused in the produce aisle and read the text.

Susan: *PLZ CALL DAISY DEAD CRAP BAD THX*

Daisy died? She was only three! Her parents, the Greenes, were two of my favorite clients—kind to us and absolutely enamored of their little Standard Poodle pup. She was their baby.

Maybe it was OK that the office bugged me this one time. I quickly called back.

"Susan, it's Jessica...What the heck?"

"Oh my God, Dr. V, it's bad. Mr. Greene called this morning to bring Daisy's body in. He can't even talk."

"Do you know what happened?"

"She got out, hit by a car, I don't know, and then Animal Control got involved...I think you should call them. They asked for you."

I put my head in my hands. Of all the people for this to happen to. Good Lord. "I'll be there in a few minutes."

I got to work and pulled up Ron and Laura Greene's phone number. A sniffling voice answered the phone. "Yes?"

"Hey, Mr. Greene. It's Dr. Vogelsang. I just heard about Daisy. I'm so, so sorry."

"Oh, Dr. Vogelsang," he whispered, voice obscured with congestion and grief. "I can't believe this is happening. Did they tell you what happened?"

"Just that she passed away, Mr. Greene."

"Laura was getting groceries out of the car. And you know how much Daisy loves the car—she thought she was going for a ride—so she ran into the front yard while Laura was inside the house. She didn't even see her sneak out."

"Uh-huh," I said, my heart sinking.

"So, Laura went back into the house and started vacuuming." He paused, choking back more tears. "Daisy hates the vacuum. *Hated* it. She always hides when we vacuum so Laura didn't think anything of her not being around. It was an hour before Laura thought to go looking for her. And by then—" he paused.

"Oh, Mr. Greene."

"She was unconscious. Someone hit her and didn't even bother stopping. And we panicked. I think she was still alive. So we called 911. I mean, what else were we going to do?"

My breath caught at the thought of these lovely people, so distraught.

"Dr. Vogelsang," he told me, "I thought they were going to send an ambulance. But they sent out Animal Control. And then . . . they wanted to arrest us."

"Oh my God. No!" I put my hand to my mouth.

"They did," he said, his voice cracking. "They said we—" He took a deep breath. "—we neglected our dog by letting her run loose and they called the cops on us. We just wanted to try and get Daisy to the emergency room if they weren't going to help us but they wouldn't let us leave the driveway. I asked them if just one of us could go and the other person would stay and they said no."

I sat down on a stool, my head in my hands. "I am *so* sorry, Mr. Greene. I can't believe they did that to you."

"They made the sheriffs come out while she lay there dying. The sheriffs refused to take a report, though. They told Animal Control it was obviously an accident."

"Thank God."

"We called them for help," he said, "and they took an awful situation and made it ten times worse. And by the time they left, she had stopped breathing." He paused. "How could they do that to us?"

"Mr. Greene. I wish there was something I could say that would express how sad I am for you and how horrible this must have been for you."

"Thank you," he said. Then, in a tiny voice that broke my heart, he said, "I don't know what to do. She was our everything."

"Do you have family nearby?" I asked. "Is there anyone helping you and Laura out?"

"They're all out of state," he said. "I just...we can't leave the house right now." He sighed. "But thank you for calling. I really appreciate it."

"Of course," I said, frustrated with my inability to say something helpful. "You guys know how much we care about you. Please, if there's anything I can do..." There wasn't much else to say.

After we hung up, I sat and stared at the wall for a few minutes. I tried to imagine what they were feeling, this couple who had, I'm not exaggerating, doted on Daisy as they would a child. They'd loved this little pup with all their hearts, made a terrible, honest mistake that could have happened to anyone, and were greeted with derision and threats by the people they called for help.

"I'm heading out," I said to the other clinic staff. "Anyone want to chip in $5 for the Greenes?" Manny took an early lunch break and came with me.

Armed with a handful of cash from the clinic crew, we ran to the store and filled up a bag with a few days' supply of quick and easy food items, crackers, pasta, a box of cookies. On top I balanced a little bouquet of flowers. Then I picked up a blank card and wrote inside, *Please take care of yourselves. XOXO.*

We drove toward the Greenes' house, which was set low on a hill amid a grove of pine trees. We looked down at the house from our vantage point up on the street: no motion. No one would see us. Manny placed the bag on their stoop, rang the bell, and scurried up the driveway before they answered the door. It was a paltry bag of groceries, but I couldn't think of anything else to do.

I grimaced driving home as I thought of this couple, too paralyzed by grief to even leave the house to get something to eat. In a world that gives you a standard one day of grieving a pet before you're expected to get back to normal—*Buck up! It's just a dog*—the loss of a pet can be overwhelmingly lonely. Doubly so when the world kicks you so hard when you're down.

They never mentioned the bag, not then, or when they came back a few months later with a new dog, Gilda, whom they loved just as unconditionally as they'd loved Daisy. But when they moved away a year later, they wrote me a card with the most beautiful words in it, words that made me glad I had become a vet. And at the bottom: *Thank you—for everything. Love Laura, Ron, and Gilda Greene.*

I hope they have learned to forgive themselves. No matter the circumstances of a pet's death, we find ways to blame ourselves, even for things completely out of our control. I'm no more immune to this syndrome than anyone else; in fact, I might be worse because we vets hold ourselves to a particularly high standard for our own pets that we, being humans, can't always live up to.

Vets have a tendency not to believe clients when they say, "I just noticed this today." How could you not have noticed this? we think, poking at a large ulcerated mass dangling from a knee, or an abscessed tooth wobbling around oozing green goo. Some things are pretty hard to miss. On the other hand, most people don't examine their pets weekly, so some subtle changes are easy to overlook. You assume everything's fine until one day it's not.

On a bright and sunny Easter Sunday, I forced my children into their rarely worn itchy holiday finery and herded them into the car to head up to my parents' house. Emmett, who never liked to stay home alone, was invited as well. We arrived, healthy and vital, and poured out of the car at the other end to start the hunt for Easter eggs.

While the kids were crawling under the hedges, getting burrs and sticks attached to their lace and tweed, Emmett became bored and ambled toward the much more interesting buffet table. Ham? his eyebrows asked. Deviled eggs. Summer sausage. Heaven. Inhaling deeply, he slid his chin down the length of the table while my father stood at the far end with a spatula ready to shoo him away, or more likely toss him some ham when I wasn't looking.

Two hours and two thousand calories later, the adults sank into the couch to sit back and relax with glasses of wine. The kids headed outside to the big wooden swing on the far side of the lawn. Emmett stayed beside me for a few minutes, then, realizing there was no more food to be had, headed over to the back door to see what the kids were doing.

He sniffed. I continued talking.

He whined. I looked up.

He jumped up on the door and scrabbled at the glass, which he'd never done. I went up to the door and let him out quickly, wondering if we were in for a night of digestive distress. Then I heard the barking.

My father has had a long-standing beef with their next-door neighbor for many reasons, not the least of which were the neighbor's dogs. Territorial and untrained, they had a bad habit of growling and launching themselves at the fence whenever someone walked by. Except now one of the dogs was in my parents' backyard, between me and the kids who were on the far side. She stood, tail raised, hackles up, staring at them. They froze.

By the time I knew what was happening, Emmett had already planted himself firmly between the kids and the other dog. My normally amiable dog was more alert and intense than I had ever seen him, twitching his tail and pushing his ears forward. Then the other dog jumped on him.

Dog the Second: EMMETT

I bolted outside, yelling for my father to grab the hose. The dog had Emmett's ear in his mouth, thrashing from side to side like a shark while Emmett did his best to hold himself still. Hearing the commotion, the neighbor popped his head over the fence, his eyes widening in alarm. I heard my voice echo in my diaphragm as I yelled for him to get over here, but it didn't sound like me so much as a distorted demon. Even the other dog paused at that.

The neighbor ran through the side gate and pulled his dog off Emmett, promising it would never happen again as he dragged the dog back to his house by her collar, yelling at her all the while. I watched him leave with a twinge of regret. Now that my own dog and kids were safe, I had a moment to say a quiet prayer for that dog's fate too. I turned to Emmett, who stood stoically with blood dripping down his neck. He had a pretty decent laceration in his ear, but fortunately it wasn't severe. Festivities over, I wrapped his ear and took him home.

The next morning, Susan helped me anesthetize Emmett so I could clean his ear and stitch up the wound. While the American Medical Association's Code of Ethics suggests that MDs should avoid treating family or close friends, veterinarians face no such recommendation when it comes to our own furry family members. The risk that our emotional reaction might cloud our judgment in a life-threatening situation is still there, but it's one we can take if we so desire. As Susan shaved the side of his head, she paused. "Hey, Dr. V," she said. "Did you notice a lump here?"

I ran my fingers along his neck. It wasn't in the right location to be an abscess or a hematoma from his fight. That felt like a lymph node. An enlarged lymph node that I'd never noticed.

"Yeah, it's probably just some inflammation from the bite," said Dr. Joff when I called him over to take a look. "Did you pull a fine needle aspirate yet?"

"I'm just about to," I said, motioning to Rachelle to hand me a needle and syringe.

I slid a small needle into the node, sucking up a cell sample to send off to the lab along with a few other tests. The bloodwork arrived back first: perfect. Urinalysis: perfect. Chest X-rays: fine. Emmett took his antibiotics, his ear sealed up nicely. The swollen lymph node, however, remained. Somewhere several states away, a veterinary pathologist was staining the slides, sliding them under the microscope. Adjusting the focus button up and down until my dog's fate came into clear view. Several very long days passed while I obsessively checked the online lab forms waiting for the result. Not wanting to worry Brian unnecessarily and feeling superstitious, I decided to keep my concerns to myself. Afterward we could have a good laugh over my unfounded worry, like I'd done about the client who thought her dog's nipple was an abnormal growth.

At three forty-five on the third day, a new line popped up in the lab results section on the computer screen. *VOGELSANG, EMMETT—FINE NEEDLE ASPIRATE, FINAL.* I held my breath and clicked on the link.

213

MICROSCOPIC FINDINGS: LYMPHOMA

No. No, no, no. I read it again and again, hoping the letters would somehow rearrange themselves on the screen to something more agreeable—hammy lop, palmy ohm—but there they remained, frozen. My sweet seven-year-old dog, the best dog I ever had, had cancer.

And there it was. We teach our dogs to "stay," but they never do.

I heard footsteps behind me, sensed a head popping up behind my shoulder. Susan read the screen before putting her arm around me and resting her cheek on my shoulder. She loved him too. I hugged her back, then started looking up the most recent research on chemotherapy protocols.

"How was your day?" Brian asked when he got home that night, as I sat morosely on the couch with Emmett's head in my lap.

"Remember how I said Emmett had a little bit of neck swelling but it was probably nothing? The results came back. He has cancer," I said, dissolving into tears as the news became solid and terribly concrete once I finally said it aloud.

Brian paused with a soda can halfway up to his mouth. "Oh. Aw, no." He looked terribly sad, but he kept it together more than I had. We both knew that though Emmett lived in our house and was part of our family, it was my heart that he picked up and carried along with him.

"So what are you going to do?" Brian asked.

I sighed. "I want to try chemotherapy."

I was comfortable with most aspects of veterinary medicine by that point, but chemotherapy was a bit beyond my pay grade; it had always been something I referred out to other vets. I recruited Dr. Farley, one of the internal medicine specialists we often sent patients to, to help me with a plan. We settled on the UW Madison protocol, which had a median survival time of nine to thirteen months. It was worth a shot: Half the dogs lived longer, half lived less. I'd take every day I could get. Dr. Farley didn't tell me what I already knew: While this would probably make Emmett better for a while, it was not going to cure him.

Emmett was a champ through it all, gamely dealing with the catheters and the long hours he had to spend on the floor with Susan while the toxic drugs dripped slowly into his bloodstream. After his first treatment, I took him home and gave him a huge doggy granola treat, which he gobbled like a champ. Unlike those for humans, canine chemotherapy protocols aren't necessarily designed to permanently eradicate the cancer so much as stave it off as long as possible; therefore the side effects tend to be less severe. For example, Emmett kept his beautiful coat. He seemed a little more tired than usual, but he was still his happy self, at least at the beginning.

After the first treatment, his enlarged node disappeared like a bad dream. I could pretend, if only for a moment, that he wasn't actually sick. We went to Dog Beach more times in two weeks than we had in the prior two years, Emmett zooming through the waves and nosing through people's unattended beach bags, running up to strangers to lean in to be petted, unruffled by his sand-encrusted exterior. We'd depart before he became too exhausted, and he'd contentedly fall asleep in the car on the way home. I watched him at rest, suddenly noticing the sunken-in appearance of the muscles of his forehead. The drugs were helping, but not without cost.

I became a connoisseur of lymph nodes during this time, obsessively moving my hands up and down his body every day, evaluating their size. Under the jaw, by the clavicles, near the armpits, in the groin, behind the knees. Rub, palpate, evaluate. I focused on that left shoulder blade where the first node had popped up, running my fingers up and down for the telltale slip of a returning swelling. We were only two months past his diagnosis when it happened. I was devastated, even though I knew the day would come. We hadn't even finished the initial course of chemotherapy.

Dr. Farley scowled in frustration when he palpated the node. "Dammit," he said, turning to me. "Dammit dammit dammit. Some dogs are just refractory to treatment. I'm so sorry." He took a breath, then said, "We could try a rescue treatment, if you wanted…" A Hail Mary at the end of a rough game. We both knew it wouldn't change anything.

"I appreciate your help," I said, and meant it. "We tried our best." Emmett wagged his tail in agreement, licking Dr. Farley's hand as he often did when he sensed someone was unhappy. "Such a good boy," I said, holding my hand out to offer him a treat.

For the first time in years, Emmett refused it. The time to say good-bye was coming sooner rather than later. For all the years he had taken such good care of me, lifted my spirits, and eased my pain: Now, as his good days were dwindling, it was almost time to return the favor.

Our quiet time together was bittersweet, peppered with regret for all the things I could have done better. "I should have noticed this sooner," I said, laying my head on Emmett. He put his paw in my arm, the way he always seemed to do to say, *I love you.* I rubbed his belly.

"I'm so sorry," I said. "You might have beat this if I had." I stopped petting him to wipe my eyes. "What am I going to do without you, bud?" He put his head back down on his paws, frustrated that I'd paused in my massage. *Less jabber, more petting, please.*

As much as I wished I could just put my head in the sand, I knew I had to start planning for Emmett's death. I saw the trajectory play out almost every day at work. As pet owners, the gift of euthanasia is both a blessing and a curse; having control over when a loved one's death will occur is an enormous responsibility. People who plan ahead, who know exactly what parameters will mean the threshold has been crossed, tend to handle things better than people who avoid thinking about it until the pet is in crisis.

So as painful as it was, I pulled out my quality-of-life assessment charts and started to consider what would and would not be acceptable for him and for us. I also had to determine how I was going to handle it when it actually came time to euthanize him. I knew I couldn't do it at work, a place I needed to keep emotionally neutral. I wanted to do it at home, a place where he felt safe and comfortable, a place where all the happy memories wouldn't be overshadowed by this one sad moment.

While I had no problem performing most of Emmett's medical care on my own, I simply couldn't be the one to administer the drugs that would end his life. Susan, who had become a dear friend to me, agreed to come to my house and perform the euthanasia. It would turn out to be such a singularly comforting experience that I would later devote my career to doing house call hospice care for others, but at the time euthanasia at home was a rare occurrence, a favor people who worked in vet clinics did for one another.

When Emmett stopped eating entirely, I knew it was almost time. He still had enough energy for one last trip to Dog Beach together, just the two of us. It was a bright cloudless Sunday and the sand was crowded with happy pups and kids throwing tennis balls. Emmett walked down the path with a wagging tail, but when I unclipped his leash, he stayed by my side instead of tearing off into the water like we normally did, and we walked.

As we sat nose-to-nose on the shore, enjoying each other's company, a man with a large camera lens slung around his neck approached.

"May I take your picture?" he asked. I looked around. The beach was full of people and dogs jumping, having fun. Why would he want a picture of the two of us just sitting there?

"I saw you down the beach," he continued, "and there's just something about the way you are looking at each other that really struck me."

I nodded, too choked up to say yes out loud. After snapping a few shots, he handed me his card. "Send me an email later this week and I'll get the picture to you," he said. "Thanks." By the time I wrote him on Friday, Emmett was already gone.

After we returned from the beach, Emmett flopped onto his bed and slept for ten hours straight. The next morning he didn't want to get up at all, and his breathing had become shallow. I sighed. He was done, and I had to go to work.

It was a very long Monday. I filled in Isaac and asked if I could have Tuesday off since I didn't think I would be in any shape to see clients. He sighed. "We're awfully busy," he said. "How about a half day?" Guess I should have done what many other people do in similar situations and just call in sick instead. Even people in the veterinary field can be terribly unhelpful when it comes to acknowledging the grief of pet loss.

At lunch, I went to Barnes and Noble with Susan to pick out a book for the kids. The only one I could find had a bunch of illustrations of dogs with angel wings zooming around above the clouds. I couldn't read past the first page without tearing up, but it would have to do. I shoved it at my husband when I got home that evening. "Can you read this to them tonight?" He looked at the title as my face wrinkled up. According to the babysitter, Emmett had slept most of the day.

"Do we tell the kids before or after he dies?" he asked. Zoe and Zach were four and two at the time. No one told me in vet school how to counsel families on this topic, and I had no idea what would be appropriate language for kids this age. The prevailing veterinary wisdom at the time was to advise people to "muddle through it as best you can and tell the kids whatever you want." I couldn't figure out how to explain to the children, "Emmett is alive right now but he will be dead tomorrow night," so I said nothing. We decided to euthanize him the next day while they were at preschool and tell them afterward, after they returned from school and he was already gone, that he had died. I know better now, but at the time I was flying blind. Brian put the book aside for the following night.

I lasted all of two hours at work on Tuesday before Susan sent me home. "They'll manage," she said. "I'll be there at one o'clock with...everything." She gave me a hug. Manny and Mary-Kate watched me leave with lowered eyes. Emmett had spent so much time at the clinic that he was like another employee to them, our clinic therapy dog.

When I got home, it was just me and Emmett for a couple hours. I gave him a sedative and snuggled up on the floor next to him. He looked at me in surprise—this was his spot by my feet, what was I doing down there with him?—but he was too pooped to do much other than put his head back down and nap.

Brian arrived home first, giving me a hug. "My dad wanted to know if he could come over and say good-bye," he said.

"Your *dad*?" I asked. "Really?" My mother-in-law was a bona fide animal grandma extraordinaire, but Brian's father coming to pay his respects was a shock.

"I know," said Brian. "But he said Emmett was something special."

Shortly after Susan arrived, standing on the doorstep with a box of drugs looking apologetic, my father-in-law pulled up. And then there was no other reason to wait.

Susan, who loved Emmett almost as much as I did, who spent so many hours cuddled up with him dispensing his chemotherapy, gently held his paw while we gave the injection. The three of us were now curled up in Emmett's favorite spot in the living room, Brian and his dad standing just a bit outside the circle, watching respectfully. I laid my head on Emmett's chest like I had so many times before, my fingers intertwined in his fur, listening to his heartbeat until it slowed down and then finally stopped. I knew when that happened that a little part of my own heart quit beating as well. "Good-bye, Emmett Otter," I said, and just like that, he was gone.

I had to cut right to the chase when the kids got home, since my face was so puffy and red it was clear something was terribly wrong. "I'm so sorry," I said. "Emmett went to heaven." They looked at me, confusion on their little cherub faces. I had been dreading this moment almost as much as Emmett's death itself.

"What? How?" asked Zach in his two-year-old lisp.

"Well, you know he's been sick, right?" I asked. He nodded. "He was very ill, and although we tried really hard to save him, he died."

"So where is he?"

"He went to heaven." The holes in their religious education were about to become apparent.

"Kevin?" asked my son, mishearing me. Kevin was currently fifteen miles away recording a podcast on digital data storage, which seemed about as far away from heaven as I could imagine.

"Not Kevin, heaven," I said. "It's...a place you go when you die."

"It's up in the clouds," my daughter interjected, her preschool chapel education kicking in. Now my son was really confused.

"Up in the clouds? How did he get to heaven? Who took him?" he persisted.

A person from the pet crematorium had come by to pick up his body, a reality I didn't think I was ready to explain. "Angels took him," I said hesitantly, thinking of the book upstairs and wondering if it covered any of this.

"Angels?" Zach asked, looking around nervously. "Where are they? Did you see them? What do they look like?"

"No," I said, sweating and wishing I had researched child psychology a little better. "They're...invisible."

"So when is he coming back?"

"Never."

"You get sick and die and go up in the sky and then you get to see Emmett and you never come back," my daughter summarized. My grief might have clouded my senses, but even so, I knew I was screwing this one up. Too late now.

My husband read them the "dogs go to heaven and wear wings and chase balls" book, but the damage had already been done. My son spent the next three months panicking every time he had a sniffle. He jumped at every small noise, convinced an invisible angel was about to drag him off into the hereafter with unseen hands. I vowed to do better the next time around. If I could ever bring myself to get another pet, that is.

Dog the Third:
KEKOA

From the time he was a little towheaded baby, Kevin lived for splashy adventures. His uncle was Elvis's head of security, and as a child he'd watch with glee when they needed to coordinate Elvis's hotel schedule. No matter where The King went, legions of girls would camp out on the streets, blocking traffic and screaming and fainting. To get around this, they would deploy one or two fake Elvises out the side doors. Then they would announce "Elvis has left the building," so everyone would disperse, leaving Elvis, very much still in the building, free to come and go as he pleased. Flash and cheekiness and just a bit of mildly diabolical subterfuge: that was the scaffolding of Kevin's youth. That never changed.

When Brian and I were planning our wedding, I had fallen in love with Turtle Island, a small private resort in Fiji. I don't even remember what magazine I saw it in, but it immediately spoke to me: a quiet, reserved, low-traffic escape from the world. "I want us to go there for our honeymoon," I said. We had initially planned on Hawaii, but this seemed more exotic. More remote. Off the grid. A way to start off our marriage with an adventure.

Shortly after I announced my intention, Fiji experienced a coup d'état. I tried to convince Brian that the country would be perfectly stable by the time we got married, but his tolerance for political unrest was lower than mine and he was having none of it. "Nope," said Brian, and we reverted back to our original plan. Although Hawaii was beautiful, we'd been there before, and it didn't compare to the images I had in my head of Fiji. Someday, I promised myself. Someday I will go.

Kevin had listened to our plans with interest. Not one to be deterred by a little thing like a political uprising, a few months after my wedding he stole my idea and took his own trip to the resort I'd found.

"How did you even manage that?" I asked. "Isn't that a couples-only place?"

"Yeah," he shrugged, tan and happy. "I just took a friend instead." Rules, schmules. Rules were made to be bent. It never would have occurred to him to let a little thing like a mandatory partnering get in the way of a new adventure.

We watched his vacation video, Kevin taking great joy in pointing out all the things I had been looking forward to. "Yeah, remember that dinner-on-the-beach thing you were talking about? That's us doing it right there. And the deserted beach? Oh yeah, that was awesome too. You really should go."

Apparently Kevin had told the island management that he was on his honeymoon because, well, might as well go all in. Neither he nor his blushing bride had any romantic interest in each other, but it made for another good story to tell, so he hammed it up. "Congratulations!" the staff cried as he strode off the plane with the other guests. He grinned, chastely holding his "wife" by the hand. So modest.

I observed with a combination of interest and envy what they got to do on the island: moonlit dinners on the beach, kayaking in turquoise lagoons, meandering through tropical gardens. Midway through the video, we watched as Kevin strode into the dining area in some sort of tropical toga, grinning at the thunderous applause. "They had us dress up in traditional Fijian wedding clothes for dinner one night," he said. It was the only time he would ever wear groom attire.

One of the activities one could partake in on the island was "purchasing" a turtle. You could use nontoxic paint to cover the shell with whatever message you wished, thus rendering the shell worthless to poachers, and release the turtle back into the ocean. "We pretty much did everything we could while we were there," he said. "I don't know if I'll get a chance to go back."

As I watched the turtle on the TV screen wade into the water, flap his fins, then jet off into the deep blue sea, I told Kevin that when I go—and I *will* go—I'm going to try and find his turtle. "What did you write on it?" I asked.

He spread his hands expansively, with a flourish. "Elvis," he said, "has left the building."

CHAPTER 19

One cold February morning, we packed the kids into the car and took an hour-and-a-half drive north to the Retrievers of SoCal rescue to meet a six-year-old black Lab named Lucy. She was feisty, glossy, and fun, and I fell for her as soon as I spotted her on a rescue website.

My husband sat sullenly in the driver's seat beside me. He was less besotted with the idea. It was his fault, I reasoned, for going off on a business trip to China for a week and not disabling Petfinder on our home computers. What else did he expect?

I hadn't been sleeping well since Emmett died. Far from being the I'll-never-love-again type, I immediately began to reflect on how much I missed that relationship and began browsing shelter websites on a regular basis. Brian tried his best to convince me of the benefits of a dog-free household: No messes. No barking. No pet expenses. No fur. It was a feeble attempt and he knew it.

He didn't outright say no, but he didn't outright say yes either. Left in this dogless limbo, I decided the only way to make forward progress was to just go ahead and do it.

I started slow. "Look at this Boston terrier!" I'd coo,

swinging my laptop around to display an elderly, one-eyed dog with a snaggletooth. He was super cute, but he was also incontinent. My husband grunted. I tried this for a week or two, then began moving slowly toward bigger dogs. Healthier ones. One by one, I'd read their descriptions aloud, casually, just, you know, looking.

I slept all of about an hour the whole time Brian was in China, restlessly tossing and turning. To keep my mind entertained during those long insomniac nights, I continued to browse the web, alighting again on the rescue group from which I had adopted Emmett. Before I knew it, I had sent in an email application, just so they'd have it on file. My fingers worked of their own volition. I barely remember doing it. And Brian, incommunicado in Asia, was sadly unavailable for consultation.

When he came home on Friday, jet-lagged and loopy, I told him, "Get some rest. We have an appointment tomorrow in Riverside to meet a Lab." I barely paused for breath. "Itsnotagivenitsjustameetingwedonthavetogetherpleasedont divorceme."

He only had the energy to sigh. Long-haul flights do have their advantages.

The dog I had requested to meet was Lucy, six years old, bouncy, and relinquished due to the terrible real estate bust that had put so many people out of their homes that year. She ran out of the kennel at warp speed, zipping this way and that, dropping a soggy tennis ball on my husband's feet, then taking a few laps around the driveway. Zoom-zoom-zoom. The kids shrieked in delight.

"Boy, she's energetic," Brian offered noncommittally. "Does she chew things?"

"It's possible," the volunteer admitted. "I think digging is more her thing, though."

Noting the side-eye I was receiving from my spouse, the rescue volunteer suggested we take a look at another dog, one who didn't photograph quite so well but was kind and sweet and might be a good match for the family. There she stood, with her hangdog face and her defeated posture and her barrel chest and her gnarly teeth, just sitting back patiently. She came over with her tail gently wagging, licked my daughter and then my son, and sat down. *It's OK*, her face said as we petted Lucy. *I just wanted to say hi.* She turned to leave, but paused, looking back from her drooped head with just the tiniest bit of hopefulness, just in case we were looking back. My heart cracked a tiny little bit.

And that is how we ended up driving home with Kekoa instead.

On the way home, I flipped through her paperwork. We would be her third home, according to the rescue. I saw based on her records that she was born on April 1. It seems a bit of a cruel joke that so many pranks have been pulled on her in the past, bouncing from home to home, never entirely sure of her security.

My home, I vowed, would be her last. I wanted to tell her: You will never be hit, shocked, or neglected again. You will have to wear silly hats (and, on occasion, full costumes) and pose for pictures with the kids, but in return you will have friends to play with, and adventures and walks and toys, and you will never doubt that you are loved or wanted again.

Tucked neatly into the back of her New Adoption Folder, squished behind her vaccination record and certificate of adoption, I found a neatly folded letter from her last owner. I paused, my palms sweaty.

"What's that one say?" my husband asked.

"I think it's a rabies certificate," I said. I looked in the rear-view mirror, where Kekoa was hanging her head over the back of the seat from her place in the hatchback and licking the top of my daughter's head as she screamed in delight.

I truly believe the volunteer had no idea that letter was even there. It was probably read on relinquishment then added to the stack of papers that came with her without further thought. Nonetheless, there it was, disclosure after the fact.

It started like this: "Dear Rescue," it began. "Please know this wasn't an easy decision for us, but Kekoa's severe separation anxiety leaves us no choice but to return her to you."

I sighed, and started a mental list of what anti-anxiety meds we had in stock. Mostly for Kekoa, but I could have used some too.

As Brian focused on the road ahead and the kids chatted excitedly in the back, I read the Long Sad Story of Kekoa. After arriving at the rescue at seven years of age for reasons unknown, she was adopted by a woman who wanted a companion for her other dog. One year later, that dog passed away, and Kekoa was no longer needed. Left in the yard while her owner was at work, she howled balefully for hours at a time, leading to complaints from neighbors and, shortly thereafter, her return to the rescue.

What with that, her unphotogenic black coat, and her odd tick-shaped body, she wasn't about to get adopted anytime soon, unless a sucker like me took the bait. I was convinced I was perfect for her despite her issues. I could keep her indoors, I thought. It's manageable.

OK, call it an error of omission if you will, but I neglected to share that silly old piddly "severe anxiety" bit of information with my husband because, well, I would handle it myself and I didn't want him to turn the car around. If I played my cards right he'd never even know she had a problem. By the time we reached the house, the kids would be hers, and she'd be home free.

I'm no stranger to the occasional lie for a just cause, or as I prefer to call it, "creative truth interpretation." For this trait, I blame my maternal grandfather Pepe, the undisputed master of what my grandmother charitably referred to as Tall Tales. I refused to go into the back toolshed for four years because of the hairy troll who lived underneath it, patiently biding his time for the day curiosity would overcome me and I would try to sneak a peek, only to be dragged underneath and messily devoured. "You know," Pepe would say ominously, "that you used to have five cousins, not four?" And off he'd go, chuckling to himself. The reason for this story? The shed was where Pepe would sneak off to smoke, and he wanted to be left alone.

At his funeral, my mother and aunt stared at each other in shock as they realized he had, for his entire life, convinced the extended family he was a captain in the Merchant Marines, only to be found out when Great-Aunt Mae slapped her knee at the wake and said, "He never even set foot on a boat! Jesus, Mary, and Joseph, that man."

I wasn't offended by his masterful storytelling. I was in awe. He never did it to hurt anyone; I think he mostly just liked keeping life a little more colorful than it was otherwise.

With the exception of sociopaths and pathological liars, most people who tell tall tales do so with a specific purpose in mind that seems perfectly reasonable to them. I'm not saying I agree or that I'm proud of my own transgressions, but I understand the temptation. I try to keep this in mind when clients lie to me, which they do with some regularity.

Sometimes they're motivated by a sense of guilt—"Isn't it nuts? This eight-pound ulcerated, bleeding mass just popped up on Ranger's ankle yesterday. I couldn't believe it myself."

But willful ignorance also plays a role, such as the time a woman who looked like she was on her way back from the church bake sale dropped off her Yorkie for possible seizures. "He's just acting really out of it."

When I went to examine the dog, the poor thing smelled like a frat boy after a bender. The stench of alcohol oozed out of his pores. The owner's relief that he didn't have a brain tumor turned into horror when I told her that her dog was drunk. "I don't understand!" she cried in dismay. "I'd never... Who would do such a thing to Winchester?"

"Well," I said, trying to be delicate, "do you have any children?"

"Yes, my seventeen-year-old son," she said, worrying at the chain around her neck. "But he wouldn't ever...no..."

Be diplomatic, I thought to myself. "Does he have any friends who come over?"

"Yes!" she said, eyes widening. "Oh, that rotten Johnny Schwarz. Wait till I get my hands on him!"

People avoid reality out of a sense of self-preservation and because certain members of the medical profession seem to excel at the art of shaming. I get this. Who hasn't told the dentist, "Oh yes, I absolutely floss three times a day and brush for a full two minutes after every meal"? These are the lies born out of a fear of humiliation, a subconscious plea for forgiveness for our transgressions. From the medical professional's point of view, though, these lies make it harder for us to do our jobs. If your dog ate a marijuana brownie by accident but you said he might have gotten into some rat bait, those are two entirely different treatment scenarios. If you really have been monitoring your dog's food like you say and he still isn't losing weight, we need to check his thyroid.

I've learned over the years to try and tone down the sanctimony as much as possible—I am less than perfect myself—and just let people know that I want to know the truth, it's OK, and I promise not to bite or pull out my Catholic nun ruler and go to town. I save that for the people who really deserve it, like the ones who try to crop their dog's ears at home using tooth floss to sew them up and then, several weeks later, bring me the infected mess to clean up.

Mr. Mackles and his chubby Bichon, Peaches, were already regulars at the clinic by the time I came on board. He usually arrived about fifteen minutes before his appointment and sat in the lobby with Peaches precariously balanced on his lap, chatting up the other clients in the waiting area in his amiable Kentucky drawl.

He was a very pleasant man, but his temperament sadly hadn't rubbed off on his charge, who was here for a possible urinary tract infection. I pushed open the door to the exam room and said hello. Peaches pulled her lip back and snarled at me.

"Naw naw, Peaches, that's not nice," Mr. Mackles said, tucking her under one arm like a football as he stood up to shake my hand. "She's just not feelin' right, Doc. I just don't know. I just don't know what's wrong." He blinked down at his lap, dotted with wet spots where Peaches had dribbled urine on him.

I had already flipped through her chart before going into the room, so I had seen the notes going all the way back from Peaches' prior veterinarian in Kentucky. Urinary issues were nothing new for her. At one point, the veterinarian had been suspicious of bladder stones and recommended an X-ray and a special diet, both of which Mr. Mackles had declined at the time.

After getting the details about Peaches' current problem, I asked Mr. Mackles what diet Peaches was on.

"Diet?" he asked, his glasses making his eyes large and owl-like as he blinked at me. "Is she fat? Does she need to be on a diet?"

"I mean, what food is she eating?" I said. "I see that"—I thumbed through the chart—"Dr. Larsen back in Bowling Green had recommended a special food for Peaches that she thought might help with the bladder problems."

"Oh, yes," he said. "She eats what's on sale. That stuff is pricey. Pri—SAY."

So I began my exam. Peaches had a tender belly for sure, and when I prodded at the area near where her bladder would be located she winced as I felt something solid scraping around. No wonder she was crabby. Mr. Mackles agreed to let me run a urinalysis, though he balked at the additional $300 for X-rays that would let me visualize bladder stones. "Can we start with the urine test?" The stepwise approach to testing is pretty common in our field.

In veterinary medicine, our preferred method for obtaining urine is with a cystocentesis, in which we insert a needle into the bladder through the abdomen to draw our sample. Though more invasive than other methods, it's the best way to get a sample without contamination from the urethra or the floor.

With Peaches sighing in resignation on her back on the ultrasound table, I placed the probe on her abdomen. I moved the probe left and right as images of her insides swept across the screen. Her bladder swung into view, a small black halo at the bottom of the screen. Adjusting the buttons and my hand so the bladder was in the center, I immediately saw exactly what I had been expecting—the telltale wedge-shaped shadow of a bladder stone, bouncing the sound waves back at the probe so that nothing beneath it was visible. I inserted the needle above the probe, watching the sliver of white as it slid into the bladder with minimal resistance, feeling the *thunk* of the needle as it hit the solid ball that was the source of all her troubles. I pulled the needle back just enough to suck up a syringe full of cloudy urine, then brought Peaches back to Mr. Mackles.

I told him what I saw, and that she had bladder stones. "An X-ray will confirm this," I told him, "and will also let me know if there is more than one stone." He didn't look too happy. "I really think she needs this," I said. He sighed. "All right. She was my wife's pride and joy, so I need to take good care of her." He looked up to see if I had heard him. "Did I ever tell you about my wife, Priscilla?" I shook my head.

Manny took Peaches to get the X-rays started as Mr. Mackles continued. "My wife had multiple sclerosis," he said, "so she was in a wheelchair."

I nodded.

"Well, we had a couple of dogs—a coonhound, lordy that dog could howl—but she liked Peaches best. Peaches used to jump up on her lap and they would just go everywhere together. They were just the cutest dang pair you ever did see. We were so happy together.

"Then, it happened." He paused, as if to gather his thoughts.

"I'm pretty sure Priscilla—we called her Prissy, but she wasn't really—Prissy thought the brake on her chair was set but it wasn't. There she was, settin' up at the top of the stairs with Peaches on her lap like always, and I heard her shoutin' for me. I got there as fast as I could, but my own knee's not too good so I had to hobble over, hoppin' and jumpin' and runnin' like I had a banshee on my heels."

He stopped again, the memory obviously painful. "She was teetering right there on the top of the stairs, just fighting to stay on. I—I grabbed Peaches—it's what Prissy would have wanted—" He took in a shuddering breath of air. "The last thing I saw was the look on her face as she went backward down those stairs. It was *terrible*." He sniffled and wiped his nose. "Peaches is all I have left. I had to come out to California just to get away from the memories."

"I had no idea, Mr. Mackles," I said, horrified at what he had been through. The logistics of the whole tragedy were just...so...bizarre. Poor man. I left to get him a cup of water while we waited for the X-rays.

As suspected, Peaches had one large bladder stone, and a bunch of smaller ones, floating about. The infection in her bladder would require antibiotics, but that stone wasn't going anywhere without surgery. Mr. Mackles looked pained.

"How much is this going to be?" he asked, and Manny showed him the estimate we had prepared.

Mr. Mackles mopped his brow with a handkerchief he pulled out of his back pocket. "As you can imagine, things have been tough," he said, "what with the move and all. Do you all offer any discounts for widowers?" I said I would talk to my office manager and we would do all we could.

After Susan helped to arrange a billing discount, Mr. Mackles agreed to have Peaches' surgery later that week. Fortunately for everyone, the surgery went swimmingly and Peaches went home without a hitch. When he came back for suture removal, Mr. Mackles reported happily that Peaches was like a puppy again. "And my house doesn't smell like dog pee anymore!" he added.

I didn't see Peaches again until her yearly exam some months later. Relieved of her bladder pain, she was much happier to see me and even gave me a kiss. Mr. Mackles chuckled. "She sure is doing well," he said. "I think that food's helping."

"It does," I agreed. After sending the stones we fished out of Peaches' bladder to the lab for analysis, we were able to recommend a food that would minimize the chances of those stones coming back. As long as she remained on it, her chances of recurrence were greatly reduced.

"The food's kind of expensive, though," he said. "Do you all... have any sort of discount? For bulk purchases?"

I turned to the front of the chart. "Susan put a discount on your chart, Mr. Mackles." I showed him the entry. "That's forever, not just for the surgery. So it will apply to your food purchases too."

He brightened. "OK! Thanks!"

"It's the least we can do," I said, as he bundled Peaches up under his arm. As he walked into the lobby, I heard him address someone in the waiting area. "We're all done! Let's go!"

I ran to the door and pressed my head against the window into the waiting area, where a petite woman in a velour tracksuit and brimmed straw hat rose to her feet. There was no wheelchair in sight.

"Does Mr. Mackles have a new girlfriend?" I asked Mary-Kate after they left.

"That's his wife," she said. "She had a weird name too... Prudie?"

"Prissy," I said dully. Mary-Kate nodded. "That's it!" I stood there for a minute, forehead resting on the glass. I'm such a rube.

Manny walked into the exam room to clean up. "Are you OK, Doc?"

I turned around with a pained expression. "Remember Mr. Mackles's story about his wife rolling down the stairs in her wheelchair and dying?"

He nodded. "Yeah, the one who grabbed the dog instead of the wheelchair handle?" That hadn't even occurred to me, but now that he mentioned it... "That was some crazy stuff right there. He's a character."

I pointed. "That's his wife there in the lobby."

Manny frowned in confusion. "Did he get remarried?"

"To someone with the exact same first name?"

When I told Susan the story, she threw her head back and laughed and laughed.

"I had no idea," I said. "I'm sorry."

Susan wiped tears from her eyes and said, "It's OK. I thought that whole story was a little over the top. Seriously, though, does he even remember he told us all that?"

I shrugged. "Are we...going to take his discount away?"

She shook her head. "It's coded as a senior discount, not a my-wife-died-before-my-very-eyes one. I would have given it to him anyway." She propped her elbows on the table and set her chin on her fist. "I want him to keep coming in. He's funny."

CHAPTER 20

Through the open window, a long string of muffled expletives and incoherent grumblings floated through the screen and settled solidly on my lap. I lifted my head to peek out the window, where Brian was standing with his camera around his neck, attempting to get Kekoa to hold still with pink Easter bunny ears on while the kids scampered in the background. Kekoa was doing what Kekoa always seemed to do, which was sit stock-still with her head hanging down disconsolately. *I'm sorry*, she said with her eyes peering up at you from above her dipped snout. *Whatever it is, I'm sorry I'm sorry I'm sorry*. She lived in a constant state of extreme remorse, even when she was perfectly content.

"What's wrong?" I asked, coming outside with a handful of treats. "Do you need me to try and get her to look up?" Seeing the treats, Kekoa perked up, the bunny ears sliding back on her narrow head.

"That's not it," Brian said, grunting as he heaved Kekoa's rear ninety degrees to the left, rotating her toward the house. Like a sack of potatoes, she endured this indignity, allowing herself to be maneuvered this way and that in search of the perfect family portrait.

Brian tapped the light meter on his camera, fiddled with some buttons, and pointed the lens at the dog. He shook his head. "It's really hard to photograph a black dog," he said, showing me the shots he'd taken so far, where she slumped like a depressed bag of coal. Wearing satin bunny ears. "I can probably fix the exposure in Photoshop, but I have to tell you, she's not the most attractive dog."

He was right. Kekoa was shaped more like a cartoonist's exaggerated rendition of a goofy Lab than an actual Labrador. Her head was disproportionately small, and her wide barrel chest was supported by four spindly legs. The total effect was that of an overinflated balloon. But we didn't choose her for her aesthetics.

When she would lumber over and plop on my feet, her skinny tail smacking into the wall with such force you'd think someone was cracking a whip on the drywall, she never seemed to notice. Such was her excitement that she paced from foot to foot as she stood near me, massive, looming, and then with the gentlest motion eased her tiny head into my hands and covered them with kisses. I tried to push her head away when I'd had enough, but then she kissed that hand too, so eventually I just gave up. Her tail never stopped wagging the entire time. I'd fallen in love.

Whenever the kids stretched out on the floor, Kekoa scurried over, thump-thump-thump, and hovered over them like the Blob. She melted onto them, all tongue and fur, dissolving into a puddle of their delighted giggles. After wedging herself in between Zach and Zoe, scooting her hips back and forth to make room, she'd contentedly roll onto her back, kick her legs up in the air, and occasionally let out a small fart.

We left the windows open and tolerated the occasional poor photograph, because, well, no one ever said *My dog's photogenic qualities make me feel so cozy and loved.* We bought one of those really expensive vacuums, because fur tumbleweeds skittering across the floor is a small price to pay for the comforting pressure of a happy dog leaning into you for butt scratches. And we kept plenty of paper towels and hand sanitizer around because as gross as a string of sticky saliva is on your forearm, it was utterly charming to be so loved that Kekoa could quite literally just eat you up.

This complete and probably undeserved adoration of human companionship came with a heavy price tag, however. Kekoa would very much have loved to have been one of those four-pound pocket dogs one could carry effortlessly into the mall, the post office, and work, a permanent barnacle on those she loved best. Sadly, as a seventy-pound sphere of gas, fur, and saliva, there were many occasions when she had to remain at home by herself, and each and every time we left she mourned deeply, as if we were heading off for a long deployment and not a two-minute trip to the 7-Eleven.

When she was stuck with no one but the cat to keep her company, she funneled her pain, anxiety, and deep, pervasive grief into "music." She sang a song of misery, a piercing wail of heartbreaking angst that shattered glass and the sanity of those near enough to hear it on a regular basis. The first time I heard her howling, I paused in the driveway and looked out the window to see which direction the approaching ambulance was coming from. The second time, I thought a pack of coyotes had broken into the house. The third time, only day seven of her life with us, Brian and I stepped out to say hello to a neighbor and heard her ballad of woe through our open front window. BaWOOOOOOOOOOOOOOOOOO! OOO! Arrrrroooooo0OOOOOooooooooo! So this was why she had lost her last home.

"Is she sad?" asked the neighbor.

"I think she misses us," I said, then, gingerly, "Can you hear this from inside your house?" Thankfully, they shook their heads no.

"Well, at least she doesn't do it while we're home," I said to Brian as he grimaced in the direction of the house. "And she's not destructive!"

The next day, I came home after taking the kids to school and pulled into the driveway, listening intently for the song of the sad. It was blessedly quiet.

I opened the front door, and Kekoa came skittering around the corner excitedly, knocking the cat aside in her exhilaration. "Hi, Kekoa," I said, reaching down to pat her. "Did you miss me the fifteen minutes I was gone?"

When I removed my hand from her head, I noticed my fingers were coated in a sticky substance. I looked down at her, innocently wagging her tail with a sheen of white powder stuck to her nose, the edges of her lips, and, when I looked down, her paws. Wondering why my dog suddenly looked like Al Pacino after a coke binge in *Scarface*, I went around the corner and saw the pantry door ajar. A mostly empty cardboard box of powdered sugar, chewed to a barely recognizable state, lay forlornly on the kitchen floor, massacred in an exsanguination of white powder. I looked at Kekoa. She looked back.

"Kekoa," I said. She wagged her tail.

"KeKOA," I said again, sternly. She plopped down on the pile of powdered sugar and continued to wag at me, licking the sticky sugar paste on her nose. It took me the better part of two hours, mopping and grumbling, to get that mess cleaned up.

The next day, I made sure I pulled the pantry door shut before taking the kids to school. This time when I returned, the house was quiet yet again. Maybe she just needed some time to adjust, I thought, opening the door. No Kekoa. See how calm she is? We're getting there, thank God.

"Kekoa!" I called again. Nothing. The cat wandered around the corner, gave me an indifferent flick of the tail, and glided back over to the windowsill.

Perplexed, I walked around the bottom floor, winding up again in the kitchen. There was the pantry door, still shut. "Kekoa?" I called. "Where are you?"

Then I heard it, the quiet thump-thump-thump of a tail whacking a door. The sound was coming from inside the pantry. I pulled the door open and out she tumbled, a pile of wrappers, boxes, and crackers falling out behind her in a landslide across the freshly mopped floor. She immediately ran over to the other side of the kitchen island and peeked back at me, her tail nervously swishing from side to side, Goldfish crumbs spraying with each shake.

I was so confused I couldn't even get upset. How the heck did she do that? She must have pushed the handle down with her nose, wedged herself into the pantry, and accidentally knocked the door shut behind her with her rear end. In her combination of fear and elation, she had devoured almost every edible item on the bottom three shelves. Fortunately most of the items were canned foods, but there was still plenty of carnage. Half a loaf of bread. A bag of peanuts. Pretzels. I scanned the bags, from which she had expertly extracted the edible bits, for signs of toxic food items and to my relief found no chocolate wrappers or sugar-free gum, two things that might have added "emergency run to the clinic" to my already packed to-do list.

Peering back in, I noticed a bunch of bananas nestled among the cans of beans and soup, the sole survivor of the slaughter. Apparently, peeling them was too much work. Surveying the disaster before me, I tried to figure out what I was going to do. That afternoon, my son looked at me thoughtfully and asked, "Why doesn't Koa go to preschool if she gets so lonely?"

It was a good idea. I debated the merits of leaving her at home to work it out or taking her in to work with me. Our office shared a building with a doggy day-care facility, so my first experiment involved a trial day there. I reasoned she would enjoy being with a group more than she would sitting by herself, surrounded by equally anxious dogs and cats in cages. The day care promised to put her in a room with the other big dogs and give her lots of love.

I walked over at lunch and peered in the window to see

how she was doing. I surveyed the room, where bouncing Weimaraners tugged on chew toys and Golden Retrievers trotted back and forth with tennis balls. Wagging tails, relaxed eyes. After scanning for a minute, I picked out a black bucket in the corner I had assumed was a trash can. It was Kekoa, hunched down motionlessly, staring mournfully at the door. The attendant walked over and held out a ball, which she ignored. Maybe she's just tired from all the fun she had this morning, I reasoned.

When I picked her up after work, the daily report card indicated that Kekoa had spent the entire eight-hour period in that exact position. "She seemed a little sad," the note said in looping cursive, "but we loved having her. Maybe she'll get used to us in time."

The following day I decided to try bringing her directly into work instead. She immediately wedged herself under the stool by my feet, a space about an inch too short for her girth. Good, I thought. In the time it takes her to wiggle out I can run into an exam room before she follows me.

Susan handed me the file for Room 1. I looked at the presenting complaint. "Dog exploded in living room but is much better now."

"I hope this is referring to diarrhea, because if not we've just witnessed a miracle."

"No need. It's diarrhea."

I popped up and ran into Room 1 to investigate the gut grenade incident before Kekoa realized I was taking off.

About two minutes into the appointment, I heard a small whine from the back hallway. Ooooooo—ooooooo. It was soft, Kekoa whispering a song of abandonment to the empty corridor. The pet owners didn't hear it, at first. The whimpers were drowned out by the gurgling in Tank's belly.

"Then we gave him a bratwurst yesterday and—did I hear a baby or something?"

"Oh, you know the vet clinic," I said. "There's always someone making noise."

"So anyway, I told Marie to leave the spicy mustard off but—is that dog OK?"

AoooOOoOOOOOOOOOoooOOOOOOO. Now Kekoa was getting angry. I heard her claws scratching at the door.

"She's fine," I said. "Excuse me a moment."

I poked my head out the door. "Manny?"

"Got it," he said, jogging around the corner with a nylon leash in his hand. "Come on, Koa."

"I'm so sorry," I said, returning to Tank. I prodded his generous belly to see if he was in pain and if anything seemed swollen or out of place. "When was the last time he had diarrhea?"

"Last night," the owner said. "But it was this weird green color and—" He paused, furrowing his eyebrow as he looked at the back door.

A small yellow puddle of pee was seeping under the door, widening into a lake as it pooled toward my shoes.

"I'm so sorry," I said, pulling out paper towels and wadding them under the door with my foot. I heard footsteps, and Manny muttering to Kekoa. "That's my dog, and she is really upset I'm in here with you and not out there with her."

Tank's owner laughed. "Tank's the same way," he said.

"He ate a couch last year when we left him alone during the Fourth of July."

"A couch?" I asked.

"A couch," he affirmed, pulling out his cell phone for the photographic proof. He wasn't kidding.

When I finished with Tank, I came back to the treatment area to find Kekoa blocked in under Rachelle's feet by the lab area, a leather leash stretched to the max from where Manny had tied it to a table. The nylon leash he used the first time sat sadly in the trash, chewed in two.

Behavior work is, depending on who you ask, one of the most rewarding or frustrating areas of veterinary medicine. On the one hand, behavior issues are one of the most common concerns people have about their pets: separation anxiety, aggression, inappropriate elimination, that always charming leg humping. Owners with a good grasp of early intervention and behavioral management can create a much better bond with their pet; it can even prevent some relinquishments to the shelter. For me, maintaining that human-animal bond for a family is every bit as rewarding as improving a pet's physical health.

On the other hand, it's hard work. If a dog has a skin infection, we send owners home with antibiotics, and as long as they remember to give the pill, boom, it clears up. If a dog has food guarding issues, the sort of problem where an owner may get bitten for approaching the food bowl, there isn't a pill for that. There's a program, one involving lots of steps that may or may not include medication but that certainly involve time and effort on the part of both the veterinarian and the owner.

I knew that in Kekoa's case, her separation anxiety related to our departure would be best managed through a gradual system of desensitization and counterconditioning, involving me leaving the home for a few seconds and then coming back, over and over until she no longer associated the shutting of the door with my departure. Unless it was the jingle of the car keys that set her off, then I would have to work on that daily. Or the sound of the car engine. I tried to discern the exact trigger for Kekoa's distress, but by the time I got to the car she had already started howling and, once I came back in, seemed to decide her call was luring me back like a siren song, causing her to redouble her efforts. She wasn't following the plan.

At work, I rummaged through the cabinet in search of the anxiety medications we had on hand. Our selection was limited.

"Are these for you or the dog?" asked Susan, giving me a playful elbow nudge.

I screwed my nose up and held up the boxes. "I don't think we even have the right dose for her size."

Susan tilted her head thoughtfully. "You know, we have Scott coming in on Thursday. I think Pilco just had a new separation anxiety drug come out this year. You can ask him about it."

Ah yes, our regular visit from a pharmaceutical company rep was coming up on Thursday. I've been in enough doctors' offices to see how it works over in the human medical field, as statuesque blond women in perfect suits with glossy hair wheeled their little briefcases into the back office to entice the physicians into giving their latest pill a try. I've heard all sorts of things about the perks and enticements offered to MDs on behalf of a friendly drug company, but all I have to go on is what happens in veterinary medicine, the dirty, hay-covered, poorer cousin. We got Scott.

Scott was amiable enough, in an IT guy sort of way. Twice a year, he ambled in with his Dockers and his polo shirt, benevolently passing out pens to the staff. In exchange for listening to his spiel about Pilco's latest drug offerings, we got sub sandwiches, perhaps, or pizza. Don't get me wrong, we were grateful for any and all free food in the vet clinic, but it's not the sort of palm greasing that would make anyone feel obligated to order hundreds or thousands of dollars' worth of drugs they didn't think would work.

As we sat eating our sandwiches that Thursday, Scott went through a PowerPoint presentation projected onto the back wall featuring close-ups of fleas, tapeworms, and weeping skin infections. Impervious to gross imagery, we plowed through our food with gusto as we listened to the risk of diarrhea after a dose of their new antibiotic, watched a German Shorthaired Pointer go from stiff-legged goose-stepping to running in the snow on their new anti-inflammatory medication, and observed a stern-faced parasitologist present a dissected heart filled with writhing heartworms that could have been prevented with Pilco's newest monthly preventative. He flipped through charts and graphs and quotes from scientific papers supporting the assertion that their drugs were superior to those of the guy coming in next month with bagels. He promised to send over the actual journal articles, should we need them. Susan took notes with her new Pilco pen.

"I bet we all have roundworms too," said Manny after the talk, thoroughly floored by the charts showing the ominous possibilities. "Can I drink some of that dewormer?"

As Scott was packing up, I walked up and asked him about Sepaxa, their new separation anxiety drug. He had touched on it briefly during the talk.

"Oh, Sepaxa's great," he said. "Eighty-five percent of the top third of affected dogs showed at least a 55 percent decrease in the worst 25 percent of their symptoms in the first ninety days." While I tried to figure out if these numbers were supposed to be encouraging, he plucked out a shiny brochure from his brief-case and then, flipping through a stack of neatly stapled white papers, pressed two journal articles into my hand. "Here's all the data on it," he said cheerily. "Let me go to the car and get you a sample. How much does your dog weigh?"

When I got home that afternoon, I read through all the papers Scott had given me before logging onto a members-only website for veterinarians to read the collective opinions of the Internet. The verdict? Worth a shot.

"Come here, Kekoa," I sang, holding the beef-scented disk, the dog equivalent of a SweeTart, in my hand. She ran up, happy as always. Her tongue snaked out, and slurp! Away went the pill. Could it really be that easy?

The next morning, Kekoa didn't come when I opened the pantry door to get her breakfast. That was odd. I called her name. Still no Kekoa. That was just bizarre. I found her sprawled out on her bed staring up at the ceiling, a surly teen-ager, stoned out of her mind. She didn't get into the pantry that day. She barely looked at her own food bowl.

"Is Koa sick?" asked Zoe, pouting when she refused to chase after a ball.

"No," I said, "she's just...resting." We were on day three of her sample box, and while the pill had stopped her anxious behavior, it had stopped most of her normal behavior too. She was a zombie dog. The brochure had mentioned an adjustment period, but this seemed extreme.

"Do you think I should cut her dose down?" I asked Dr. Joff.

"Nah," he said. "Sometimes they take a few weeks to adjust."

That night, I watched Kekoa amble listlessly into the kitchen for her evening meal. She looked even more depressed than she usually did. Brian caught her chewing through his laptop case trying to get at a granola bar he had zipped away inside, and she was too tired to even run away when he started to wave his hands and yell. I knew I should probably give it some more time, but I felt terribly guilty putting my dog on psychoactives when the main problem was that I didn't have a lock on the pantry door. So we installed one.

That was her last day on Sepaxa, when I joined the large group of clients known as "poorly compliant." I ended up incorporating a rather involved process of behavioral modifications when I was leaving for extended periods, namely rolling a Kong toy down the hall to keep her busy while I sneaked out the back door before she realized I was gone. Without the cue of the front door to set her off, she often thought I was somewhere in the house and she just hadn't found me yet, and settled down. For the most part.

It's one of the most consistent life lessons in this field: You can recommend whatever you want to a client, but at the end of the day they're going to do what they want to do, and hopefully they don't hurt the pet in the process. I reminded myself of this on a regular basis when clients decided that my medical recommendations, which they'd paid $45 and thirty minutes of office time to receive, weren't worth the price of admission. Such was the case with Lady.

I surveyed the appointments for the day, hoping I could manage to get out right on schedule. Brian had a rare evening work event to which I was actually invited, but if I wanted to be able to go I needed time to get home, greet the babysitter, hose off the smell of the clinic, and be at the restaurant by seven thirty. It looked straightforward so far: a spay, a cat neuter, a couple of dentals, ear infections, fleas.

So far, so good, but I had learned not to count on anything in this place. The first room of the day was a new client, and I sent Manny in to get an initial history while I texted Brian: *Day's looking good so far. Will keep you posted.*

Brian responded with a link to the restaurant, the fancy sort of place we rarely dined at. I couldn't remember the last time I went somewhere nice. I made a mental note: We need to do some more date nights. I thought about the contents of my closet: khakis, more khakis, and Dockers. Nurse shoes. Buttondowns. I frowned, wondering if I even had anything to wear. I set down my phone as Manny came out of the room with his mouth pressed into a thin line.

"What's that look for?"

He shook his head. "She kept calling me Jose."

"Jose? That's not even close. Did you correct her?"

"Not after the second time."

Poor Manny. "So tell me about the dog."

He sat down with the file. "OK. Lady is a five-year-old Doodle, started throwing up last night. Happened about four times overnight."

"Did the owner take the food and water away?"

"I forgot to ask."

"How's the dog look?"

"A little depressed. Temp's OK, heart rate is 130."

"Is she spayed?"

"Yes."

"Diarrhea?"

"Forgot to ask." Manny must have been really put out. Forgetting important bits of medical history was unlike him.

Manny and I entered the room, where a middle-aged woman in a fleece pullover sat with her Goldendoodle's head in her lap. "Oh, I'm glad you're here, Doctor," she said, patting her short brown hair. "I'm so worried about Lady."

"Nice to meet you both," I said. "So Lady has been vomiting since last night?"

"Yes," she said. "As I was telling Jose"—he poked me in the back—"she started about six last night and kept puking every few hours. It was very robust." She paused, and I realized she was about to give me a reenactment. "It sounded like this: HUUURRRRGHHH. You know that noise, right? I'm really worried."

"Oh, that's not good. Did she eat anything unusual last night?"

"Not really. Just her normal dog food."

"Did you continue to offer food and water after she started vomiting?"

"Well, I took her dog food away," she said, rubbing her dog's ears, "but I thought she would be hungry after puking up her dinner, so I gave her some queso fresco."

"You gave her *queso fresco*?"

"Yeah, don't you eat Mexican food? It's a kind of cheese."

"I'm familiar with it," I said drily. "It's just that cheese is an unusual choice for a dog who's been vomiting."

"Well, it's a very bland cheese," she said defensively. "It's not like I gave Lady a block of pepperjack."

"I understand," I said, "but the concern is that all cheeses—even the bland ones—have a lot of fat in them, and they can be upsetting to a dog's stomach. Especially if they're already vomiting."

"I do it all the time," she insisted. "It's bland. I know Mexican food is usually spicy but this one isn't *at all*. Right, Jose?"

"It's bland," Manny agreed, "but my momma gave me chicken soup when I had the flu, not nachos."

Heading this one off at the pass, I sent Manny out of the room while I examined Lady. She looked a little depressed, her gums were a bit tacky, and her stomach seemed a little tender. I relayed all of this to the owner.

"I'm *so* worried," she said. "Is she going to die?"

"I hope not," I said. "Any chance she got into something she shouldn't have?" Besides cheese.

"No," she said.

"No toys or anything that she might have chewed up?"

"Toys? Well, she is a terrible chewer. She ate my shoe a couple of days ago."

I grimaced. "It wouldn't be a bad idea to do some blood-work and X-rays to see if there's anything going on in there," I told her.

"Is that expensive?"

"I'll have Manny give you an exact estimate before we do anything."

"Can it wait? Money's really tight."

"Well," I said, "it would be really helpful to have that information, but if you can't do that right now you can keep her at home for the day and watch her. Don't give her *anything*. Let her stomach rest and see how she does. If she's still vomiting, or if you try to feed her later and she vomits it again, we definitely need to take X-rays."

"I'm just so worried," she repeated. "Can I give her anything to help her feel better?"

"We can give her some fluids under the skin," I said. "That would be a really good idea."

"So can I give her Gatorade at home?"

"No," I said. "Nothing goes in her mouth. No food, no water, no Gatorade, no cheese."

"Tums?"

"*Nothing*. Anything we do for the next twelve hours needs to be through an IV or under her skin."

I gave Manny the estimate for the workup and fluids. "If she declines it," I said, "tell her she needs to come back by four thirty if the dog is worse so we have time to get everything done. And tell her one more time not a thing in the dog's mouth." Manny presented her with the estimate, which she declined. He reported back that she asked him if he didn't agree that queso fresco was bland, though.

I sighed. The rest of the day went according to plan. The surgeries were up and running around by three, no one needed a late-afternoon sedation, and even Dr. Joff was in a good mood. Four thirty came and went. I texted Brian: *Looks like the coast is clear. See you at 7:30.* He responded: *:D*

At six, I started winding up the day. The last appointment, a wellness check, came and went without incident. At six fifteen, Mary-Kate came into the back with a sad look on her face. "Lady's here," she said.

"Lady? I told her she had to come back by four thirty. What..."

"She said she's still vomiting and she's really worried."

I looked at my watch. "Put her in a room and have her sign the estimate."

Mary-Kate cocked her head. "She said she isn't signing anything and she wants to talk to you."

I went into the room, dragging Manny along behind me.

"So Lady's still vomiting?"

"Yes," the owner said. "Three more times. I'm really upset you didn't tell me I should have done the X-rays this morning."

"Did you take her food and water away like we discussed?" There was a pause. "Yes."

I palpated Lady's stomach. She belched, then before I could pull back vomited a large quantity of chicken noodle soup on my head and shoulder.

I sat up, carrot pieces dripping off my arm. "When did you feed her?"

The owner fidgeted. "This afternoon."

I looked at her.

"She was hungry!"

"Well," I said as I went to the sink to scrape off the food. "It's really hard for me to tell if she's vomiting because her stomach is irritated or if it's because she has something else going on. Every time you feed her it's going to upset her stomach again. But at this point I do think she should get the workup done."

"You should have said that this morning, you know."

Manny handed me a paper towel, patting my hand as he did so. "I always leave the final decision up to the owner," I said, "and although it's getting late, we can get this done now, because I think Lady needs it."

"I'm so worried," the owner said, yet again.

"I know. So should we start? My techs are leaving for the night in just a few minutes."

"Do you really think this is necessary?" the owner said. "Why is she vomiting so much?"

"That's what I'm trying to figure out," I said. "The blood-work and X-rays will help us rule out some of the possibilities. I don't know if she has a shoe in her stomach, or if she has Addison's, or—"

"No offense," said the owner, "but I think I'm going to take her to my regular vet."

"Tonight?"

"Tomorrow. First thing."

Manny and I looked at each other. "Are you sure you want to do that? She's been vomiting for twenty-four hours now."

"I know," said Lady's owner, "and you still haven't told me why and I don't like feeling strong-armed into expensive tests. So I think I'll let my regular vet deal with it tomorrow."

That settled, we left the room. I looked at my watch: six forty. I can still make it, I thought.

"Are we wrapped up for the day, Susan?"

Susan gave me the thumbs-up. I texted Brian: *on my way*.

As I was opening the front door at home, my cell phone rang. Work.

"What's up, Mary-Kate?"

"Lady's owner is here. She said the dog vomited again in the car and she wants to do the bloodwork and X-rays now."

It was seven o'clock. Our last appointment slot was six. "Did you explain," I said, taking a breath, "that the staff is gone for the day?"

I heard a raised voice in the background. "She wants to know why you're gone if you're open until seven."

"Mary-Kate, tell her—"

"If I go to a restaurant and it's open until seven that means I can walk in at seven and sit down!" said an angry voice in my ear. "This is the worst customer service that I ever—"

Mary-Kate came back on the phone. "Ma'am, please don't grab the phone out of my hand. The doctor is gone for the day."

"We're all gone, Mary-Kate," I said. "Give her the number to the emergency clinic." Then I hung up, willing to suffer the consequences.

I took a lightning-quick shower, threw on the first clean set of clothes I could find, and headed back out the door. At seven forty-five, I pulled into the parking lot of the steak house and ran in, realizing belatedly that I hadn't changed my shoes. Hopefully there was no vomit on them. I scraped the top of my shoe on the doorstop, grimacing.

I saw Brian in the back and trotted over to greet him, taking in the crowd of well-dressed executives sitting with their nicely groomed spouses.

"Hi," he said, leaning over to give me a hug. As he did, he whispered in my ear, "Is that a noodle in your hair?"

CHAPTER 21

When Brian and I moved into our current home, we made a deliberate decision to remove as much carpet as possible. It seemed like a good idea at the time, but of course hardwood comes with its own set of issues, namely its tendency to turn the house into a vast echo chamber and the Freddy Krueger–like scars etched into the flooring by a dog with no traction. So we compromised, putting a few area rugs in the places we spent the most time. Kekoa was grateful for this, settling onto the rug with a satisfied sigh wherever there was a foot she could sit upon.

It was one such foot that made the discovery that she'd been peeing on the rug, when I sank a barefoot toe into it and removed it with a slightly sticky slurp. I knew that slurp. It was the exact one I remembered from my parents' living room in Taffy's later years, when they had just given up on housebreaking her and told people to avoid the rug entirely.

I sank to my hands and knees and sniffed the floor like a bloodhound. Eeew. There. Flipping the carpet back, I saw not one but three telltale circles. Brian is going to kill me, I thought. Well, after he kills the dog.

After bringing Kekoa to work to run a full complement

of tests, I determined she probably had a mild case of incontinence, which wouldn't be unheard of in an older spayed female. I dutifully brought home her bottle of meds, crossing my fingers that it would work before Brian noticed something was amiss. In the meantime, I attacked the rug like a soldier on a mission, determined to eradicate all olfactory clues. Let's face it, though: No matter how many suction devices and enzymatic cleaners you have at your disposal, pee smell never really goes away, not entirely.

It didn't help that my husband has a super-nose. My sense of smell was dulled from years in the clinic, a necessary defense mechanism when you deal in the smell of wet fur all day. Brian, on the other hand, works with computers in offices with air filters, leaving his sinuses fresh as a daisy to come home, inhale deeply with his nose in the air, and bellow, "It smells like dog in here!" I tried the Axe body spray approach a few times, spritzing some form of pet odor destroyer air freshener or another in the room before he got home from work, but all that did was make the house smell like a dog covered in putrid air freshener. Brian would start sneezing, then ask me what I was trying to hide. All I could do was clean, every day, and use lots of baking soda.

To my husband, his home was his castle, and the animals were his subjects, existing under his benevolent dictatorship. Yes, you might abide in his kingdom, but only by his rules: No fur tumbleweeds skittering across the floor. Don't bring fleas into the house. And for God's sake, don't do anything that smells bad. All I had to do was maintain the illusion that this was totally doable in a house full of pets and kids. If I could keep a lid on those, we'd all get along just fine. If he knew Kekoa was defiling the rug on a regular basis, though, there's no saying what might happen.

I thought things were getting better with her new medication, but it was hard to tell since I couldn't smell a single thing to begin with, and I never actually caught Kekoa doing something wrong. All I had to go on was the presence or absence of pee spots on the underside of the rug, and I hadn't found one in weeks. Victory.

One cold and foggy morning, I padded downstairs and heard Brian, who had woken up before me, muttering to himself. I peeked around the corner apprehensively, and there he was, on his knees with the corner of the area rug flipped up, attacking it with a SpotBot.

"Oh hey," I said, edging over to him. "Did the kids spill orange juice or something?"

He looked up at me and rolled his eyes. "It's dog pee. Just like every other time I've cleaned it up this month."

I paused. "You've been cleaning the rug?"

"Yes," he said, motioning me to move so he could scrub where I was standing. "You were doing a terrible job so I just started doing it myself." This was very likely true. Cleaning has never been my strong suit. "She's doing better on whatever you're giving her, though. We might not have to replace this whole thing after all."

"I didn't know you were doing that," I said. "I thought you would...be more upset."

"I'm not thrilled," he said, giving me a don't-think-I've-forgotten-this-was-your-idea look. "But when she sleeps in

Zoe's room she keeps her from having nightmares, so I guess I'll deal. Dopey dog." He sat back and wiped his brow.

What do we forgive when we love our dog? Everything. Fortunately, that seemed to also extend to spouses.

I first became suspicious that something was about to be dropped on me when Brian started cleaning the dinner dishes without prompting.

"Thank you," I said, and waited.

"Of course," he said, waving his hand in my general direction. "Anything for you." He continued to collect dishes, puttering around for a few more minutes before turning on the hot water to drown out what was coming next.

"Oh, hey," he said. "About our anniversary next week?" Here it comes.

It happened every year. Each July, right around our wedding anniversary, Brian would suddenly realize that two major life events were about to collide and he would need to figure out how to avoid a major disaster. The first event, obviously, was celebrating the day we were married. The second event was Comic-Con. Only one of those events could be moved to an alternative date.

It was hard for me to put up much of a fight, knowing that he had no intention of missing Comic-Con anyway and was simply trying to allow me the illusion of giving him permission to attend each and every last second. After all, going to the convention with his friends was a part of Brian's life long before I was.

The San Diego Comic Convention began in 1970 as a small gathering of comic book fans, which is the way Brian remembered it from when he first attended in 1986. Over the years, Comic-Con has grown to a massive celebration of all the popular arts, drawing over a hundred thousand visitors to the downtown San Diego convention center. Despite the fact that the initial comic book collections on which the con was founded were now stuffed in a small dank corner, pushed aside to make way for Hollywood studios and toy booths, Brian had remained a loyal attendee.

Attending Comic-Con was always a singularly strange experience given the diverse interests of those who participated. Some people, old-school Marvel fans like my husband, were there for the comics and the panels with beloved sci-fi authors. The kids in their teens were usually there to see the latest tween vampire movie stars, lining up and shivering on the chilly waterfront at three a.m. to make sure they could find a seat in the auditorium. A large contingent attended for the opportunity to walk around in steampunk Victorian finery or Princess Leia costumes without judgment. At Comic-Con, for one brief shining moment, the geeks truly did inherit the earth.

This is what drew Kevin, of course. These were his people.

One of Comic-Con's signature events was the Masquerade, where all the impeccably attired attendees would come to vie for costuming awards. The first year Brian and Kevin had attended together, they dutifully sat in the back and watched person after person parade across the stage, pose, and shuffle off to the side to make way for the next competitor.

"When's the party?" asked Kevin.

"This is the party," said Brian.

Kevin sighed. "Do I always have to figure this stuff out myself?" he asked.

"What do you mean?"

"Look around," said Kevin. "Tons of good-looking women in skimpy costumes and this boring show is all we have to offer them?" He smiled, a twinkle in his eye. "We can do better."

In 2002, Kevin rented out a loft downtown for the same night as the Masquerade. He purchased booth space at the Comic-Con and sold tickets to the inaugural "X-Sanguin" event, promising more debauchery than the Masquerade, better music, and adult beverages.

By the next year, word had gotten out that Kevin's party was the only good show in town. When the cast and crew of the wildly popular Lord of the Rings franchise came wandering by the X-Sanguin booth, Kevin motioned them over and handed them a pile of free tickets.

"You have to come to the party tonight," he told me gleefully later that day. "We're having the dudes from Lord of the Rings come and party with us."

"No way," I said. "They're not actually going to come."

Kevin leaned back and opened his hands expansively. "Of course they are. What else is going on tonight?" He pulled himself back forward, steepling his fingers gleefully. "Were you there last year in the VIP area? Mark Hamill showed up." He paused expectantly, then rolled his eyes at my blank expression. "Luke Skywalker. We got Luke Skywalker. Geez, Brian, school your woman."

"We'll be there," said Brian.

There was no bigger feather in your geek cap in 2003 than to say you rubbed elbows with the guys from the Lord of the Rings, and true to his word Kevin delivered. I dutifully showed up in a medieval princess costume rented for the occasion and found Kevin sitting with Gollum, Frodo, and Merry. Not people in costumes, but the actual actors. After some small talk, they headed out, leaving Kevin to the person he was most excited to meet: Richard Taylor, the head of the special effects company Weta Workshop who was responsible for the Academy Award–winning effects in the film series. Taylor was one of his heroes.

"He invited me to New Zealand!" he whispered when Richard left to see the rest of the party, quivering with excitement.

"No way," I said. "How'd you swing that?"

Kevin just grinned. The King of the Comic-Con needs no reason. He was just the kind of guy whose enthusiasm couldn't help but win over everyone he met. True to his word, Richard did host Kevin in New Zealand, giving him a personalized behind-the-scenes tour of the biggest movie franchise of the decade. There were tens of thousands of slathering Lord of the Rings fans who would have sold their grandmothers for an invitation like that, but Kevin was the only one I know who could actually pull it off through the sheer force of his charisma.

Unlike Kevin, I had always viewed my own personal eccentricities as a hindrance I needed to work around, or at least try to hide. It took many years for me to accept that they might actually work to my benefit, and even longer to believe that there might be a person out there who not only coped with but actually liked the fact that I watched every episode of *Star Trek: TNG* and idolized Carl Sagan. Going to the con with Brian was a nice way to reinforce that connection, even if I only lasted a day before saying, "I'm good. You go with Kevin the rest of the week."

We've always had a good give-and-take in our marriage. In return for regularly postponing our anniversary, yawning through Chargers games every Sunday in the fall, and allowing Brian to hang concept art from *The Fellowship of the Ring* on the wall, I asked only one thing in return: Let me do my thing with the animals. That was more than enough to balance the scales.

CHAPTER 22

Living with Kekoa was like having an unpredictable crazy aunt in your guest room; you never knew what each day would bring. She lived with her emotions on her sleeve: soaring elation, undying devotion, miserable agony. I had to give her credit for that, experiencing life with the intensity turned to eleven at all times, though I often had to remind myself of my admiration when the extremes of emotion pushed her to dark deeds.

When I was in veterinary school, one of the ways I passed the time in between pharmacology assignments was watching *Sex and the City*. A mind flush, if you will, stepping out of the world of smelly path lab dissections and into a more sparkly world of purses and footwear. During this time I became obsessed with one thing: Jimmy Choo shoes.

They were beautiful. They were delicate. They were completely uncomfortable. In short, they were the complete opposite of my boring basic daily footwear, which in those days was Doc Martens. All I wanted was one pair I could take out on the rare occasion I got off campus to go somewhere fun, even if I could barely walk in them. I could fantasize all I wanted and make my dream pair as ridiculous as possible, because a $500 pair of unwearable shoes was way outside the budget of a typical broke vet student.

My junior year in school, I got my lucky break. Brian and I were in Las Vegas for a weekend getaway, and he had a windfall at the craps table. Miraculously, he got out while he was ahead and pushed a couple of large bills into my hand. I headed straight to the new Jimmy Choo flagship store at Caesars, a mecca for people like me about to make impractical impulse buys, wandered past the sky-high gladiator sandals and straight for the clearance rack in the back. This is how I got my first and most loved Choos, a delicate pair of taupe sandals with a defect that made the left shoe squeak when I walked, hence their bargain-basement price. I didn't mind. I was used to squeak toys.

I took them out only for rare special occasions when I didn't have to walk too far, so all these years later they were still in surprisingly good shape, until that one fateful New Year's Day.

The night before, I had worn them out on the town for New Year's Eve and wandered through the front door barefoot in the wee hours of the morning, dangling them in my hand. I dropped them by the front door before heading up to bed, glad the kids were safely at my parents' house. I remember that very clearly; that, and Kekoa's baleful expression as I gave her no more than a minute or two of attention before turning in. She had not been thrilled about being left behind.

The next morning, the first thing I noticed as I walked down the stairs was that my shoes were no longer in the entryway. Perhaps Brian had put them away, mindful of his investment. Kekoa ran up, tail wagging, giving my hand a lick, and as I reached down to pat her a strange whiff of something unpleasant hit my nostrils.

In slow motion, my eyes swept across the carpet and quickly landed on the offensive pile of dog poop on the carpet. Did the stress of the New Year give her some GI distress? Or did she eat some more LEGOs again? It looked like something weird was sticking out of the heap.

As I drew closer, the true horror of the situation slowly dawned on me. That little foreign object was not a stick or a toy but a sad wooden stiletto pump poking out of the top of the heap, the sole firmly pressed into the pile of excrement. The heel, waving in vain for help. The second shoe fared even worse, drowned at the bottom. Kekoa dragged my shoes away from the front door as if to blame them for my absence the night before, and just to drive the point home pooped all over them so it wouldn't happen again.

Brian came downstairs to investigate the choking noises I was making. "Bah ha ha!" he said, trying to lighten the moment. "Now you have Jimmy Poos!"

After screaming and carrying on in tongues for a few minutes, I pulled out some gloves to see if there was any hope left for my prized soles. Brian shook his head as I tried all the techniques I could find online about the deep cleaning of shoes. I thought back to Emmett's accident in Brian's office and the diaper-eating incident, wondering what I had done to so anger the gods of dog poop, if they somehow held all those thousands of doses of anti-diarrheal medications prescribed over the years against me. It is a question without an answer.

After several hours of sweating with saddle soap, shoe polish, and wire brushes, they were still in sorry shape. Being a pale beige, they bore some permanent stains. You had to look closely, though—maybe no one would notice. "What do you think?" I asked, holding them hopefully up to Brian.

He picked one up, then wrinkled his nose. "They still smell like poop," he said.

I eventually sent them off for professional cleaning, where they fixed the odor problem, if not the discoloration. "Oh, you're here for the designer shoes," the woman at the dry cleaner said. "They're gorgeous." She held them out and winked conspiratorially, clearly unaware of their checkered history. "I tried them on before we sent them out. I hope you don't mind."

Just this once, I didn't.

Most dog owners have a woeful tale about a treasured possession destroyed by the dog. A first-edition *Game of Thrones* hardcover devoured by a canine who is clearly still angry about the Red Wedding. Valuable baseball cards. Cash, usually in larger denominations. Car keys, new iPhones, you get the picture. If the ingested item requires surgery to extract, that just adds insult to injury.

Sometimes these items are wrecked by a dog suffering from separation anxiety or boredom, as is often the case when people come home and find their couch cushions shredded or a door knocked off its hinges. The cases I see most often in the clinic, probably because they are the dogs usually in need of medical attention, are those who prefer to eat the evidence. Labradors are notorious for swallowing just about anything that can fit in their mouths, a phenomenon known as pica, though pretty much any dog can go through a thought process modern medicine has yet to decipher, one that makes him say to himself: *Hmm, that knife looks good. I'm going to swallow it.*

Fortunately, the majority of items we see are much more banal. Socks and rocks were the items of choice in my clinic. Perhaps owing to our warm Southern California climate or the blessed evolution of fashion, pantyhose have fallen out of favor with both women and the dogs who love them, so I've been spared the sight of a perfectly happy-looking dog trotting in with a nylon foot dangling from his rear end.

The decision about what to do when a dog presents with something other than food floating in his stomach depends on a lot of factors. Is it something toxic, like a battery or zinc-containing pennies? Will he likely pass it on his own, like the dog who pooped modified LEGO creations for a week, or is it likely to cause an obstruction? Or perhaps it is something the owner simply can't bear the thought of having to retrieve on the far side of the digestive process, like a valuable piece of jewelry?

I used to think the stories of jewelry-thieving dogs were urban legends or at least exaggerations, but it happens all the time. I was once almost the victim of one myself.

One of the larger national service dog organizations has a facility in San Diego, and it's not uncommon to meet someone who is a puppy raiser either out and about, or in the clinic. These kind souls volunteer their time and effort to take in these puppies and guide them through their first twelve months, only to have to return them so they can continue their training at the dedicated facility until they are ready for place-ment. During that first year, the puppy raisers are responsible for socialization, training, and the cost of the dog's food and medical care.

I always love seeing service dogs in training in the clinic, in part because I just enjoy puppies period, but also because it's fascinating to see how well behaved these pups tend to be due to the heightened training regimen many of them go through. It was with this expectation in mind that I swept into a room with a four-month-old Labrador puppy, Joey, waiting for his rabies vaccine.

Before I even got all the way into the room, Joey pounced on my shoe and started going to town on the laces. "He's teething something fierce," said his raiser, Mrs. Taylor. "He's gone through every toy in the house and a few pairs of shoes."

"He's a feisty little guy, that's for sure," I said, leaning down to pet Joey. He play-growled at my hand and launched at my finger.

Mrs. Taylor regarded him fondly. "I've been raising pup-pies for this group for years now," she said, "and I've never had one who got into as much trouble as this one. He ate a rock last week and I was sure he was going to need surgery, but he threw it up before we could come in." Pause. "Joey. No. Joey. Come here," she said, trying her best to distract him from my foot by waving a squeak toy in his direction.

He was slick and flexible in the way of all wiggly puppies, bending ferret-like around my hand as I tried to take his tem-perature. He attempted to get my hand away with no luck, then turned around to give me kisses instead.

"Aw," I said, taking the thermometer away. "Good boy. We're almost—" and that is when he launched himself at my face. I believe he was attempting to give me a free nostril piercing or at least a small playful nibble, but I turned my head aside just in time.

"Joey!" cried Mrs. Taylor, as I stood up, rubbing my ear.

"I'm fine, he didn't hurt me," I said, running my finger over my earlobe. "But he pulled my earring out." And that was no small feat, considering I was wearing small diamond studs with a safety back on them. He had managed to hook his teeth just so on the top and bottom and yank it right out. I knew better than to tempt fate with anything enticing like shiny dangly earrings, especially when I worked with cats on a daily basis, but I'd figured little studs were safe. Wrong.

Our eyes turned to the floor to see where the earring had fallen. I got back down and rubbed my hands on the floor, quickly finding the back. Joey and I were now nose-to-nose, and this was when I noticed him quietly rolling something around on his tongue, like he was savoring a fine vintage of Cabernet.

Mrs. Taylor noticed it a split second later and we froze, two officers approaching a jumper on the edge of the bridge. "Joey," she said, inching toward him. "Don't do it."

"Come here, Joey," I said in what I hoped was a reassuring voice, holding my hand out. My husband had given me those earrings a month before for our anniversary, and I wasn't looking forward to explaining this one to him. *See, he didn't mean to eat my earring—no really, I was just standing there and he yanked it out . . . no, he's a good dog, really, future service dog . . .*

Joey cocked his head and regarded us as his jaw worked, deciding whether he should swallow his new treasure or spit it out. We surrounded him, slowly. Mrs. Taylor launched herself at him and tackled his hind end. "Quick!" she said. I slid my hands over his head and pop, open his jaws went and out came the earring, slightly slobbery but otherwise none the worse for wear.

"Good boy," said Mrs. Taylor wearily as I disinfected my earring with some rubbing alcohol. I sensed this was not the first time she had staged an emergency intervention with Joey. She nodded to me. "We're still working on 'Drop it,'" she offered.

"That sounds like a good plan," I said. By this time he was rooting in the garbage, pulling out a dirty paper towel to shred. "I'd love to hear how he does in his service dog training."

Mrs. Taylor shook her head, laughing. "I'm not quite sure he has the temperament they are looking for." She distracted him with another treat. "But he sure is a great dog either way."

And because I had my earring safely in hand, I could agree. I don't know if he ever made it through service dog training, but I'm sure whatever he ended up doing, he did it with great gusto.

CHAPTER 23

I had come a long way from the scrunchie-wearing kid in a hand-painted denim jacket that kids used to throw pencil erasers at on the bus, at least on paper. Now I had a Bedazzler and a graduate degree, so I felt I'd moved up in the world. Still, those early experiences imprint themselves deep in our psyches, and all it took was one peek at the pictures in my junior high yearbook collecting dust in the garage to plunge me back into all those old feelings of inadequacy and self-doubt. So I rarely looked at them; there was no point in revisiting old hurts.

When the ten-year high school reunion invitation arrived in the mail, I shrugged and tossed it in the recycle bin. My friend Mieko, the classmate who'd introduced me to my husband, was attending and did her best to convince me to join her.

"It'll be fun," she said. "Don't you want to see the old gang?"

"What old gang?" I asked. "I kept in touch with everyone I wanted to keep in touch with." All three of them. It seemed like a lot of effort for the off chance of a little schadenfreude in case one of my old tormentors had wound up in prison. "I'm good. Let me know how it goes."

"All right," she sighed. "I'll be sure to let you know if any of the cheerleaders got fat."

"Please do," I said.

Mieko dutifully reported back several days later that the reunion passed uneventfully and miraculously, everyone was still alive. "The women pretty much look the same," she said. "But the guys all went bald." Everyone was in middle management and no one was doing anything exciting, either good or bad, as far as she could tell. A bunch of people loosely bonded by geographic proximity in the hormonal excesses of youth, trying to stuff themselves into their old letterman's jackets. Getting together in the hope that someone else's story was more interesting, or better yet less interesting, than their own.

By the time Mouth Breather Dan showed up in the hospital one busy Saturday afternoon, he hadn't entered my mind in eons. Susan came walking briskly into the back with the red patient folders we reserved for emergencies, clutching a small, bloodied Chihuahua to her chest. I looked up from the Cocker Spaniel whose ear I was currently spelunking, put down the otoscope, and met Susan at the exam room table.

"Car?"

"Dog park incident." Sunny weekends and crowded parks often led to such emergencies.

Ah, there on the side, a puncture wound. Susan placed an oxygen mask over the dog's face while I did a quick assessment to see how badly she was injured. Pink gums (good), racing heart (to be expected), superficial lesions, normal femoral pulses, breathing well and without the telltale muffled sound of a collapsed lung. So far, so good. As my eyes traveled down to her leg, I noticed that it looked substantially more swollen than the other one. I gently prodded at it. She yelped.

"All right," I said. "She doesn't look like she has any penetrating wounds to the chest or abdomen, but her leg is worrying me. Can she stand up?" The scared dog looked up at me, trembling at the trauma of her awful day, and refused to stand up. "We need rads and some pain meds to start," I told Susan, then listed off the treatment plan I wanted to run. While Susan put together an estimate for the owner, I grabbed the chart so I could go out front and talk to him.

Cookie Arnold. Owned by Daniel Arnold. Hah, I thought as a little neuron in the back of my mind mused, Remember that guy from junior high? Same name! Weird!

I looked at the address in the file—one town over from my junior high. It was entirely possible that I was about to come face-to-face with my eighth-grade tormenter, and I had no time to wonder what I thought about the situation. I pushed the door open and strode out into the waiting room. "Mr. Arnold?" I called. At the back of the room, a man turned around and started to walk toward me.

Had I not seen his name on the chart, I probably wouldn't have recognized him. But there he was, same features stretched and distorted under a mask of age. Same height, but definitely an expanded radius. A slightly receding hairline framed a face worn by years in the sun. His T-shirt read ARNOLD FLOORING, and as I squinted at his chest to get a better look at the logo, a small pigtailed head emerged from behind his back.

"Where's Cookie?" the little girl asked, sniffling. "Is she OK? I swear I just looked away for a minute, Dad, you have to believe me—"

"It's not your fault," he said, patting her shoulder. He turned to me. "Did you get to look at her yet?"

"I did," I said. I put out my hand. "I'm Dr. Vogelsang," I said, relieved that he wouldn't recognize my married name. "Please, have a seat."

In all of the revenge fantasies I had nursed in my late teens, none involved a meeting at which our identities and histories were completely irrelevant to the situation at hand. And here he was, not an escaped convict, not a desperate loser bleeding out failure for me to enjoy, but just a completely normal person with a cute daughter who was worried about their dog. Average people having an adult interaction.

I looked into his eyes waiting for a jolt of adrenaline, flashbacks, desire to vomit, any of the lurching gut responses I'd lived with on a daily basis all those years ago. I waited for it, and felt absolutely nothing. A memory with no nerve endings, like scar tissue. Huh.

"What's your name?" I asked the little girl.

"Gina," she said.

"OK, Gina," I told her, reaching out and taking her hand. "Cookie got shaken up a bit, but I don't think she has anything life threatening." She exhaled in unison with her father. "Mr. Arnold, this is what I want to do to check her out."

The next day he took Cookie home with a sack of meds and strict instructions to come back for a bandage change in three days. As far as I know, he never did make the connection.

Dog the Third: KEKOA

Mouth Breather Dan—or just Dan, I suppose I should call him now—had grown from a typical bully-type kid into a typical standard adult, one who cared for his family and by all accounts was trying to be a good parent. I imagine if I were to see him in a PTA meeting he would fit right in, backslapping the other dads and throwing his hands up in frustration at the Chargers' performance against the Raiders the night before. Fitting in just comes more naturally to some people than to others. I was still working on it.

As I suspected when my kids were in their infant play-groups, I had a slightly different take on parenting than many of my peers. I was somewhat laissez-faire in their child-hood, figuring if they wanted to go outside and play in the dirt with the dog, that was fine and they could come get me if they needed anything. I was shocked to learn that other parents had been busily plotting their child's college admis-sion trajectories and were beginning with piano lessons, soccer coaching, and math tutoring at four years old. I had already blown it.

In an attempt to be a part of the team, I volunteered in my children's classrooms, nervously telling other kindergart-ners to pull the crayons out of their noses and wiping finger paint out of perfectly coiffed pigtails. It seemed like I was always missing the boat: I got my daughter a Dora backpack when all the other girls had moved on to Rapunzel; I brought in cake pops when gluten-free agave-sweetened Rice Krispie Treats were all the rage; and despite sitting on the outskirts of the PTA coffee klatches, I was never quite able to penetrate the inner circle. I thought my love of dogs might be an inroad to conversation and camaraderie, and followed the lead of other moms by taking Kekoa with me for a walk when I picked the kids up from school. The schnoodles and maltipoos were uniformly disgusted by Kekoa's ungainly demeanor and bulk, I guess, and after the PTA president tossed the principal a meaningful look I was told dogs weren't allowed on school property at any time. I stood a foot away on the sidewalk as she planted herself between me and the bus circle.

"What about that dog over there?" I asked, pointing to a Yorkie being carted around under his armpits by a second grader. His bow quivered in terror as excited children surrounded him.

"He's being carried," she replied curtly. "He's not actually *on* the property." My interactions with the principal only went downhill from there.

My last attempt to fit the mold came on Valentine's Day, when I sat my kids down and declared instead of just buying cheap lollipops from the grocery store for their annual classroom valentine exchanges, we would do a real, actual craft. I'd show them I could use the Martha Stewart website too, and all would be well. Fifty dollars in craft supplies and two and a half hours later, my kids and I proudly surveyed the fruits of our labor: two classrooms' worth of little cutesy matchboxes, painstakingly covered in festive red and white scrapbook paper and ribbons and filled with conversation hearts. They were adorable. We were so proud. I divided the pile up in two, plenty for each child to distribute to all their classmates, and sent them off to school.

The day after the holiday party, my phone rang. I looked at the number—the children's school. Panicking that someone was injured, I picked up the phone immediately and was horrified to hear the principal ask for me.

"This is she," I said. "Is everything all right?"

"Well," she said, inhaling, "I hear that you sent some... crafts to school yesterday for Valentine's Day. Matches, I think?"

"Well, matchboxes," I said, confused. "Oh my God. Did we accidentally leave matches in one?" We were so careful to empty them out!

"No, but there have been *multiple* complaints," she said, speaking slowly and enunciating every syllable.

"Oh," I said. "Why?"

"Well, there's the sulfur residue, for one," she said, drawing it out with the distasteful drawl one would commonly reserve for toxic-waste-covered cigarette butts. "And then there's the simple fact that they were matchboxes, which one of the mothers figured out when she disassembled your... contribution." As if I were trying to sneak contraband onto campus.

Perplexed at the outrage, I said nothing, so she continued: "There's a warning on them to keep them away from children, you know."

"The warning," I said, taking a deep breath, "was about the matches, not the cardboard they came in."

"Nonetheless," she said. "Those remaining were confiscated and thrown away. You have to think about the message you're sending the children."

I thought of my children and the message she had just sent them, and me. I pictured her grimace of horror as the PTA president indignantly ripped the paper off the craft my child had worked so hard on, and them shaking their heads at my nerve in trying to turn their little princes and princesses into chain-smoking pyromaniacs. I have a message for you too, woman, I thought to myself, but I'm too much of a lady to say it out loud.

My kids came home, embarrassed and upset. They wanted to know if they needed to apologize to the class. I gave them a hug and said absolutely not. The only person who needed to apologize was me, for putting them through that. What was I thinking? Who cared what these strangers thought? I didn't need to try to fit in any more than Kekoa needed to look or act like a designer mutt. That never would make me happy. I was proud of my funny-looking flatulent dog and my hands-off parenting and my incendiary crafts, and if they didn't like it, fine.

"Should we throw these away?" my son asked sadly, gesturing to the leftover boxes.

"Don't you dare," I said.

My children and I used up every last bit of paper and boxes on a new project I dubbed "Passive Aggressive Crafting 101." When we had the boxes in hand, we sold them to friends and family for $10 each. We donated all the proceeds to the Josh Project, a program that donates a stuffed dog and a book about being in the hospital to children's hospitals around the country. If the worst imminent threat to your child's life is the possible sulfur exposure from holding an empty matchbox, I figure, you have an awful lot to be thankful for.

As an added bonus, my daughter's Girl Scout leader pulled me aside a bit later and said if I wanted the troop to do the matchbox project as a group, she was all for it. "It'll have to be at my house, though," she said. "We can't do it at school. The principal already hates me enough as it is." It was the start of a beautiful friendship. By the way, she's a dog person too. Somehow we always manage to find each other.

CHAPTER 24

We all loved Mr. Mansoor at the clinic, almost as much as Mr. Mansoor loved his two Miniature Schnauzers. Somewhere along the way, Mr. Mansoor and his wife had divorced, he retained custody of the dogs, and his dedication only intensified. George and Gracie were his family, and a more kind and loving trio I have never seen. He was also a chef, and every time he came in for a visit he brought along some delight he had concocted the day before: Pastries. Kebabs. In the vacuum of the vet clinic, where time is always short and most of the hardworking support staff squeaks by on wages much lower than their level of dedication deserves, the gift of food is always gratefully accepted and invariably consumed. Mr. Mansoor was a delight, not only because he was an excellent chef but because he was a kind soul.

"May I feed my dogs chicken?" he asked. "I'd like to cook some for Gracie and George."

"Of course," I said. "I want to come over too." We laughed. I outlined what was safe and what was not when it came to cooking for dogs: chicken breast, yes, raisins, no, and so on. He'd take notes and share with me what recipes his dogs particularly appreciated.

I was surprised to see Gracie's name appear on the computer screen on a quiet Tuesday afternoon. Normally Mr. Mansoor scheduled his appointments for the morning, before his shifts began.

"Emergency," Mary-Kate told me as she hurried into the back. "Gracie. They're in Room 1."

My heart sank.

"What happened?"

"I don't know, I just wanted you to get in there. It's not good."

Skipping my usual protocol of sending a technician in ahead of me, I grabbed Susan and hustled into the exam room. "Mr. Mansoor. What's going on?"

Sobbing, he held Gracie in his arms, wrapped in a blanket. He told me that had taken George and Gracie for a leisurely hike, allowing them off lead in one of the quieter areas where they were unlikely to encounter any other people. By the time he saw the coyote, it already had Gracie in its jaws. He screamed and threw rocks until the coyote dropped the dog and drove over as quickly as he could, but the damage had been done.

When someone dies, be it pet or person, there's a subtle but unmistakable dulling of the twinkle that lets you know the spirit has fled the flesh. I knew before I even reached the table that Gracie was gone, but I put my stethoscope on her chest anyway.

An entire conversation transpired between us without a word. A grimace, a pained wrinkling of the forehead. There was nothing to be done. The last tiny bit of hope Mr. Mansoor had been holding on to disappeared as his eyes darkened and his face fell. He sat down hard on the exam room chair, trying to catch his breath.

As professionals, we are taught to maintain a certain distance from clients, both physical and emotional. Not everyone is comfortable with proximity, and no matter how distressed a client is, they may not want a hug or even a hand on their shoulder. It's not a law, just a general code of conduct, which of course I bend on a regular basis depending on who is in front of me.

I didn't feel right just standing there over this wonderful client who looked so alone, so I sat down next to him on the bench. Susan gently tucked Gracie's legs into the blanket, rewrapped her snugly, and gave her a little kiss on the head before quietly slipping out of the room. Mr. Mansoor put his head down and cried while I sat with him.

There are times you need to be alone and times you most desperately need not to be, when you need someone there, not to do anything but simply be present. That is what I did. Working in this field you gain a certain level of comfort with death and grief, not so much a collegial affinity, really, but a realistic acknowledgment that yes, this is as much a part of the job as the new puppy visits, and part of doing this job well means recognizing that you are a pylon in a rough harbor.

There are things I do know: the physiology of death, the uncertain guilt of an owner experiencing relief that his pet is no longer suffering; and things I don't: No two situations are ever entirely the same. You'd think that since veterinarians deal with more death and grief than most other professionals we would get some sort of basic counseling in how to help owners handle grief, but that didn't happen, at least when I was in school. There were just too many other things to learn. Helping clients with death is a by-the-seat-of-your-pants thing, and some people are exponentially better at it than others. Experience helps.

I wasn't around death very much in my childhood. My first experience with it came back in Massachusetts, in the form of a baby swallow that had landed on my grandparents' porch with a broken wing. I squatted down next to Babcia in the garage as she attempted to nurse it back to health in a little shoe box. I had utter faith in her healing skills, having seen her fix neighborhood cats and scabby-kneed kids with proficiency and a good helping of Old World methodology: poultices from the garden, some whiskey on the wound, kind words.

But in this case, it was not to be. Despite our ministrations, the swallow died the next day, and I cried as Babcia buried it in the garden. She was with me the next Sunday as I emerged tearfully from morning mass.

"What happened?" she asked, wiping my cheek.

During Sunday school, I had asked Father O'Brien to bless the little bird in heaven. He pinched the bridge of his red nose and explained, in a patient tone, that animals don't go to heaven. "Only humans are made in the divine likeness," he said.

I was sad for the bird, and massively disappointed that there were no animals in the afterlife, since I had already resigned myself to the fact that there was no pony to be had in this one.

I repeated his words to Babcia and her face darkened. "God marks the dropping of every sparrow," she said to me, patting my cheek before standing up. There was about to be a Bible-Off. She squared her shoulders, straightened her pearls, and patted her hair as she strode into the vestibule. She came out a few minutes later, a satisfied smile pulling at the edges of her lips. "Father O'Brien doesn't know everything," she said, gesturing to the ceiling and the large figure of Jesus solemnly watching over us. That afternoon, she pulled out a small vial of holy water she had smuggled out from the font at the front of the church and held my hand as we sprinkled it over the little bird's grave. "*Dopóki si znowu nie spotkamy,*" she said. Until we meet again.

Death and I parted ways for many long years after that, then sprang back in like a wound-up coil. I lost both my grandfathers fairly close together in my adult life. I loved them equally fiercely, but they could not have been more different. Nowhere was this more apparent than in the last few days before their deaths.

Pepe, my mother's dad, was the first of my grandparents to pass away. A heavy smoker, he had been told since he was sixty that he'd be dead of lung cancer within a year, and like a couch potato mutt who eats nothing but junk and lives till he's twenty, Pepe simply decided that he would like to keep on keeping on for another twenty-five years or so, thank you

293

very much. And he did, with his cigarettes and his Dunkin' Donuts buddies, merrily watching the world go by until at last his habit finally caught up with him. He did finally quit smoking after the first round of radiation therapy, but it was too late. I flew back to Boston on the first flight I could book when the hospice nurse told us to come and say our good-byes.

I went straight from the airport to his house at ten at night. I walked up the driveway, brushing a light drift of snowflakes from my shoulder, and pushed through the door to where the rest of my family sat vigil around his rented hospital bed.

Pepe, barely conscious under the influence of all the morphine he was being given every four hours, turned his head toward me as I walked out of the shadow into the dimly lit living room. His face, always so full and wrinkled up in a big smile, was now drawn and pale, sunken cheeks sagging on his bones. His eyes, always so bright and twinkling, were nearly closed, concentrating on the rattling intake of breath.

"We're so glad you could come," said my aunt Michele, pulling me into an embrace before scooting aside so I could join in the bedside vigil. I put my hand over Pepe's, the fingers that had always tickled me under the chin after telling me a particularly spectacular tall tale now bony and weakened.

"Hi, Pepe," I said, bringing his hand to my lips. He squeezed my fingers.

"I love you," I said, wishing I had something better to add. My sister was always the talker in the family. Chatty Kathy, Pepe called her, and here she was gently talking to him about all her wonderful memories of twirling in the snow while he laughed and came up with various nicknames for her.

My mother pulled me aside. "Would you help me with his medicine?" she asked. My grandmother trusted no one without medical training to rub his gums with the morphine-soaked sponge, meaning my mother the nurse had been taking care of him round the clock. I was happy to have a job to do; while my mother and aunt caught some much-needed sleep, I dosed the drugs and my sister dosed the company.

Death isn't what scares most people, not really. Death itself is actually quite boring. It's the moment right before that makes most people panic. In this sense, hospice providers are true angels, smoothing over some of that uncertainty by letting you know exactly what is going to happen. What I learned from watching Pepe's hospice nurse, Tammy, I would carry over into my work as a veterinarian, trying to re-create that sense of order to wrap around people living in chaos.

The next day, his hospice nurse let us know his time was very short. That rattling quality to his breathing, his refusal to swallow water, those were signs the body was shutting down. "It's close," she said before she left. "Please, call me any time day or night if you need me to come back." Pepe had spent the day unconscious, murmuring to unseen friends, occasionally letting out a pleased smile or grunt.

My mother and aunt were determined to let Pepe know that he didn't need to stick around for their sake; that he was free to cross over with their love and blessing. "Go to the light, Dad," my aunt said gently, and it became a mantra. "Go to the light. It's OK. We love you." As his breathing slowed, they continued to encourage him.

After half an hour or so, he let out a soft groan and his eyes fluttered open. "Go to…" my mom's voice cut off as he sat halfway up, looked her right in the eye, and said, "NOOO!" then flopped back on the bed. Everyone sat in shocked silence for a second, then burst into laughter.

"OK, Dad, sorry, we'll shut up," said my aunt. "Take all the time you want."

In the end, it was my beautiful cousin Jenn, who had cared for him so often in his illness, who was sitting quietly with him in the early-morning hours when he left. The key word, of course, being *quiet*.

My dad's father, Dziadziu, on the other hand, had been waiting patiently to die for at least the last two decades of his life. "I'm going to be the first one to go," he said to me when I was six, only to outlive all three of my other grandparents. "I'm going to die any day." He said this so frequently I was convinced he would one day preside over my own funeral, slamming the door on Al Roker when he showed up to wish him a happy two hundredth birthday.

After the horrors he had witnessed during World War II, I knew death was not something Dziadziu feared. What he feared was a bad life, something he managed to escape and elude for many years after immigrating to the United States.

When Babcia died, he died too, except someone forgot to let his body know. His heart kept on beating, day after day, when the wife he lived for had already departed. He stared out the window with a pipe in one hand and a glass in the other, waiting. After a year or so of this, his body started to wear down under the weight of his own gravitational pull.

He refused nurses and doctors. "Just let me go," he muttered whenever someone suggested a trip to the cardiologist.

When he fell unconscious on the living room floor, he was unable to tell anyone to leave him alone, so he ended up in the emergency room, where doctors failed to find anything wrong with him. He gradually came to, surrounded by family and doctors. He peered wide-eyed at the bright light in a momentary burst of happiness, then, realizing he was still alive, his eyes narrowed and he scowled.

"Good news, John," the doctors told him. "You seem to be perfectly fine, so go home and we'll follow up with your internist tomorrow."

Like Pepe, he too said "NOOOO!" Unlike Pepe, he was determined to head in the opposite direction. With no further ceremony, he set his brow in a determined line, sent the doctors a triumphant smirk, and died.

As I sat with Mr. Mansoor, I pondered all of these events while he remained in his own internal mourning place for a bit. Eventually he looked up at me and took a deep breath. "Doctor," he said, "do you think dogs go to heaven?"

Most dreams come and go in my consciousness, fading before I've even fully awakened. But every once in a while, one sticks, an image so intense and evocative that years later, I can still close my eyes and picture the scene.

Shortly after Dziadziu died in his hospital bed, I dreamed I was sitting in a train station somewhere in the past, dark and shadowy. Only one other man was there with me. An old steam engine pulled up, and the door opened. The man gingerly got up, adjusting his cardigan, and walked toward the door. A woman's hand reached out to him, as he stepped up to meet her. The doors closed and the train pulled away, leaving me alone on the platform.

I told my father about this dream at Dziadziu's funeral, and my dad—not one for new-agey dream analysis—looked at me strangely. "Really?" he said. "You dreamed that."

"Yes," I said. "Isn't that weird?"

"You know," he told me, "Dziadziu met Babcia on a train from Poland to the work camps."

No, I had not known that. We shuddered together, a rational mind's attempt to shake off the unexplainable, and my father poured us each a glass of wine.

Some months later, I had another strangely realistic dream. I was standing on the side of a road in the mountains, enjoying the scenery. A car pulled up, a big shiny chrome-wheeled beast, and the passenger window rolled down. It was Babcia. "Hello, my little babushka!" she sang in her full voice, and I reached in to kiss her on the cheek.

"Is Dziadziu in there?" I asked, trying to see into the driver's seat.

"Yes," she said. "But he doesn't want to talk." Typical.

I felt a wet nose on my hand and looked into the backseat. It was Taffy, puffballed and glowing, enjoying the car ride.

"You found Taffy?" I said, overjoyed.

She just smiled and rolled up the window. Again they left me, driving into the mountains. I woke up sniffling, my cheeks still warm from the late-summer sunshine in my dream. When I close my eyes I can still see the car, a massive green boat of a Buick, chugging away into the hereafter; Taffy peering out the back window, tail wagging.

It was this image that came into my head before Mr. Mansoor finished his question. "Yes," I said. "I do think they go to heaven."

"Perhaps I will see you again, my Gracie," he said to his pup as he pulled the blanket up and over her silver fur, and laid his head on her chest.

"I hope so," I said, and sensing that the time was right, I left him alone with her to say his good-byes. I thought I had it all figured out by that point, but not long after I realized I still had plenty to learn.

CHAPTER 25

The next to last time I saw Kevin he was at a Comic-Con booth, standing next to a woman dressed like Xena, selling tickets to his X-Sanguin party. I was following Brian around at my annual one-day Comic-Con walkabout, but after a few hours the convention center smelled like BO and Mountain Dew, and I was cranky and ready to head home to Kekoa and the kids.

"Just one more quick stop," Brian said. "I need to say hi to Kevin at the booth."

I drummed my fingers on the table, impatiently waiting for Kevin to finish describing the custom-designed getup he'd worn to Burning Man to Brian so we could leave. "Are you guys coming to the party tonight?" he asked. "It's a bar crawl, and everyone has to wear a Santa costume. We're renting one of those double-decker London buses!" My husband looked at me to gauge my reaction before turning back to Kevin and shaking his head. No Santa Bus tonight.

Kevin coughed into his elbow, then looked at me and said, "Hey, can I ask you something about Niles?"

Ten years after his tumultuous arrival, Niles was still alive and well in the Workman household. I had predicted they'd be sick of him in a month or two, but a decade later he was the most loved and spoiled Jack Russell on the planet.

"Ask away," I said, brightening up. He had a question about Benadryl dosing, which I was happy to answer, and then we were on our way. Kevin did that all the time. He didn't really need your advice, but he wanted you to feel involved in the conversation so he'd draw you in with a query or a compliment or a gesture. He made everyone feel likable, a rare and generous personality trait much more common in the canine than us primates. The last thing I heard him say was "You should come tonight! You'll regret not going!"

He was right, of course.

Most of us live our lives trying to balance the scales between what we give and what we take, but wind up squarely on the "taker" side of things. It's human nature to take things, to accumulate. If we fail to replenish the energy we dole out, like all finite resources, the well eventually runs out when there is simply nothing more to give. Maybe this is why dogs don't live as long as we do. They give so generously of themselves every waking moment, depleting their reserves a little more each day. It exhausts the soul.

Kevin was tired; we knew this even then. He was worrying about his father, whose Alzheimer's was progressing, and lying awake thinking on things in the early-morning hours when he should have been fast asleep. "Don't worry," he said as his cough progressed into a deep hacking reverberating in his chest. "It's nothing." And so it continued, until his reserves were completely depleted.

The next time I saw Kevin was in a hospital bed, after that

persistent cough progressed to something worse, a pneumonia he ignored for a little too long before finally agreeing to get it checked out. He went in for a bronchoscopy—a simple procedure, he said. They just needed to figure out the source of this cough, no problem.

He never woke up. Now he laid in a coma in the intensive care unit as we all came to the horrible realization we had too many debts to repay, a hollow well to refill, and it might be too late.

Brian had gone on his own to visit regularly since Kevin's admittance to the hospital, his mood a little less hopeful each time. Finally, he asked me to accompany him. That's when I knew how bad it had gotten.

A man who lived such a grandiose life deserved a much more fitting exit than a boring old pneumonia: smothered by a manatee in Hawaii, maybe, or accidentally run over by a snowmobile in Antarctica. "Maybe he caught something at Burning Man," his friends suggested, and the doctors said, "It's possible." Whatever the reason, our happy existence ground to a halt with startling rapidity as we found ourselves, without warning or the chance to say good-bye, staring at his quiet form in the sterile cocoon of the hospital suite willing him to open his eyes and come back to us.

Kevin's hospital room was Grand Central, stuffed to the brim with family and friends, all of us struggling to wrap our heads around what was happening. Some people read to him. Others filed his nails. As far as I know, Kevin is the only person in the world who managed to hold court and command a room even when completely unconscious.

We waited our turn to greet him. "Keep fighting," Brian said, patting his dear friend on the shoulder before stepping back and allowing me a moment.

I walked up to Kevin, distraught at the sight of him lying so still. I picked up his hand, remembering how he used to pick me up and shake the crinkles out of my spine as a form of greeting. I put it to my cheek, wanting to believe he would awaken at any moment and start talking to me about Niles, or some old embarrassing secret of my husband's, or anything at all. I rubbed his hand between mine, and it was gray and waxy. He had always been so warm; this was all wrong. In that part of our brain that separates what we hope from what we know, I took in all that was going on around me and I knew: This was my chance to say good-bye.

"I'll keep an eye on Niles for you," I murmured to him. His mother, Betty, perhaps the strongest person I've ever met, was in the corner of the room consoling his friends and chuckling at one of the bawdier stories about her son. "We love you, dude."

A week later, he was gone.

One of Kevin's favorite places to visit had been Lions, Tigers and Bears, a sanctuary about an hour from my home that housed, well, lions, tigers, and bears—mostly castoffs from zoos and former pets that had outgrown their cages. "How is it that you've been there ten times and I didn't even know this place existed?" I asked him once. He just laughed and gave me directions. It was here, at a home for mistreated animals who had nowhere else to go, that we held his memorial event.

Betty had expressly forbidden a somber funeral service, so this was instead billed as a celebration and family barbecue. On a sunny winter afternoon, his friends gathered in the bright chilly air, sharing stories of varying degrees of appropriateness while the tigers roared their approval. I almost got peed on by a lion who could, amazingly enough, arc a stream of urine about five feet backward through the layers of fencing with what must be stunning urethral musculature.

I heard a familiar laugh behind me as I skittered backward, almost knocking over Betty in the process.

"They did that to Kevin his first time out here too," she said. "Stunk up his car for a week." She smiled the best she could and marched off to where a small group of friends was starting to sniffle, smacking one of them on the back of his shoulder. "Hey now. I said no crying. It's a beautiful day."

We tried to follow her orders, with middling success. Brian inherited boxes of VHS tapes from Kevin's home studio, a running documentary of all the living he had stuffed into too few years. Every night he would pop one into the VHS digital converter he bought specifically for this job, forging a path through grief with one purposeful task after another. Kekoa followed him around every night that he did this, though I can't say for certain whether it was because she sensed he needed her by his side or because he usually ate a bowl of pretzels while he worked with the tapes. Probably both.

As the nights wore on and Brian got more tired, pretzels would drop from his fingers with increasing frequency. Sometimes one would bounce and land in the box of videotapes, and she would have to get up to dig it out. I happened to see her doing this late one night and caught the slightest hesitation in her left foot before she placed it solidly on the ground. I drew closer, wondering if her left ankle looked swollen compared with her right. I got out a piece of string and wrapped it around each side to compare. Yes, it was bigger.

I didn't waver from my usual MO of keeping this to myself until I had a better idea of what was going on, mostly because I kept hoping, like always, that perhaps this was another false alarm. *You again?* I thought the radiologist would sniff, debating whether or not to write a stern letter to the radiology teaching department at Davis reprimanding them for my poor education. "Don't you remember Hornof's Hock? That rare but completely normal incidental finding in black Labs where the left tarsus is larger than the right? Geez."

In she went the next day, while I listed in my head all the reasons the X-rays would absolutely, positively come back normal. She's feeling fiiiine, I thought. She's not limping. She's eating well. She lets me palpate it.

My friend and colleague Kristen saw the X-rays pop up on the computer screen before I did. After this many years in the unpleasant world of life-and-death diagnoses, I found the body language of Big News pretty easy to interpret. When one is waiting for confirmation or rebuttal of a poor diagnosis, there are really only two results: Good (smile, reassuring pat, moving in toward you with strong eye contact) or Bad (the sigh, the pause, the standing back, the looking to the side).

Kristen walked over, hesitated at the doorway, and pressed her lips together.

"It's cancer," I said.

"It's cancer," she said. The X-rays were pretty clear on that.

Brian, as always, left the decision about what to do next up to me. You'd think after this many years of seeing the best medicine had to offer that making the decision to do everything would be easy. After all, shouldn't I do everything I could? Aggressive treatment, a leg amputation potentially followed by chemotherapy or radiation, could extend Kekoa's life by an average of two to eight months. The cost? Around $5,000, plus the recovery from a major surgery. For the many people who want to go the distance, I am so glad that modern veterinary medicine offers such amazing cutting-edge treatment. But it's not the only choice.

I decided, after some soul searching and discussions with my colleagues, that I would focus on palliative care and skip the chemo/radiation/surgery process. I wanted to make happy memories in the time we had left. In addition to pain management, I started a bucket list for Kekoa. Being the couch potato that she was, she had no interest in heading to Dog Beach or taking in new vistas on a hike, and I was too worried about her leg to chance it anyway. But she was a foodie through and through, so we did a Bucket of Food List instead. Each day, a taste of a new ingredient: healthier items at first—sweet potato, kale; as she progressed, the food got more tempting— a bite of hamburger, bacon, ice cream. And this cancer didn't affect her Labrador-size appetite, so she got to enjoy all sorts of forbidden delicacies.

The kids must have wondered why Kekoa was getting so

much people food when it had always been against the law of the land, but they couldn't quite bring themselves to ask. We played a let's-pretend-this-isn't-going-on thing for a while— not because I wanted to hide things from them, but because I wanted to save them from the anticipatory grieving process as long as possible. My daughter, for sure, knew something was up. She was eight by now, and like her mother she was quiet, perceptive, and sensitive to the changed mood around her.

"Why'd you bring Koa into work today?" my daughter would ask, watching as I carefully unloaded Kekoa's substantial bulk from the car to save her having to jump onto her affected leg.

"Checkup," I'd say.

"Is that another bottle of medicine for her?"

"Yes."

"Can I give her a treat?"

"Sure."

I didn't know it at the time, but Kekoa was setting the groundwork for my future work in pet hospice care. She was loved, spoiled, and managed as well as medicine allowed me to, for the next two months. I didn't want to acknowledge it was time to say good-bye—I could convince myself we had a few more good days or a week, but I knew, as the waves of panic and nausea washed over me, that this was the moment I had been dreading. I steeled myself for the gut-wrenching truth that the kids deserved to know what was going on, and be given a chance to say good-bye.

My husband once again took one for the team. As I stood

to the side and hiccuped, he explained to the children that Kekoa was very sick, and we were going to euthanize her the next day.

I remembered how badly I had done this the last time, so now I had a plan.

We stated it very clearly: Kekoa is sick and she is going to die, and a vet—not me—is going to give her a shot to help that happen painlessly and peacefully. It's going to be very sad and we will all cry, but this is something we have to do.

We cried until we couldn't cry anymore, and once I could talk again I put my arms around my kids and asked them if they understood what we just told them.

My son nodded sagely, wiping her eyes. "She's going to Kevin."

I paused. After Emmett died and Zach had misheard the destination, my colleagues and I started using "Gone to Kevin" as a euphemism for a pet dying, the idea of Kevin as a vague benevolent dog handler somewhere in the sky. But I stopped saying it once my actual friend Kevin died.

My son repeated, with more certainty this time, "Kekoa's gone to Kevin. With Emmett, right?" My daughter nodded in agreement.

I started to respond, and stopped myself. I pictured the first version of the afterlife in what I had shown them in that old book back with Emmett, dogs with white feathery wings jumping around beside St. Peter, on clouds with tennis balls in their mouths.

Then I thought of Kevin surrounded by dogs up in the

hereafter. "Chick magnets," he would say knowingly while feeding them steak and letting them sit on the leather couch. This was a guy who used to buy those one-pound Hershey bars to hand out on Halloween; he liked to spoil everyone around him. I know which afterlife Kekoa would prefer.

"Yes," I said to my children. "Kekoa's going to Kevin. And he better take good care of her." My husband, fist pressed to his mouth, said nothing as he hugged the kids tighter.

I don't remember much about that last night except for the fact that none of us got much sleep. Kekoa was the exception, snoring away with a full belly and a hefty dose of pain medications. Even in her deep slumber, she thumped her tail on the floor whenever she heard my voice.

The next day I asked the children if they wanted to be present when Kristen came for the euthanasia. "Absolutely, positively not," they said, so Brian ushered them out the door to the park, leaving me alone with her. As the door closed behind them, I felt one last time the old familiar sting of her manticore tail whipping against my leg.

I looked down at her trusting eyes, thinking to myself, Just call it off. Tell Kristen you changed your mind and Koa's good for another few days, and in that moment I realized fully why my mother walked out the door without Taffy all those years ago. It's so much easier on us to not make that decision, to just let them die on their own—even if that means they spend the last days in the excruciating physical pain of bone cancer or struggling to breathe with a failing heart.

One of the tricks grief counselors teach you is to imagine

what your pet would say to you, if he or she could talk. Looking for reassurance, or resignation, anything, really. With Kekoa's head in my lap, I told her, "I'm worried I'm letting you go too soon."

She licked my hand, carefully and thoroughly, getting her tongue fully around each finger like she was scrubbing in for surgery. When she first came home with us, my daughter had teasingly called her Licky. I was going to miss those sticky, sloppy, pungent kisses.

"But I don't want you to be in pain."

She sighed, rolling on her side.

"Can you forgive me?"

More kisses.

Trust and love were always all she had to offer, and now was no different. I had her permission to do what I knew would be best. So I sat on the floor cradling Kekoa's head in my lap, feeding her treats until Kristen arrived, lost in memories and wondering why doing the right thing still, after all this time and experience, hurt so much.

Kristen came with all the medical items necessary for a gentle passing. I provided the optional items: classical music and food. I sat cross-legged on the floor and held a bowl of chocolate chip ice cream, with bacon sprinkled on top. We both cried.

Bacon and chocolate: two things I would never recommend feeding your dog, unless you want to kill him or her. I laughed ruefully when that thought entered my head as I watched Kekoa nibbling the forbidden items. And that is the last thing she heard: a bemused "Oh, Kekoa."

She went off to find Kevin with her face still perched on the edge of the ice cream bowl, the taste of ice cream on her tongue, my voice in her ears, and a gentle hand on her head.

We used to joke that the pitch of her howl could pierce the veil between this world and the next. Sometimes, in the still of the night in that hesitation between sleep and wakefulness, I pause for a breath to listen for that plaintive wail. I haven't heard her yet. Clearly, Kevin's keeping her busy.

EPILOGUE

One of the many benefits of living with a dog, and more specifically a retriever, is having your own living, breathing, organic Roomba. Aside from the fur issue, our floors were pristine, even with two kids who seemed to get as many cracker bits outside their mouths as they did inside.

It was strange that this was the first thing I noticed in the absence of a dog, that suddenly we needed to clean the floors. I would sweep through my tears, cursing the universe and mumbling about this sudden onslaught of crumbs. It was the first argument I presented to Brian for adopting another dog immediately, though he saw right through that charade. "Look at the floors. A dog would take care of this."

"Not yet," he said.

"But I miss having a dog!" I pleaded. "This is what I do. I am good at dog. It's my thing."

"I think you need a break from dogs. They always get cancer," he said. "Why don't you pick a dog that doesn't get cancer?"

"It doesn't work that way," I told him. "Besides, you love what you love." It was a question I had asked myself, long before I actually ended up falling in love with retrievers—breeds in which half of them die of, you guessed it, cancer. Years of laughter and love and wet licks, a joy debt we pay with one painful smashed heart at the end. And yet, it was still worth it. It was always worth it.

"Just wait a little while," he said. "Enjoy your break."

There was no enjoyment to be had in the absence of a dog. I took no pleasure in the respite from picking up dog toys, which was never really a hardship. Going to the pet store was still a necessity as the cat persevered, having outlived every non-human creature in the house by that point, and I teared up when I had to walk past the dog food aisle. My husband was unmoved by my words, so I decided to communicate in a medium he understood: photography.

I emailed him a picture of the little engraved box of ashes, sitting by the door waiting for me to come home. "Not enjoyable." The next snapshot: the box with a dog treat balanced on the lid. "Not the same."

There was no response. I couldn't figure out if he was trying to extinguish my melodrama or was merely consulting a therapist for advice on when I should be committed, so I backed off. For a little while.

About a month after this exchange, Brian informed me he was going on a half-day bike ride the following afternoon.

"Who are you heading out with?" I asked.

"Some buddies from work," he said.

I paused, my hand hovering over the pan of sauce I was stirring. Brian's mountain bike, purchased shortly after a doctor's appointment that scared him long enough to acquire the bike though not enough to actually ride it, was sitting in the garage, as pristine as the day he brought it home. To my knowledge it hadn't traveled more than fifty feet in the two years he had owned it.

"Are you sure you're ready for a six-hour ride?" I asked. The mountain biking trails in the hills above San Diego were remote and viciously hot this time of year. "Aren't you supposed to work up to a long ride?"

"I'll be fine," he said. "The guys I'm with know what they're doing."

"But do you?" I asked. "Do you have all your hydration ready?"

He pointed to a lone, tiny water bottle. I panicked. He was going to die.

I spent the next two hours puttering around the house, pulling out CamelBaks and containers of Gu from my stash. "You need one bottle with electrolytes and this one with water," I told him. "Is this enough Gu? Maybe I should run to the store. Do you have sunscreen? What are you going to wear?"

"Really," he said. "This isn't necessary. I'll be fine. I swear."

But I couldn't stop worrying, because I knew how hot it could get out there, and how quickly someone could get heatstroke, and how spotty the cell phone reception was in the backcountry.

I should take heart in the notion that my husband is a terrible liar and has no idea what constitutes a plausible falsehood. In this case, though, I wasn't suspicious, just very gullible.

Epilogue

The next morning, after grumbling as he loaded his bike into the car, I fretfully watched him drive away. I hope he remembers to Gu every hour, I thought to myself. I should have asked him for the cell numbers of his work friends.

I went about my day, doing the standard weekend activities with my kids and running loads of laundry. Around three o'clock, Brian rolled back in while I was on the phone with my sister.

I looked up. He didn't look sunburned. Good. Limbs intact? Yes. He waved to me, indicating I should come outside. I waved back, pointing at the phone. In a minute. He nodded, hugging the kids who were running up to him. "Hang on a second, guys."

He went outside for a minute, then came back in. "I really need you to come outside."

"Can I call you back?" I said to Kris, getting concerned. I knew it. He had a concussion and was confused. His bike was crumpled into a metal pretzel and I needed to help him extract it from the car.

I followed him out the door, the kids running ahead. The back of the SUV was open. The kids screamed. What horror awaited? I picked up the pace. I rounded the back of the car, and there I saw a small, very fluffy, slightly overwhelmed-looking twelve-week-old Golden Retriever puppy.

I started crying, and through my tears and little choking hiccups, I said, "Please tell me...you did not get this dog... from a pet store," because, even in my emotional state, responsible pet ownership was the first thing that popped into my head.

"Seriously? You think I haven't been listening to you all these years?" Brian said, before spilling the beans: He had been researching Golden Retrievers for the last couple of months. He called and spoke to breeders, looking for a puppy from a line with a strong history of good health, knowing my inclination was to bring home the old and infirm instead.

I don't usually advocate springing a dog on a person unannounced, but in this case I let it slide. He was the last of his litter to find a home, too gangly and the wrong color to qualify as a show dog, the rusty-colored last-born in a family of creamy catalog-ready Goldens. He was perfect for us.

And thus we've embarked on yet another journey, this time with a goofball named Brody. He is as guileless and innocent as they come, experiencing the world anew each day with awe and wonder. When I open my eyes in the morning, inwardly groaning at the list of tasks awaiting me— cleaning, grocery shopping, shuttling children to school—and briefly fantasize about disappearing for a week or a month into the Bwindi Impenetrable Forest to live with the gorillas, he is always there, nose-to-nose with me, breathing in contentment and grateful for the life he is living at that exact moment.

Brody is five now, the children's dog as much as mine, a permanent thread woven into their lives and their glimmering childhood memories. Right now, they think he will live forever. He has such a short time to make such a big impact, kissing and gnawing and snuggling his way into every nook and cranny of their day, and when one day he is gone, so too will be a piece of their hearts as well as mine. I know this now all too well, but I also know that rather than fear and dread that moment, I need to treasure the one I have now.

The pain of the loss is the price we have to pay for all the wonder we accumulate building up to it, and as much as we forget this in our distress our loved ones aren't really gone, not entirely. Their mark on us lives on, the myriad ways they make us better people just by being themselves, a truly phenomenal gift. Which explains why we keep going back for more.

When I first read Charles Dickens's classic *A Christmas Carol*, all I could think was that the Ghost of Christmas Present reminded me of nothing so much as a dog. A beaming, happy ball of energy so intent on living in the present he could barely remember the moment before, since he was too busy enjoying the now of things. Every time he reentered Scrooge's field of vision, he had aged just a little bit. And in the blink of an eye, one brief hour, he was gone. When I researched the author's life, I learned that Dickens did in fact have dogs, Newfoundlands to be exact. It explains a lot about that spirit. After Kevin died, I was trying to explain what he was like to a friend and used the exact same comparison.

I think Kevin would understand I mean it as a compliment to call him a dog in human's clothing—full of love, brimming with life, and gone all too soon. There will never be another friend like Kevin, for his unique characteristics were so very rare in the human race. But for him, and for Taffy, and Emmett, Kekoa, Brody, all of them, I can honor them by striving just a little more to live like they did: with joy, unabashed and open, reminding myself and others that our flaws do not make us less, but ever more worthy of being loved just the way we are.

ACKNOWLEDGMENTS

The author would like to acknowledge:

That in order to preserve the anonymity of people who came to me for help, I have changed the names of both the clients and their pets, as well as identifying details of their visits. I also changed the names of my co-workers, and pretty much everyone who isn't immediate family.

My friends and colleagues who stayed with me when we were covered in anal glands, fending off dysphoric cats, and laughing when the only other option was to cry: Carrie, Moises, Audrey, Libby, Betsy, Anne, Kristen; you guys are the best. Amber, I would have strangled at least fifteen people with an oxygen hose if it weren't for you. You're amazing.

Caroline, Janet, and Kristen, who convinced me I was not alone in this world of pet authors. Your friendship, support, and overall fabulousness sustained me through a great deal of doubt. To the veterinarians who encouraged me to write and smash a few molds here and there even though vets don't do these kinds of things: Marty Becker, Andy Roark, and Lorie Huston, thank you. And of course, I might not be here at all if it weren't for the author of the Nerdbook, Sophia Yin, my pocket mentor for so many years. The Nerdbook was only the

Acknowledgments

first of her many contributions to the field. Please tell Kevin when you see him that you had a Jack Russell too.

All my pawcurious readers who have stuck with me through all these adventures both good and bad, and to those who always stepped up when I asked them to yet again support one of the many causes important to me: Annette, Cathey, Jeanne, Lisa, Jane, Summer, Karen, and everyone who has taken the time to comment, contact me, and share your stories. They matter.

My editor Emily Griffin, who single-handedly changed my mistaken belief that editors were scary people wielding red pens with impunity, and my publisher Grand Central for taking a leap of faith on a debut author with Yet Another Dog Book.

My agent Steve Troha and his assistant Nikki Thean, for not only forgiving me my absolute cluelessness about the publishing process but also for endless patience and excellent guidance in bringing this idea to fruition. I couldn't have done it without you! Please don't ever show my first proposal to anyone.

Betty and Ron Workman, for their unconditional support of this book as well as every endeavor Kevin's friends have undertaken. Betty, you are a woman of unimaginable grace and kindness. Now I know where Kevin got it from.

My family: My husband, Brian, who has never batted an eyelid at any of the myriad twists and turns my life has taken in pursuit of being a Real Author; I wake up every morning grateful for your love. Also my beautiful children, Zoe and Zach, who make me joyful and proud every day; my parents,

Acknowledgments

Mitch and Pat, who always assumed I could do it, whatever it was; and my in-laws Stan and Julie, for always being there for us. My sister and best friend, Kris, who is much funnier than I am. I love you all.

And lastly, the big cheese himself, Kevin Workman, who was never afraid to let his freak flag fly. Rock on, brother.

ABOUT THE AUTHOR

Dr. Jessica Vogelsang is a veterinarian, mother, and big-time dog person. Dr. Vogelsang worked in emergency and small animal medicine before settling into her current practice providing in-home hospice care for dogs and cats in San Diego with Paws Into Grace. She is the founder of the website pawcurious.com, and her writing has been featured in or on Yahoo!, CNN, *Ladies Home Journal, People Pets, Outside* magazine, and *USA Today*.